THE CHURCH GROWTH SYSTEM (PIE)

PIECES OF THE PIE

TO HELP YOU AND YOUR

CHURCH GROW.

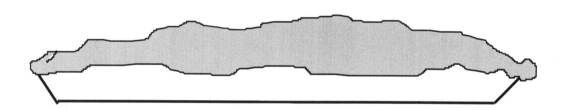

By
DR. MICHAEL R. HOUSEHOLDER

Fishnet Publishers
Knoxville, TN

The Church Growth System (Pie)
Practical Ingredients for Church Growth
A Church Growth System to help you, and your church grow

Written by Dr. Michael R. Householder

Church Growth Pie

Copyright 2003 by Dr. Michael R. Householder
Revised edition Church Growth System 2013

Requests for information should be addressed to:

P.O. Box 20606
Knoxville, TN 37940

Library of Congress Cataloging in Publication Data
Householder, Michael, 1955-

ISBN # 9781491069653

Printed in the United States of America

About the Author

Dr. Michael Richard Householder was born February 3, 1955 in Knoxville,

Tennessee. At age ten, Mike decided to follow Jesus Christ as his Lord and Savior and he was baptized. Mike studied at and graduated from:

- Johnson Bible College in 1977 with a B.A. in Bible and ministry,

- Lincoln Christian Seminary in 1981 with an M.A. in Philosophy,

- Cincinnati Bible Seminary in 1983 with an M.Div. Theology,

- Fuller Theological Seminary in 1992 with a D.Min. in Church Growth.

Throughout his ministry, Mike has been a minister in Indiana and Tennessee, a professor at Platte Bible College, and an instructor in the LAMP program at Johnson Bible College. Also, Mike and Jacque were missionaries in Russia and Poland between the years 1993 and 2000. Since 1995 and currently, Mike is the Director of Global Church Growth Discipling Ministries.

At age 17, Dr. Michael R. Householder was called by God into full-time Christian service. At that time, Mike was not certain what this service would be or where it would be carried out but Mike was willing to allow God to lead him. While at Johnson Bible College, Mike was given the opportunity to work for TCM as an intern in Eastern Europe. This was a life-changing experience for Mike. He recognized that God was calling him to be involved somehow and someway in foreign missions around the world.

Between 1975 and 1994, God began laying the foundation for the ministry that He had planned for Mike. Mike joined and guided five short-term mission trips to Eastern Europe between 1975 and 1988. In 1980, the first year as being a minister at a church located in Indiana; Mike began discipling and baptized 60 people. This is when Mike realized something needed to be done to help new disciples continue their growth in their new life as disciples of Jesus Christ. Therefore, Mike began developing his material, "Walk in Discipleship" series. Then in 1992, God opened an opportunity for Mike to begin leading a fulltime ministry in Russia.

In 1995, Mike founded Global Church Growth Discipling Ministries. Also that year and with Poland being on his heart, Mike and his wife Jacque moved to Poland. However this move would be a short-term move because in December of 1999 Jacque discovered she had breast cancer. This brought Mike and Jacque back to the United States for her treatment. Her cancer is now in remission.

Subsequent to the move back to the United States, Mike has continued to be actively involved with foreign missions, world-wide. Churches in Russia, Poland, Mexico, Antigua, and America have all been trained in the principles of discipleship and church growth.
In 2004, Global Church Growth Discipling Ministries was incorporated into a 501c3 mission

Other titles by the author

The Christian Church in Poland: A History of Church Planting with Strategies for Future Beginnings. UMI Dissertation Service: Ann Arbor, Michigan, 1992

A Walk in Discipleship Volumes I & II
(Discipleship Manual in Spanish available)
Fishnet Publishers: P.O. Box 20606 Knoxville, TN 37940

10 Steps to Spiritual Growth
Fishnet Publishers: Knoxville, TN, 2000
(Also available in Spanish, Polish, Italian, and Russian)

"The Most Precious Thing in the World" 1998
(Evangelism Booklet and guide): Fishnet Publishers
Knoxville, TN
(Available in Spanish, Polish, Portuguese, Malamyam, and Italian)

"My Pact with God Journal" 2005

"Children with His heart" Volume one 2012
A devotional book that looks at all the hearts mentioned in the Bible.

Acknowledgments

I first want to thank all those who have mentored me over the years. I also want to thank those who have been willing to follow, and those who have challenged me to be better as a person and leader. I especially want to thank Marie Garrett Bob Bolser, and Jim Knowles for their help as editors and proof-readers for this project. For Leonard Wymore for his friendship, encouragement and sentiments in this work. And for the leaders, preachers and churches that have used these principles in their churches.

Dedication

I wish to dedicate this to all those who have been willing to be discipled by me, and those who will be, God willing. For without a doubt each one has also helped me in my growth over the years. For I am just one beggar serving the Lord, and helping other beggars to find the food of life and how to acquire and share it with others.

Contents

Foreword
By Leonard Wymore

Friend and fellow Servant in Christ: May I invite you to prepare yourself and those that study this book with you, to be open to creative thinking and constant renewal under the leadership of God's Word and the Holy Spirit.

This book reviews a number of concepts and projects to which most of us have been exposed to, but I am confident that you and others will find many new refreshing and challenging insights into the ministry of the church.

Dr. Householder's purpose with this book is to review what it means to be a New Testament Church- not just the theory or theology but also the practicality. We will find concepts and suggestions to help revitalize the local congregation and advice about how to reach, teach, win and nurture new converts.

This book is actually a WORK BOOK. The author provides information, thought and practical observations on the essentials of church growth. The discussions of the essentials are fair and balanced. You may not always be in position to implement all the concepts but they are worthy of consideration. Each practitioner must seek his or her own course of action by study of the Word of God and in prayer responding to the leading of the Holy Spirit.

This book covers the familiar aspects of church growth and at the same time provides thoughtful suggestions regarding the evaluation of traditional patterns and offers guidance in implementing scriptural admonitions in today's history and culture.

The information and encouragement for beginning a new congregation is very helpful and follows scriptural examples. Discipleship is an important concept for all congregations to consider implementing. The discussion and ideas of a discipleship ministry is worth the study by all who plan to see the church grow.

I recommend that you study and put into practice the scriptural, thoughtful and experienced recourses offered in this book. The author has shared these with us in personal candor and honesty. Let us use and share these with gratitude. Paul the Apostle, exhorted us in Ephesians 4:16 "the whole body... knit together... each part working properly... builds itself in love."

Preface

Some may ask, where did this book come from? You know there are usually some event, or series of events, that prompt an author to write a book. These events started back in 1979 for me. I had just finished a youth ministry and felt the move to become a minister. So, I was called to be a minister of a small rule church in Indiana. The church consisted of 30 faithful members. As people came to see the new preacher I would immediately visit them in their home and initiated a home Bible study. In the first 6 months God used me to baptize 30 souls and then another 30 in the following 6 months. Therefore within the first year the church had tripled. Wow the lord was really moving.

But what was I going to do with them? In the past I have seen that most churches <u>assumed</u> and consumed, and not assimilated their newcomers. What do I mean here? Most churches assume that those who join or become Christians will just fall into place and become a part of the status quo, and if they do not, then they will end up somewhere else, that is the way it usually happens, so it is not big deal in the long run, people just come and go.

Others just <u>consumed</u> the new ones coming in. That is, they expected and encouraged the newcomer to get involved in what the church needed and wanted at the time. The problem is the person was usually not considered in the process. Is the person mature enough to take on the responsibility? Is he or she gifted in the area of need? Does the person even have the desire in that area? So after a year or so the person is burned out or discouraged and leaves because they did not have a spiritual foundation and maturity to get involved in such a ministry.

True assimilation is different. To have healthy assimilation there must be discipleship and mentorship before you ask anyone to take on a major responsibility, especially in the realm of teacher or team leader.

At this point I began looking for material to disciple these people and hopefully those of the original group. In 1980 there were very few models and materials available. The navigators had some material, and I used it at first, but found it was very shallow in my humble opinion. So I began developing "A Walk in Discipleship" I began working with 3 men and 3 women in two different groups in hope that they would then teach others. To be honest I was too new at this, and there was a lot to learn and mistakes to make. But after five years those whom I baptized were still in attendance. It was unusual that no one moved away, but it was true.

About two and half years into this five year ministry two of the elders approached me and said, "Mike we do not like how things are going, there are to many people and we like it the way it was. And be assured it will be." Well I lasted another two and half years before I was approached again. At this point I had suggested that the congregation go to two services, or build on, but that was not an option. One of the elders told me, "I helped my dad nail the nails in this building and it was not going to be altered." I decided then to move on and not split the church, although I had explored the idea, but key people hoped the elders would change. A year later I was back in the area and to my dismay, horror, but not surprise, the church was back to its original number. All who I baptized were now scattered.

Why does these kind of things happen in most of our churches? Why do most churches never grow? Why do churches end in splits and controversy? Why are so many ministers and elders so ill equipped, and are at each other's throat?

I then began to think about why this happened? I searched and studied and came to a number of conclusions, conclusions that would be the foundation of this book and now my ministry. In a statement, and be assured it will be mentioned later and looked at in depth, ninety percent of most church problems stem from how elders or leaders are chosen and groomed. This of course also includes the preachers and pastors too.

I hope and pray that out of my hurt and disappointment, and out of my success you too can begin your ministry, or begin again with a fresh approach that I hope will help alleviate or curb the problems we have in the church.

But am I talking about Camelot? Am I talking about a pipe dream? Read on and you make the judgment.

I first wrote this book under the title of: "The Church Growth Pie", pieces of the pie that is missing or needed to make a successful church. But as I internationally trained various ministers and ministries I see that most do not truly understand what is meant by "Pie" So in this edition I have changed the name to the "Church Growth System." This of course is more descriptive of what I am trying to accomplish. I am not suggesting a bunch of new programs for the church, but an intergraded system that will, if followed, grow your church and keep the backdoor closed.

I have also noted that churches and ministries that implement part of this system have limited or no change in their situation. But those who have made a commitment to implement the whole system have seen great success. So, I encourage you and your leadership to consider the whole system. I and Global Church Growth Ministries will help you and yours implement this system in your church. We will not come in and tear down what you're doing, but rather keep what you're doing right, and help you augment it with the entire system.

Therefore, I encourage you, as you read through this book, that it will help you in your ministry and the ministry of the Church in your community, and around the world.

Introduction
Finding Camelot

The idea of Camelot has always been a dream place, the hope of a perfect, peaceful, well run kingdom. The hope and the dreams seem to always be dashed when humans, reality, and time set in. As a believer and disciple, we should also look for and strive for the development of a Camelot. Jesus prayed for His newly emerging kingdom to have peace and unity, but again human involvement and free will proved to be hindrances to its total fulfillment. Now some may say Camelot is just an ideal that can never be reached, just a dream, a fairytale. Historically, this has proven to be true. For centuries, men have tried to create a perfect society, but end up self-destructing. In almost every case, their Camelot was based on false assumptions and foundations. Now you will expect me to say that is where the church and its foundations are different. You may be on the right track, but there are some limits. We must first decide if Camelot is possible, or a dream that needs to be swept away with reality. This is where faith comes in- faith that it is possible to have a Camelot in this day and time. The closest example of there being a Camelot is the community of the first church in Acts. Acts Two shows us that Camelot is possible, but that it is humanly impossible and hard to sustain. It is humanly impossible because it took the added power of the Spirit to see the possibility.

Or, is it more believable to believe in a future Camelot in a different space and time? Will we only realize Camelot when Christ returns and sets up His kingdom on earth and in heaven? This sounds believable if you believe in the possibility. This future hope, however, should not deter or lessen each disciple and church from striving to create a Camelot here and now. The formula and the power are available; it's the human element that stands in the way. It's the lack of faith, not the lack of power. It is the lack of teaching and understanding, not the lack of truth. Camelot is about individual responsibility and corporate unity that produce the possibility.

What limits the likelihood of Camelot taking place are the introductions of other foundations and outside influences into the kingdom. As far back as the Old Testament, God warned His kingdom not to allow outside forces to destroy His potential Camelot. Today, the same thing happens when the church allows outside influences to run the church. The Church, as we see it in the New Testament, is not a business or a democracy. It was and is a kingdom, and Jesus is our King. The leaders or Elders sit at His roundtable. The church is His bride, and Sir Lancelot is His pseudo friend who tries to woo the bride away from time to time. At times, Lancelot seems like one of us, but he never was. He befriends the church and tries to destroy the kingdom. He may be in the form of a carnal member or leader of the church who does not have a kingdom mindset, who should have never been a leader, who leads out of the flesh and not the Spirit. Each congregation has, from time to time, a Lancelot who tries to lead others in the church astray. It is up to the acting roundtable in each church to protect the kingdom and be sure that the wishes of the King are carried out and fulfilled in their part of the kingdom. In Camelot, each knight had jurisdiction or responsibility over certain regions in the kingdom, much like each congregation. Now, of course, we cannot always take illustrations to their conclusions, but it is important to realize that there are times individuals like Peter allowed Satan the opportunity to guide their voice and actions. The point being made here is that the church is in a battle. I have also seen that the church, especially the American church, has taken on the form of American democracy rather than Biblical models of form and operation. In so doing, I think the church has circumvented the process, and many times put in action a system that is doomed to fail or that creates the possibilities of failure.

I was just at a church recently to share with them our mission's idea on what we could do to help the church in their discipleship and shepherding programs. I was to first teach their Bible study and then meet with some of the Elders to share what we do so they could decide if they would want me to help them in their church growth. The church had been in existence for about a year and a half and was a split (illegitimate birth) from another church in the community. Basically it was not a new church, but part of an old church moving to a different location. It was made up mainly of the senior citizens' group of the former church. In this process, one of the wealthier men put up $150,000 to buy the existing building. At that point, they had four Elders, one of whom was this generous patron. At this meeting, this Elder was in the hospital. He asked another member, not an Elder, to sit in and be his representative. In actuality, there was a trust or power problem between the Elders. In the process, one of the Elders told the representative that he had no right to just show up and expect to represent an Elder. Then the representative shouted, "I have a right because he is the President of the corporation." Right there and then, as I heard this statement, I knew the problem. Maybe in the eyes of the State and on paper this man was the representative, although the board should still be a plurality of leaders, but in the eyes of God and in light of the Bible, we have a major problem when one man tries to control and pull his weight to have his or her own way. It was great that a soul loved God and churches enough to give that kind of money to buy the property; however, when he gave it, he gave it to God; he should have put it in God's hands. The church is not an organization that any one man can or should control, even on the local level. It seems that the attitudes and seeds of conflict that were in the old church are now in this new church. When man wants and tries to get possession of the church, problems will arise and division will follow.

How could this happen? Why does it happen today? How can a church solve this problem? How can a church prevent this problem from ever arising?

These are some of the questions I hope to answer in this book. As I have and continue to travel, I am amazed at the lack of vision and understanding there is about the structure and polity of the New Testament Church. The brotherhood I associate with prides itself on being a New Testament Church, but I have even found in many of the churches that they have lost or never had a clear view of what it means to be a New Testament Church. Time after time, I have seen that churches are run like businesses, corporations, or democratic institutions. This has been the biggest detriment to the growth and health of the church today. Democracy has become the mode of operation, not Biblical models.

I hope in this book to accomplish a number of things, while at the same time, fulfill one main purpose. I hope to help each leader and church understand what it means to be a New Testament church- not in theory or even heavy on theology, but rather practically. I hope to share some practical principles on what it will take to revitalize the existing church while also helping the church know how to reach out to new converts. I hope to help the reader develop the tools that will grow the church and to help each church and believer know how to disciple and shepherd. I also hope each leader will realize his or her responsibility, and seek to get across that 90% of the problem is determined by how leaders are chosen and groomed. I hope to suggest some ways that the new church can get started on the right path, hopefully derailing any future pitfalls that usually befall the church today.

I hope to help the church be healthy, and to present the pieces of the Pie that will help it grow. Any missing piece will hinder that growth. I hopefully pray this book can help answer some of these questions and problems, as well as others that are issued along the way.

Dr. Mike

PART ONE

Church Growth Ingredients

Section One: The Ingredients

I heard a story once about a little church that Sunday after Sunday prepared the communion table by placing a piece of white linen over the elements. During the ceremony, the two serving Elders carefully and reverently removed the cloth, folded it, and set it aside. One Sunday morning the cloth was soiled, and the person preparing the table, a new member, left it off. Well you would think the earth had come to an end. The debate went on from house to house about this atrocity. Then, during a church meeting shortly thereafter, the debate heated up about the importance of that little white cloth and how for years it was the tradition and how no one could remember it not being on the table. Then the eldest lady in the church spoke up and set things straight. She said when her father was alive he told her that years ago they had open trays for the bread and juice and they decided to put this cloth over the elements to keep the flies off of them.

Oh, what things we do allow to make us the way we are! Traditions that should have never been formed creep up to master us. The foundations we have will determine what result or structure we will end up with. A house, a person's health, an organization, and a person's soul will also be determined, in part, by their past and by the foundations made earlier in their life. The same is the case, no matter how old the person is, when they decide to follow Christ. The foundations that are laid in their first two years of following Christ will set the habits and the stage for who they will be. So, it is important to have the right foundation or ingredients in the beginning.

Once you put salt instead of sugar in your pie, your outcome is set in stone. Now, thank God, there is hope in the church and in each individual. In the fresh new pie (church), we can see to it that it starts off with the right ingredients. The results will almost be assured that it will turn out to be good. Only if an outsider comes in and tries to spoil it will you have a problem.

In the ready-made pie, it is possible but difficult to make the pie as good as it could be. In this case, some of the wrong or forgotten ingredients need to be removed or added. With the Holy Spirit, conversion, and the willingness to go back to the Bible and its principles, any church can do it and glorify God if they have the will and desire.

That's what this first section to the book is all about. Helping the new church begin with the right ingredients, and the established church, if it desires to remove the ingredients that hinder a good growing church and add those ingredients that will make it as God wished it to be.

If you are of good faith, willing, and have a humble heart, God can use you to make a difference in your church and those around you.

Purpose of the Church
Chapter One

In the movie, A Knight's Tale, the main character wanted to be a knight. He had been the aide of a knight since he was a little boy. The time came for him to take on the mantle of a knight when his knight died after a joust. Although he had to claim he was of royal blood to participate, he actually was not qualified by the standards of the day to fight as a knight. Because he had developed a relationship with the king, however, he was made a knight with all the honors. Although we are not of royal blood by birth, we do become royal by our relationship with Jesus, our King, in our new birth.

In Ephesians, Paul is telling the Gentiles, at first, that they were once not a part of the royal Kingdom, but through the blood of Jesus and His acceptance, the Gentiles are now included in the Kingdom. So it is obvious that the gospel is for the whole world, and we must share this joy and option for life with others. Paul understood that his purpose was to bring the Kingdom to the Gentiles. He also shared that the purpose of the church was to reveal this great mystery through the church. Ephesians 3:10 explains the mystery for which the Hebrews had searched – for centuries - and the Jews today still try to understand. In this passage, Paul is not crystal clear, but I think he is saying that God will work through a group of believers by the supernatural presence and power of God Himself. Through this work, powers and miracles will be done and the gospel preached. It will also demonstrate to the angels, both good and bad, that His special work is done through the people of God in the church, not by the angels. This is why it is a mystery to the angels. The mystery is that, through the church, the will of God will be done, Jesus proclaimed as Lord, and the world evangelized. It is no longer the children of Israel by natural birth, but the new children of Israel by the new birth. It is not through the nation of Israel that the truth will be revealed, but through the Church of new Israel.

> **The purpose for the church is to help aliens of this world to become citizens of the new eternal kingdom.**

The purpose for the church is to help aliens of this world to become citizens of the new eternal Kingdom. But it is more personal than just a Kingdom; we become a part of His household, His family. We see this clearly in Ephesians 2:19, where Paul says we're now fellow citizens in His house. He also says we are growing into a holy temple through the Spirit. Each individual who follows Christ is made into a "building block" that, combined with others, make up the church. Later in this chapter, we will see the purpose of each "living block" in God's building.

Whatever God will do, He will do it through the church. This is a blanket statement, but can you agree with it?

Even when we see a lot of corruption in the church, can the church be His only means? It seems the answer is "Yes". In prior times, God spoke through the Fathers, then the Prophets and inspired men of God. He then spoke through Christ and Apostles. In a real way, God still works and speaks through these means, but not without the direct participation of God's newest messengers, the Church, the called out ones.

The problem arises when the church fails to see its purpose in full. Through the Church, Jesus wanted the mystery of centuries revealed to the worlds, above and below, and this has not stopped for us today. I am afraid, however, that much of the church today has either forgotten what God truly has in store, or has truly missed its awesome responsibility to be the light and harbinger it was intended to be. I don't want to start off in a negative way, for there are congregations that are being faithful to their calling; but, there is so much more for them, especially for those who sometimes seem to have no clue, or who have lost their true prime directive, to learn and think about. In many cases, the problems are not rebellion against God and His church, but ignorance and apathy. With ignorance, there is hope through enlightenment and discipleship, but with apathy, there is need for prayer, for repentance, or new birth.

I said that it is through the church, but what about all of the para-church organizations? Does this create a problem for the idea that God will work only through the church? Why has there been a proliferation of para-church groups, doing work that perhaps the church should've been doing all along? Most para-church organizations have come into existence in just the past 150 years. Do we consider these organizations a part of the church overall? If so, then this would solve the problem, but the reason all these organizations have come into existence is that the local church has not been doing all it is supposed to do.

And where do they fit in the church? At this time, I am the Director of a para-church mission with the sole purpose of helping the church train its leadership to fulfill its intended, God-given task. Now the interesting thing is, if I do my ministry well, I will work myself out of a ministry, because I'm merely doing what the church should be doing, which is the case with most para-ministries. Their ministry is legitimate, but if the church as a whole followed the Bible, as it should, there would be no need under this philosophy. Another way of looking at our ministry is that we are all a part of the Church. Most para-church organizations like ours lend their ministry to the whole body. Were Paul and his team a para-church organization? Of course, they were set aside by a church to help other churches get started and to continue to help them in their development through encouragement. Except for the authority of his apostleship, our mission is doing the same type of ministry. If you look at most para-church organizations, they too are helping in some aspect of the church's mission. Is this wrong? In one sense no, because believers were doing the work as a whole. On the other hand, if each local congregation was doing its part, would we even need most of these organizations, (which, if you checked their history), were initiated because local churches were neglecting some needs as a whole?

> **One of the problems is that most local churches fail to realize their whole scope of ministry.**

How are we to reconcile this today, or should we be concerned about it at all? Can the two work together and be in God's plan? If the church is made up of individual believers and they work together for God's kingdom, then it is the church. The problem arises when the para-organizations are in competition with the church. One organization exists (not to be named) that has worked with students on college campuses around the world for years. In the past, it hasn't always encouraged the students to become a part of the local church, and in some cases, an anti-establishment attitude has been created. This could be dangerous in the long run, for in fact all students must graduate or quit their campus life at some point. If they weren't encouraged or directed to become a part of the church while in college, then they most likely won't make that jump later. This, then, is counterproductive to the church. Any para-church organization that doesn't feed or help the church is in the end, more of a hindrance than a help.

One of the problems is that most local churches fail to realize the whole scope of their ministry. One reason is, they have a misunderstanding of who they are. When I was a little boy, I was taught this little rhyme by some of my teachers: "Here is the Church, Here is the Steeple; Open the door, and here are the people." Now being a songwriter, I am keen on putting things to rhyme, but in this case, it is better to skip the rhyme, and be Biblically correct. Anyone who uses this rhyme is teaching something misleading about the church. It has helped in the establishment of the idea that the church is an organization. It has propagated the notion that we should invite people to the church, meaning the building and services. I would suggest a non-rhyming verse that is Biblical: "Here is the church building, and the steeple is optional, but open the door, and here is the church." The church is the people and community, not a building or organization. This is where we have gone wrong. If we see the people, then the world will see that the focus is not on churches and denominations, but on loving people who gather together to worship God and love each other as the church.

What should be the goal of each church and individual? **God's desire should be our desire.** God's purpose should be our purpose, both individually and corporately. God's desire is that all men be saved. This should also be our desire, as it was Paul's. Because of what God

> **God's purpose should be our purpose, both individually and corporately.**

desired, Paul became a preacher and teacher, so that every man he contacted would have a chance to be saved. Also of great importance, every man or woman should learn to pray, lift up holy hands, become holy, and do so without any wrath or dissension. These and many other things are God's will for us all. I Tim 2:1-8

The Church is not the object of business or ministry, the world is. Do you agree or disagree? When we understand this, we'll be well on our way to understanding the purpose of the church. Jesus came to seek and save the lost. He wanted to see this fulfilled through His Great Commission, but do we see the purpose and have the compassion? Our visible and invisible worship and compassion for God and man will determine:

1. **Our commitment to the Great Commission.**
2. **Our willingness to sacrifice.**
3. **Our compassion for the lost, and our concern for the saved!**

Some may ask: "Why be concerned about numbers and growth?" Except for companion-ship, the purpose of marriage between two persons is to multiply and grow the family of God. Likewise, the church must see that its purpose is to grow in quantity and quality. So - why be concerned? First of all, God is! Jesus' purpose was to seek and save the lost. Second (and also obvious), man needs salvation. More growth means fewer people in hell, and more with us in Heaven. Why do we not see this, or practice it, if we do see it? Third - we are God's only way now. Fourth - time is running out. Each day hundreds, if not thousands, goes to the grave without Christ. Today is the day of salvation. Today may be your next-door neighbor's or your brother's *last chance*. Do we really care?

But if we grow and grow, we'll become 'too big'. Wherefore some have said, "I like small churches; big churches lose the close atmosphere." Is this always true? The problem with this idea is that again, the church loses its purpose and focus. The local congregation is not in existence to be a social club for a select few. It is not to be limited because you like warm fuzzies on Sunday morning. It is in existence to be the light of Jesus and to convert the world. If each local congregation is not doing or trying to do this in its community, it's failing. It is disobeying the commands of God. It is being selfish and nearsighted.

How does a church prevent the loss of this closeness from happening? Some places to begin are: Shepherding, providing group ministries, taking care of everyone's needs. As we go through this book, you'll see some examples and methods of how to continue to grow numerically and still meet one another's needs.

Some leaders have replaced God's purpose for the church with personal agendas. Traditions, politics, selfish desires, and misinterpreted or mindless procedures have replaced basic principles and goals of the original intent of God's church. This, as we've seen, will lead others to start para-church organizations, new churches, or denominations to fill in the gap. Let us now look more clearly at the purpose.

Purpose Defined!

First, I want to look at the purpose of the church as a whole, or as a group. We must see the responsibilities of the church as a whole, as well as of each individual who makes up the whole.

PROCLAIM- Colossians 1:28 and Matthew 28:19, 20

Matthew 28:19, 20 - The purpose of the Church can be narrowed down to two main elements. Also, all other activities in the Church should fall under these two categories found in this passage. As we explore these two areas, we'll also see the purpose of this book. The church will be healthy and growing if it follows these two *prime directives* **found in this passage.**

Go and make disciples! Jesus says to "Go." What do you do when you go, but to seek out those who are in need of the gospel message? We are to go to them, not expect them to come to us. Although this is the common way of evangelizing in the church today, i.e., inviting and expecting the world to come to us (thus soothing the conscience) it is not the most effective way. Our obligation

> The world doesn't know our words or our way of life, and so to invite them to church is like trying to teach a fish to breathe air!

is to go to the lost world, both far and near. Could we expect a fish to live out of the water? The world doesn't know our words or our way of life, and so to invite them to church is like trying to teach a fish to breathe air! It might work on some rare occasions, but it's not the most effective way. In Section Two's chapter on evangelism, we'll explore this in more depth.

In the Old King James Version, the translation is "Go into the entire world and teach." Today "teaching" isn't as powerful an idea as it was back when these words were written. Today when I say *teach*, the concept is one of sitting in a classroom, listening, maybe taking notes, and maybe even remembering 20% of what is said, the next day. Today, we're taught, (we seem to think) by merely sitting in the presence of a teacher. Over the past few hundred years, missionaries and churches have gone into a majority of the world, operating under the assumption that if they teach people about Jesus, then they have fulfilled the Great

Commission. If some accept and receive Jesus, that is a bonus! Even that isn't enough; it's not what Jesus truly said, or meant. Therefore, the Old King James Version has done more of a disservice in this passage than any other aspect, except maybe not translating *baptize* as immersion, because it has given workers a false assumption that they've fulfilled their work when they've merely preached the gospel (and *maybe* gotten some converts.)

> The result is, many have "received" Jesus, but most have not become His true disciples.

The result is, many have "received" Jesus, but most have not become His true disciples. The command in the Greek, and in most recent translations today, is translated "Go make disciples," not "Go Teach." This is totally different in its meaning and in its results than just "teaching." *To make something* means there is raw material, and there is an end result from that material. When you make a disciple, you must have raw material, either a new believer or non-believer. Your result is to take that new person and help him/her become a mature and solidly founded disciple, or follower of Christ. This takes more effort and time from the church, but in the long run will produce a more committed person, and will set the groundwork for healthy disciples and churches in the future. If a person understands all he has to do is believe (note: the Bible never uses these words, and so neither should we), then any future behavior or action is logically irrelevant. On the other hand, if the person is taught that he or she is to be a follower or disciple who obeys, the chances are much greater that that person will be willing to obey God and live a Christian life.

In the past few years, discipling has become a key word and goal within some churches. For me, my eyes were opened by Dietrich Bonhoffer's book *The Cost of Discipleship*, and Juan Ortiz's book, *Disciple*. Bonhoffer was a prophet in his own time, but it would take a few more decades before some of his views caught on. As I travel all over the world, it seems that most people are not heeding Bonhoffer's call and instructions.

The first part of making disciples is the proclamation, the preaching of Jesus as the only way, and life. This is becoming increasingly less popular in society and even in some mainline denominations. When there is pluralism in the church, then there is no great urge or need for proclamation. To do so would be "politically incorrect", or "harmful to the causes of unity and brotherly love". This attitude comes at the cost of the truth and of God's will.

The Body of Christ must see that the preaching of Jesus in both word and life is the only way the world will have a chance to learn the truth, especially now when "pseudo-churches" are becoming more prominent and getting media attention. What will result is overall disintegration of the truth and importance of the Bible as God's word. When the truth becomes marginal, the church becomes irrelevant.

TEACH them to observe!

In Colossians 1:28, Paul tells fellow believers that they should proclaim Christ through their word and life. This is an illustration of Matthew 28:19. The Colossian passage describes how the Great Commission is to be carried out. We have seen that the first part of making disciples is proclaiming Him, and the results are faith and baptism, as is clearly stated in Matthew. The second part of making disciples in Matthew is to teach each disciple to observe what has been commanded and taught. A statement of faith is not enough. That faith must be acted out in every day life. If Abraham had said to God, "I have faith that you will provide a lamb. There's no need to take my son along," what would God have done? He would not have seen Abraham as righteous and would have condemned his lack of faith. This unfortunately rep-resents our faith today. Faith has become a mere acceptance of some doctrines and beliefs, and not an experience in a relationship that has an outcome that changes the life of the believer, or disciple in an ongoing lifestyle.

　　"Teaching the disciples to observe" is a lifelong process, beginning in evangelism, and continuing throughout the disciple's life. If they are taught up front that a part of being a believer is being an obedient disciple, the process will be much easier. The first two years are *so import-ant* in the new believer's life as a disciple. If they do not see discipleship and are not taught the spiritual disciplines in the first two years, they will likely not develop them later; (if they do, it will be much more of a struggle.)

> **"Teaching the disciples to observe" is a lifelong process, beginning in evangelism, and continuing throughout the disciple's life.**

　　The problem is, most existing churches don't have any means or methods to see that this happens. The common way is to tell the new convert that he is encouraged to come to church and participate in the studies and activities. There's no real mentoring in this scenario. I suggest in my later chapters that, if you shepherd and disciple the new convert from the beginning, then he will develop a firmer foundation and will stay in the church.

UNIFY - Ephesians 4

　　The Church is *all about* unity. One of Jesus' most important prayers was all about unity, but sadly, when people hear of the church, they often think of conflict and division. We will see in the chapters on leadership in Section Two that one of the main functions of the leadership at every level is to promote and preserve unity. Why is unity so important? Everything we do will be hampered or nullified if it ends in disunity. Just think of how many endeavors or projects for God ended up in disunity. When this disunity happens, either abandonment or a greatly diminished out-come results due to the lack of cooperation between the members.

　　The greatest tragedy is that disunity brings about the destruction of faith in many people's lives. To those who are already in the camp of the Lord, disunity may be destructive to their faith, even to the point of apostasy and the shipwreck of their faith. To others outside the faith, disunity may destroy any chance of them reaching out to those who are not in the kingdom of God. Why should anyone want to join or be a part of something that is constantly in disarray or not unified in his or her group or task? People of the world have enough problems and disintegration in their lives, without having to deal with another group of people who are infighting. Why bother and create more dysfunction in their lives? It is important to realize that the individual is to strive for unity in all of his/her relationships in and out of the church. The leadership within the church is the gatekeeper of unity among its members. As God is unified in everything, we also should strive for unity within the Church. One of the purposes of the church is to show the world that

> **The leadership within the church is the gatekeeper of unity among its members. As God is unified in everything, we also should strive for unity within the Church.**

we can be unified in God and with each other. It is obvious that the church has failed in this area, but we must try - in each situation, in each church, in each relationship, and in each generation. We can continue to make excuses, but now is the time in every place, with every person, to strive for unity in Christ. You cannot expect it in the world, but with the Spirit and our will, we can strive for it, and pray for it in the church and in our own relationships. We're not talking about *unity at all costs*, and it is not unity based on compromise of the truth of God. It is unity in faith, purpose, and love. As the leadership, the individual, and the church as a whole leans upon the Word and Spirit, then unity can be realized.

   Remember - *not unity at all costs.* Most issues are not a matter of faith, and so in these cases, make an effort to preserve unity. But if the conflict is over things such as Jesus' virgin birth, death and resurrection, then unity is not possible, even desirable! Even in these latter issues, make an effort to be a witness - and by all means, do everything in love.

RECONCILE - 2 Corinthians 5:18-21

   The church is __all about__ reconciliation! In verse 18, we see first that God reached out for us when we could not reach out to Him. It was through Himself in Christ that he reconciled us to Himself. Is that not awesome and mind-boggling? Only in His perfection could He offer Himself for our imperfection. We needed reconciliation to God, and Jesus was the only means for that to happen. Although this is true in every aspect, something has been missing in its deliverance to the masses.

   As is seen in Ephesians 3, the mystery of Christ's sacrifice is revealed to the world through the church. It is through the church that God and the world will be reconciled. Paul says in verses 14-17 that, because of Christ's love, He died for us. In verse 18, Paul said, "all these things (that is, that he died for us and we are now new creatures), are a gift from God. Then Paul said, "God, who reconciled us to Himself through Christ, and gave us the ministry of reconciliation." He goes on to say that we are ambassadors for Christ. It is clear that one of the main purposes of the church is to be ambassadors by being reconcilers. How do we do it?

   First, we must realize that Jesus is the only means for mankind's reconciliation. This may seem to be obvious to most conservative disciples, but to a lot of believers today, it seems they aren't so sure. (Now, they may not *say* it is not a priority, but their actions say something different.) If the church does not say (and act) as though reconciliation is its purpose, then that congregation (or individual believer) is not in the will of God, because reconciliation is God's will, and it should be ours, period.

   Second, the church must see that it is only through the church that this message will be delivered to the world. I don't understand why some people can be so motivated, and others not. Usually it is the fault of the leadership, not "discipling the disciple" (and/or the whole congregation) about the importance of us being reconcilers. Usually in this case, *the leaders them-selves* are not reconcilers or evangelists. This is why it's so important that leaders only be chosen from those who are qualified, knowledgeable, and committed to the will and Word of God.

   Third, the church, that is every believer that makes up the church, is to be God's ambassador, God's representative. This is not an option or just a good thing to do; it is *the purpose of the church,* and the sum of all its parts. To whom are we to be ambassadors to, each other, transfers or the world? No; to the world, the lost, those in need of God's reconciliation. We are the only Christ that someone may ever see. It's not our message, nor our agenda, we bring to the world, it is God's. We are His mouthpieces, His only means of bringing man to God through Christ. But, we may be the one who prevents someone from that reconciliation. If we are unwilling to be his ambassadors, many may go to their death - *with their blood on our hands*. God could have chosen another way, but he didn't, and we, the church, must come to grips with this and repent about not fulfilling this purpose of the church.

Fourth, we must be reconciled to God ourselves. How can we go and preach and try to reconcile, when many in the congregation still need to be reconciled? The first

> **How can we go and preach and try to reconcile, when many in the congregations still need to be reconciled?**

reconciliation is to God. The church or congregation is unfortunately not reconciled to God. Many think they're in a right relationship with God, but they are fooling themselves. Most are saved, but there is a need to continually come to the throne of God and be reconciled. Justification happens when we choose to follow Christ. Sanctification is a lifelong reconciling with God that needs to be done each time we sin, or wrong one another.

Fifth, we must be reconciled to each other. Is there someone in or out of the church who needs to be reconciled with you? This lack of reconciliation between you and others may stand in the way of your reaching out to them and others. This is where being hypocritical may come into play. If we are out there preaching reconciliation with God while having problems with, or even hating, our brother, how can we face the world? The world will see through it and ignore our message and us. It is a crime and a shame that we may stand in the way of another's salvation due to our lack of reconciliation with our brother and with the world. Let's say you complain about your worldly boss and can't get along with your co-workers. You will lose your witness, until you get your act together. Let's say you cannot get along with your family at home. This will hurt any witness you may have with friends and co-workers. Knowing the church's purpose may make us aware of the responsibility and, therefore, help us change our actions and reactions.

PRAY – Proverbs 15:29; Matthew 21:21, 22

To pray is to communicate. Without this communication with God, the church many times ends up like some of the churches in Revelation, who lost their first love. Only in prayer does a church keep the fires going and the communication doors open to God. Why should prayer be a part of the purpose of the church? Isn't prayer merely something we do, not what we are? One of the traditional beliefs about why we exist or were created is because God wanted to have companionship with others. Some would say He needed to create; I have some problems with that. If He needs us, that would indicate a flaw in His self-sufficiency. Within the Godhead there should be enough fellowship without the need for any outside subjects. This does not negate the fact that God has the right to choose to create as a matter of will and want.

Besides all this philosophizing, God desires our prayers and communication, and we need them also. So a part of our purpose is to communicate with God, and He with us. The bottom line is, we're talking about relationship, not just acquiring benefits. Herein lies the problem with most believers and their churches. Is a church (or individual) that is "doing" - but not communicating with God - in His will, and pleasing to Him? If we fail to fulfill our purpose of praying, then all the other areas will be short-lived or powerless. The church must also be "about the Father's business" in training and helping each disciple to learn how to pray and communicate with God. It is <u>our lifeline</u> with God!

Outreach – Acts 2:42-47

What does it mean for a church to have an outreach into the community? At first, you might think evangelism, but you can have evangelism without really reaching out to those in need. You can get on the street corner and preach the gospel but fail to reach out to anyone in your audience. It is true that when a congregation or individual reaches out to someone, the result may be a repentant heart and a saved soul, but let us refine the process more clearly. Outreach is to have compassion for someone in need, with the intent of meeting that need. Most churches fail when they reach out for numbers or decisions, not really intending to be compassionate. The goal is mercy and benevolence, not just evangelism. But just reaching out and meeting physical needs, without caring about their spiritual needs is also short-sighted and not at all what Jesus intended. He came to seek and save the lost, but in the process He had compassion on the people and took care of people's needs. So, both aspects are important ministries, and part of the overall purpose of the church as is illustrated in the church in Acts. They reached out to each other by meeting their physical and spiritual needs equally. The result of all this compassion was a great evangelistic outreach into the community as confirmed by the daily conversions the congregation had.

> **Most churches fail when they reach out for numbers or decisions, not really intending to be compassionate. The goal is mercy and benevolence, not just evangelism.**

Of course, the church cannot take care of all the world's needs - neither did Jesus, 100% of the time! He could have, but he'd have thereby put us in a position we could never reach. But for those "true believers" in the church with a genuine need, it seems to be a mandate that the church care for them. What is a genuine need? Widows and orphans are certainly prime candidates for help. This, though, calls for a commitment of support as <u>long as they need it</u>. There are those who have a genuinely urgent need resulting from some tragedy that's no fault of their own. They need help, but there is a limit to this help or benevolence; when the need is met, the help is ended. Creating dependence through ongoing help after the need has been destroys personal responsibility, and God does not want that to happen. (This, in fact, is what has happened with the current welfare system.) If recipients are willing to be trained or helped, then the church can help as much as possible. While preaching in a church in Indiana, a man approached me and asked for help from the church. He said he was out of work and needed help. It just happened that the Sunday before, one of our farmers in the church made the announcement that he needed help and was hiring. I told the man, and he contacted the member. Two weeks later, I ran into the man and asked him how the work was going and he said, "Well, I figured it out, and it was best for me to quit because I would make more money on welfare than farming."

If a person is able, there is a Biblical admonition for a person to work. The church should not offer handouts to lazy and unscrupulous individuals, in or out of the church. The main thing is that those in genuine need are to be helped, and those who are users should be taught a lesson and be helped with the means to take care of themselves.

Failing to take responsibility can result in even ignoring personal responsibility for sin. If people do not take responsibility in life issues, then they won't in spiritual issues, for both issues are tied together. A true disciple will not manipulate, use people, or find excuses to be lazy. He or she will be responsible, for that is the right thing to do.

> **Failing to take responsibility can result in even ignoring personal responsibility for sin. If people do not take responsibility in life issues, then they won't in spiritual issues, for both issues are tied together.**

Most churches fail to truly reach out into their community for a number of reasons. First, they never have seen outreach modeled. Since the government has taken over the role, and since churches seem to stay clear of the social element, it has been quite a while since churches have been involved. Now some efforts, such as the Salvation Army and inner city rescue ministries have succeeded, but far too often the local church regards them as something someone else does, so they don't have to be involved. Second, churches may not be equipped and motivated to do outreach in the community. Most ministers or leaders have not been trained as well. The far bigger problem, however, is they've not been motivated to the point where they see the need and are moved to do something. The result is they've abdicated their responsibility, so the State, or someone else, has stepped in. Third, they just don't want to be bothered by all the work it will take. This is the most damning reason of all. A church I was working with was moving into a new facility in the inner city. I suggested they might open up a soup kitchen at least once a week to reach out into the community. My response from one of the elders was, "That brings in all those needy people, and it is just too much work, and a mess taking care of them." Some just do not have a heart. "Someone else will do it, and if they don't, we still won't." How does Jesus view your congregation; as a passer-by, or a compassionate Samaritan?

Should each congregation be expected to be responsible? Yes, at least in part. What if the church as a whole, that is all the churches, were doing their part all across the land? What would be the results? I think two things would come from it. First, no Christian would ever need welfare. I might even go as far as to say the welfare system, as we know it, may never have been started. Second, more souls would be saved, and the church would not have the mark on it that it does. The reason the first church grew was, it took care of people's needs within the congregation and, therefore, brought more people in contact with the church and the gospel, and people were being saved daily. Suppose each church did something in its community through benevolent outreach, and multiply that by the number of churches and communities across the nation and the world. What impact would that have on the needy and on the growth of the church?

What will it take to grow the Church?

1. It will require the church to wake up and see that it is our responsibility to have benevolent outreach. Not to be like those who passed the needy man in the street, but rather like the Samaritan. Too often we seem to believe that we have the right doctrine and are doing all we need to do by proclaiming the gospel and saving souls. We want to help people in the future, in the eternal bliss of heaven but fail to realize that when we do give a cup of water or a bit of food to someone now, we're doing it for Christ! Christ was, and is, compassionate towards mankind. He wants His church, His disciples in the 21st century, to care like Him. When the disciple or congregation reaches out, people will be drawn into the eternal kingdom. The disciple and the congregation must always be open to new ideas and needs around them. What you did for the last person may be different than for the next.

2. It will take a strategy for each situation. The needs in each area may be somewhat different, but similar enough to build on other strategies elsewhere. The approach in the inner city may be different than in the suburbs or countryside. What may work with one person may not work with another. What may open up the heart of one to see, may close the heart of another who is blind.

3. It will take cooperation between churches. At this moment, the second largest church in the nation (in the thousands) and its mother church (in the low hundreds) are partnering together to reach out into the community near the mother church. The outreach has developed over the years into a more ethnically diversified area. The mother church is being assisted by its larger daughter (with funds and expertise) to reach out into the mother church's community. It may take a number of sister churches coming together to reach out and make an impact on the community or city they are in. Anything good done for others in the name of Jesus is good in the sight of Jesus, but it is important that it is done with the motive of love for them, first as a person, and second as a soul. But you might say their soul is more important than their physical situation. That may be theologically true in the long run, but in their eyes, physical need outweighs any- thing else.

4. It will require rethinking the purpose of the church in this area. What if there are no souls saved when you give a cup of water or a bag of food? The seed has been planted, either in their heart, or in the heart of someone who may be watching. Give - and God will give the increase.

5. It will take the development of people and ministries to meet people's needs. This is where the process will fail or succeed. We can preach, share the need, raise the funds, and cooperate with other churches and still fail if we don't motivate, and raise up men and women to develop and implement the ministries needed to meet these needs. The whole reason the seven deacons were chosen was because there was a need that was not being met. Ministries such as a food pantry fill this need today.

6. It will take the funds to support it. In most cases, herein lies the problem. Some may say, "We don't have enough money to do our own church projects and take care of those in need at the same time. Benevolence will have to wait." Here, working together with other churches will help. The point is not who gets the credit, but that the ministry gets done. At this point in history, (which may change with the next President), Mr. Bush has proposed an "Faith based Initiatives", in which the federal Government will designate funds to religious groups to help the needy. As long as there are no restrictions on the believers and actions, this may prove to be a possible solution to the problem.

SEND- Roman 10:13-15

The church is not to be self-absorbed with its own desires and grandeur, but to be concerned with sending others into the entire world. World mission is the church's mission. I have been a full-time missionary on the field in Russia and Poland for seven years, and am still on full mission support at this time. But it's hard for people interested in going into mission work to gather support and to keep it. I would say that 80% of those who would

> **The church is not to be self-absorbed with its own desires and grandeur, but to be concerned with sending others into the entire world. World mission is the church's mission.**

love to go on the field have been frustrated and discouraged to the point that few ever make it to the field. It usually takes 18 months to raise support. Over the years, I've known mission recruits, even at 18 months, failing to have the full amount needed. Even our mission, after 10 years, has not reached 100% of our needs and goals. Is there a better way? Some denominations require the churches to send their money to a clearinghouse, where some committee decides who gets to go. Others have no cooperation between churches, and the mission candidate is on his or her own to raise funds. To do this, the person has to be a salesman and a wonderful public speaker, or, if blessed, find someone who'll do it for him. But if he or she isn't, and can't find someone to tell his/her story, the chances are next to impossible (s)he will get enough to go. What if the work he'll be doing doesn't require this type of person? What if he doesn't have these gifts of fund raising, but has the gifts needed to do the work where he's been called? Too bad; he will have to stay at home. This is sad, and I feel it isn't in God's will.

Let's look at Paul in this situation. Paul would never have made it. He himself said he was not eloquent in speech, but he was the most successful missionary ever. How many people like Paul do we have out there who are qualified for the work, but not for fundraising? There must be a better way. Well, let's again look at Paul and his situation. His home church sent both him and Barnabas. Does that mean the elders put their hands on them and said "We send you now, go find the means to do it"? I think not. I believe their sending church supported them on at least their first journey. They sent them on their way with the means to do the work. This is another model that's being done in a number of churches today, known as "living link" support. That means the home church or sponsoring church supports them fully, or sees they have their needs met. In some cases, a church may be able to give 100% of the needed support. The church may see the missionary as a part of its staff and budget it in. It is a "no brainer" to add on staff after staff, especially as the church grows. This same idea must happen if the church is going to grow worldwide.

Another variation on this is that a home church, or "sending church" guarantees the candidate that the church will supply the amount needed after the person goes and raises as much support as possible. This is done with time limits and assistance from others in the congregation. This will take away a lot of anxiety that could be spent on preparing to go.

If the purpose of the church is to send, then why are we not doing it? Every church must have a part in sending someone, or a number of 'someones', to the field. Most churches are small and often can't provide full support for any one missionary on their own, but they should do all they can do. I would surmise that every person who's trying to go on the mission field has a home church of some kind, either the one in which they were brought up, or one in which they are now growing and challenged. These are the churches that must get behind their Timothy's, encourage them, and send them out into the harvest.

> **If you're concerned about souls, God will give the funds for both.**

The church is not fulfilling its purpose if it is not involved in sending others. The sending of others is the only way the world will know, and it is up to each congregation to be a part of helping and encouraging men and women to go, not just verbally, but financially as well.

I just heard of a church that cut some of its missionaries because they were into a building program and needed the funds. This is a sin. Where is the faith? This heresy must stop. If a church chooses buildings over souls, that is wrong. Oh, they say, "We are concerned about the growth of our congregation. We want to see people saved in our community." This is nothing but an excuse and a copout for your own projects. If you're concerned about souls, God will give the funds for both. If you have to cut or stop funding new missionaries to build a gym for fun and games, you had better check your priorities and repent. I know of preachers who circumvent missionaries from coming in because it might cause a problem and take away funds for their pet projects. God forbid this type of motive. Don't limit God, and don't rob Him or His called ones.

EDIFY- Ephesians 4:12-15

How many times have you heard, "No one really cared for me at that church". All they are concerned with was their cliques," or, "When I was sick, no one bothered to call on me," or "All they care about is what they can get from me." Have you heard this? Have you said this? Have you or your church ignored these statements of people?

One of the main purposes of the church's existence is to provide an atmosphere in which people will be naturally edified. What does it mean to _edify_, and who is to do the edifying? In Ephesians 4, we see a glimpse of what it means to edify. In verse 12, we see that the saints are to be equipped to do the work or service for the building up of the body. Now the "building up of the body" is what it means to edify. How does this happen? The best means is through discipleship, mentoring, and a good, consistent shepherding program. Now these are not to be just programs, but a means to help people grow and be fed, to encourage and come alongside other disciples, to be there when they need it, and to be admonished or directed when they need instruction or correction.

> **Many churches have split, and people left churches, over personalities and gossip, more than over any debate on doctrine.**

Building up, not tearing down is the phrase that describes the goal. If you were to keep a tally or list of all the comments made in the church about people, what would you find? Would you find more statements that were negative and critical, or positive and uplifting? I know in my experience, sadly, it may be the first. This would be different in each individual church, however, and it may only reflect a few who have a negative attitude at any one time. Now if you added what people said about the preacher, staff, and leadership that may make the list even more lop-sided toward the negative. If you look closely at the church in Acts 2, you will see that it was an edifying church at all levels.

I'm not saying that you overlook sins and disobedience in the church, but I am saying that when you think there is a time for discipline, do it with love and the intention of building up the brother or sister. When Paul was suggesting discipline in the Corinthian church, he was quick to teach that the discipline was for the purposes of restoration and building up, not tearing down or getting even.

If you, or someone you know, derive pleasure from gossip or tearing others down, you or they have a problem and need to repent and check the "log in your own eye". Many churches have split, and people left churches, over personalities and gossip, more than over any debate on doctrine. This should not be so. It is usually so when the church, and especially its leadership, fails to practice the God-demanded task of building up. There is no excuse for a discipled Christian to have these attitudes, or at least continue these attitudes throughout their

Christian life. I can understand it happening with a brand new believer, but for the most part, it comes from those who've been in the church for a long while. They are either ignorant, thoughtless, careless, or simply unsaved.

The bottom line is, do you love your brother? If so, treat him as such, and as you would want to be treated. Hmm, what a novel idea! If the church doesn't see its purpose as building up, then it will end up neglecting its purpose and spiral into tearing down. The church that wants to be healthy and grow will build up, not tear down.

How is this best done? Teach them to observe, and nurture them until they grow.

> **Strategy to work from: 1 The leaders must sit down and evaluate their purpose statement. 2. If a purpose statement doesn't exist, develop one based on the prime directives in the Bible. You might use the above acrostic as a guideline.**
>
> **3. Devise a plan to implement your purpose statement. 4. Commit to follow it.**
>
> **5. Encourage and equip each other to fulfill it.**

What is the Purpose of each Child of God?

First, to fulfill our Godly callings! We see in Ephesians 4 that each child of God has two callings or aspects of purpose to fulfill in his/her life. In verse one, Paul very clearly states that each believer has a calling to which he is called. This is the first of the calls, and it is expected of each disciple, regardless of who he is. We are called to "walk in a manner worthy of our calling." What is that calling? It is our call to be His disciple, His child of God. Each of us, when we meet the Lord, has a choice to either follow or run away. He is doing the calling, He is doing the drawing, and we just make the decision to follow that call. That being the case, we must do it in a worthy manner or way. Verses 2 and 3 show each of us how this is to be done in our daily life and walk. We've been called to be heirs with Christ, to be adopted children in His kingdom, and therefore, should be dedicated to walk in a humble and loving manner. It is a calling in which we worship Him and live to become like Him in all aspects of our being. Fulfilling this calling results in one's salvation and sanctification. In my book, _The Most Precious Thing_ you learn that the call is to be a disciple, a follower. In making this commitment to follow you then restore that most precious relationship with God through His Son.

> **The focus of the first calling is on our relationship with God; the second is on our relationship with man. In both cases, each disciple has the responsibility with those callings.**

The second calling we see in this passage is somewhat different, but related to the first. The first is general but not secondary, and applies to all; the second is more on an individual basis. It is each disciple's personal calling, ministry, or purpose. The text introduces the idea that Christ gave gifts to men. He explained by giving an example in verse 11. He gave some to be Apostles, prophets, etc. This calling is for the benefit of others. The first calling is for our benefit. Now it is true that when we share and help others, we are blessed, but the focus is on others. The focus of the first calling is on our relationship with God; the second is on our relationship with man. In both cases, each disciple has the responsibility with those callings.

> **Encouragement: 1. Every believer and disciple must see the existence of both callings. 2. He or she must be discipled in order to fulfill the first. 3. He or she must be taught what gifts are available. 4. Each disciple should be taught and directed in discovering their gifts. 5. They must be given a place and opportunity to use them.**

Secondly, it is our worship. God has created us, and hopes we will worship Him with our whole heart, in Spirit and truth. His highest pleasure is our genuine worship and dedication to Him. But in many cases, people who attend church feel that the church is there for them. Now they may *say* they're there for God, but their attitudes and actions say something different. I think all of us who have been a part of the church have, at some time, been guilty of being more focused on our wants than on worshiping God and building community. When a person comes out of church and complains about everything and everyone, where is that person's priorities and true worship? The worship service is not about what I like, although that may be important; it's about what God likes. Ron Dunn, in his sermon on "God is the Audience," made this point quite clear: "God is our object of worship, not man." When we complain, then our focus is not on pleasing God with a true heart, but on what keeps our interest.

> **Maybe sometimes we need to ask ourselves if God is going to sleep during our worship times and if we're wasting His time?**

Maybe sometimes we need to ask ourselves if God is going to sleep during our worship times and if we're wasting His time? If you remember more of what you didn't like and more of what others were doing and saying than what good was said, then maybe you need a checkup of your motives and priorities. Now of course, some church services are boring and unfulfilling, and this is most unfortunate. This, too, is an offense to God. God wants our best, not our leftover effort and enthusiasm.

The bottom line at this point is to realize that God wants our worship and dedication. This is part of our purpose as His creation. A mistake made in most of our lives is the inordinate stress upon formal worship on Sunday. The fact is that worship should be 24/7, not periodically, whenever we feel like it. Yes, this is easier said than done, but this 24/7 commitment still should not derail us from working towards this attitude. The only way we can improve on our worship time and quality, is if/when we are taught, shown, and most importantly, develop a heart for God that naturally leads to this kind of awareness and worship.

> **Attitude Adjustment: 1. Remember whose you are, and act accordingly. 2. Remember that what you do or don't do may affect others' worship and dedication. 3. God is our audience; He is listening and watching. 4. True worship is your calling, not an option.**

We will look more in-depth later into how a growing church and individuals worship, in Section Two's chapter on "Worship."

Power for the Child of God!

In Ephesians 3:11-21, we can see a glimpse of the Godhead's purpose as directed towards each of us. This is one of the most interesting and uplifting passages in the Bible. Again, we go back to the mystery of Christ's coming and His revelation through the church. By fulfilling His purpose, we now have the privilege of fulfilling ours. How can we do it? Well, we now have access through faith to God through Christ. Because of this, we can fulfill our purpose by going before God. We now have the ability to bow our knees in His presence. Wow, what a blessing! We also have been strengthened with power through the Spirit in the inner man. Wow, the presence of the Spirit within us! Then it goes on to say we are grounded in love because Jesus dwells in our hearts through faith. Wow, once again - the presence of God *in us*! That's not all. It says we will be filled with the fullness of God. And what are the results? We will be able to fulfill all that He asks because He is the power that works within us. If God is with us, then who can be against us? Who can keep the church as a whole from living out its purpose? Who can foil God's plan for your life and the people around you? It is you, it is I, and it is those who fail to follow God's purpose for our lives and the life of the church. Each of us chooses whether God will fulfill His intended purpose in our lives; it is not the devil who makes us choose, but those who lack the faith, and who fail to live out our purpose.

> **Who can foil God's plan for your life and the people around you? It is you, it is I, and it is those who fail to follow God's purpose for our lives and the life of the church.**

We don't have to settle for that defeat or those results. We have the power in us, and we have the means through the church God established to encourage, build up, and equip one another to fight the fight and be victorious in our quest to fulfill God's intended purpose for each individual and each congregation. So, let us not get in the way of God and His purpose.

Conclusion: In the next chapter you will discover what it takes to be a healthy, growing Church. When this is discovered, you're well on your way to fulfilling the purpose of the church!

The Healthy Growing Church!
Chapter Two

Church Growth Ingredients

What does a healthy growing church look like? Well, what does a healthy person look like? Good color, energy, good muscle, bones, good thinking processes, good eyesight, etc. Along those same lines, certain factors can tell us if a church is healthy.

Church growth is usually the natural result of church health. If the church is not growing, there's a good chance it isn't healthy. If a child of 10 isn't growing, that indicates that there's a problem. The only excuse for a church not growing would be if the church were in a pending ghost town. If the town is dying, naturally the church will suffer the same demise.

> Church growth is usually the natural result of church health. If the church is not growing numerically, there is a good chance it is not healthy.

The obvious question is, what defines a growing church? This is has been a heated debate for some time. Is it spiritual or numerical growth? Which is more important? Can we be overly concerned about one without neglecting the other? These are all-important questions for those involved in the life of the church. The churches that are growing, or are concerned about growing, usually have no problem with this debate. Typically, it is those churches that are satisfied with where they are that become defensive about the debate. They argue that spiritual growth is more important and that we shouldn't be concerned about numerical growth. But, as we will see elsewhere, Christ's commission is concerned about both - it isn't an either/or proposition. I propose that, if you are healthy spiritually, you can and should be concerned about numbers. Why? Two reasons should convince us. First, Jesus came to seek and save *all mankind,* and His wish is that they all hear, and come to salvation. That's a big number! Secondly, since every person is in need of salvation, if we aren't concerned about numbers, then we aren't concerned about people! The simple fact is that all will experience eternal punishment, unless they follow Jesus. They can't do this if they don't hear. If the church isn't concerned about numbers, then we will aid in people's destruction. A body, whose cells don't continually replace themselves with healthy new ones, will die.

To see if a person is healthy or alive, we check his vital signs. Does he have a pulse, and is the pulse strong? What's his blood pressure? What is his temperature? How does the heart beat? What do the fingernails tell us? So - what then are the vital signs for a healthy church? Peter Wagner gives us a list in his "Seven Vital Signs of a Healthy Growing Church." I would like to take the list and expound upon them.

Seven Vital Signs of a Healthy Growing Church
C. Peter Wagner

1. Good pastoral leadership
2. Biblical priorities being taught and lived
3. Evangelistic/Missions minded
4. Consistently growing larger
5. Celebration, Congregation, Cell
6. Mobilized laity
7. Unified Unit

       I was blessed to have C. Peter Wagner as my mentor in my doctorate program at Fuller Seminary. In one class he wrote these 7 Vital signs. I would like now to expand on these.

1. Good pastoral leadership! Different churches have different structures of leadership that guide the church. In Ephesians, the list of leaders includes apostles, prophets, elders or pastors, evangelists, and teachers. Whatever the makeup, the leadership needs to be visionary and Biblically sound.

       Sometimes a church grows numerically, simply on the personality of the preacher. If he falls or leaves, the church may fall. The strong church that has continued growth will not only have strong leadership but all the growth elements in place. The leadership that is concerned about the health and shepherding of the flock will help the church to have healthy growth. As we saw in Chapter One, when the leadership understands and commits to fulfilling the purpose of their roles and the overall purpose of their congregation, they will be in God's will, and He will bless that church.

> Pastoral leadership is a leadership that looks after its flock in all areas of its need. Every elder should be a pastor over some part of the flock, …

       Pastoral leadership is a leadership that looks after its flock in all areas of its need. Every elder should be a pastor over some part of the flock, or he'll become a controlling person, or find himself doing mundane things in the church. If only one person is expected to shepherd the whole flock, then only a limited amount of shepherding can be expected, for one man can only do so much. It's best that leadership is spread out so that the congregation may grow. More on how to be pastors and shepherds will come later in Section Two.

2. Biblical priorities being taught and lived! You might assume that every church has its priorities right. It's true that some churches don't major on promoting and implementing Biblical principles. Some focus on social themes, and don't really open up and apply Biblical principles. Some churches focus on emotionalism rather than content in their sermons. Studies have proven that churches focusing on social issues, at the expense of strong Biblical teaching, tend to decline. Churches focusing on moving their people by emotional means tend to grow numerically, but their spiritual growth is shallow. But, let's not make the mistake of assuming that just because a church teaches the right doctrine, it will produce healthy growth. A church that puts *all three* elements together in the church life will grow. A church that's concerned about the surrounding community, allows the Spirit to move in its members, and teaches the members how practically to put Biblical principles into practice, will grow consistently and healthily.

3. Evangelistic/Missions minded!

In most churches, this would be seen as two different areas: evangelism in your community, and missions in other countries. But, as we saw in the first chapter, making disciples includes both.

The congregation that is not winning souls is not going to fulfill the Great Commission in its area. Further, the congregation that doesn't help other missions will not help in the worldwide effort to fulfill the commission.

Each congregation must evaluate its growth during the past couple of years at least. How many additions, how many transfers, and how many people are still in the congregation after two years? Some churches have many new members, but mostly by transfer. This is not kingdom growth, but kingdom shifting. The Church did not grow; it merely shifted its members. Only conversion growth tells us if the church is growing. And those who are still in the church after a couple of years or so tell of our spiritual growth. The congregation that has no infusion of new blood will not have healthy growth.

4. Consistently growing larger!

I truly believe that a healthy church will grow in numbers, unless there are outside factors such as "land-lock", or "ghost town" conditions. The idea that "it's okay to be small for smallness' sake" is in direct opposition to the entire New Testament mission.

> Only conversion growth tells us if the church is growing. The congregation that does not have an infusion of new blood will not have healthy on going growth.

Why do churches want to stay small? Usually, it is for selfish reasons by some of the people in the church. Usually, it involves people who want to have control over what happens in their church. Notice I underlined *their* church. This is because they feel, for some reason, that they are the owner, protector, and boss of the church. If the church grows, then they will lose control and, therefore, they suppress anything that will help the church to grow. They usually won't acknowledge this, but it's un-deniable in what you see taking place. In each of these small churches, there's a threshold that the attendance will reach before the sabotage begins. If some leave, for any reason, then the next avail-able people coming through the door can fill their places. Lucky them! But once the spots are filled, others are not as welcomed. People who say, "I like small churches," will, in some cases, do what they must do to keep it small! This is sad, but true. This may even involve the preacher, as well. In order for a church to grow, it requires more than the preacher or staff doing the work. When the church operates, as it should, it will equip everyone to participate through using his or her spiritual gifts. This gives more opportunity for more people to come into the mix. The preacher, who does not want to give up any power or ego to help others find their place in ministry, may be sabotaging his own efforts. He wants to do it all, because it feels good, or because he's so insecure that he's threatened by the idea of giving up any leadership to others, fearful that he may lose control.

In some cases, a preacher or leader does not have the experience or the personality to grow a church. His personality is such that he can work well within a small group but will never be able to affect or feel comfortable with what has to be done to get the job done.

A church with this 'small-time' mentality, simply because they like smallness, cannot be in God's will. It is God's will, and pleasure that we "Go and make disciples". To make disciples, you must get them, gather them, and keep them long enough to teach them. If you do this, then you will grow, unless you drive others away in the meantime. Sacrifices must be made for growth, and most churches don't want to make them in order to grow.

A church in Florida decided they were comfortable with attendance of around 650. By most standards, a church of 650 is a large church, but by today's standards, it's more accurately considered a medium one. They decided that, when they reached this number, they would split off 150 to start a new body in another part of the city. Then when they grew again, they would repeat the process. At one point, they had started nine other churches. In most cases, each child is larger than its mother, but in total, all together they are on the verge of "mega-church" proportions. Few men are mega-church ministers, but many ministers can handle a medium sized church. God can use any group. The same type of strategy could happen with a smaller church. A church of 300 could stretch to 350, then split off 50 to start a new church.

5. Celebration, Congregation, Cell!

It is important to note that, if any one of these components is missing, the overall health of the church may suffer, or at least not be as potent as possible. Celebration can happen in the cell, but on a very limited basis. If anyone thinks everything can be accomplished in the cell, he is mistaken. The cell has its place in the church, but it is not capable of celebration on the "whole congregation" level. Many cells, which should be contained within family structures or sectors, make up the congregation. It's only when all come together, that you get true celebration. All these aspects put together will promote a healthy, growing church.

6. Mobilized laity!

A church that has mobilized laity is a congregation that's using its giftedness. In this congregation, there is no longer the 80/20 split of workers and non-workers. The goal of every leader is to see that everyone participates in some way, and helps each person discover his or her giftedness - and use it.

It seems that, in most cases where this isn't taking place, those who are not active or happily involved, usually end up complaining and putting down those who are. Those who want to do nothing and complain should be encouraged to go somewhere else and do nothing! I know this sounds harsh, but we're talking about a potential cancer that will eat at the congregation and keep it from its mission and, at the same time, keep it unhealthy. But the church that makes the goal to train and empower every member to serve through his/her giftedness will see growth. It cannot be any other way. You will have more ministers at every level; more needs being met, and more outreach and discipleship being accomplished.

> Nothing destroys momentum and growth like divisiveness and selfish agendas. When the body is divided or not in harmony, growth suffers.

7. Unified Unit!

Nothing destroys momentum or growth like divisiveness and selfish agendas. When the body is divided or not in harmony, growth suffers. When there is discord, growth is impossible because people are unable to grow while they harbor ill feelings or pursue selfish agendas at the same time.

Most churches have the dream of reaching new people and getting them involved in the church. But, when a church has a reputation of infighting and problems, then people will not want to be a part of such a group. Why should they change their problems for those of a group of strangers, or souls masquerading as representatives of Christ? This is a grave problem that most churches are not even aware of. In some cases, some of those involved don't have a clue; sadly, in others, people don't care, as long as their felt needs are taken care of. This should not be, for it is God's Church, not the people's church.

What is Unity? I like - and stand on - the premise: "In essentials unity, in opinions liberty, and in all things love." This mantra, upon which the restoration movement began, "In essentials unity," is still fresh and needed today. The first thing one must do is to be sure to know the difference between what is *essential* and what is *opinion*. This, of course, is where the rift comes: agreeing on what are, and what are not, the essentials. This, of course, is where churches have split and denominations have developed. How can we come to an understanding on what are the essentials that we need to stand on and the opinions that we should not divide over?

The essentials are based on finding the truth that counts. It is not just truth, but truth that is the base and foundation of the gospel. The essentials are the elements that are the very foundations of our salvation and our centric view of who Jesus is. The kind of music you choose, or the elements of how you worship, are insignificant compared with how you understand, and what you believe, about the deity of Jesus. How you see Jesus determines your essentials.

Unity is not 100% agreement, nor is it always compromising to the point that you give up everything. It is not unity at all costs. It's true that, because we're human, we'll have conflict. It's unavoidable, because we are all free-will beings with the right to our own opinions and views. That being the case, we will all, at some point, have conflict with those with whom we come in contact in our daily walk. The conflict isn't the problem; it's how you deal with it, and with the people who are involved. It isn't the conflict that's most destructive; it is unresolved conflict that causes problems.

Where does disunity begin? Philippians 1:27.

> It isn't the conflict that's most destructive; it is unresolved conflict which causes problems.

Most problems and divisions in the church today are not a result of false doctrine but of personality and selfishness. Almost 90% of problems that arise are due to personality problems or conflicts. If we resolve these, then we will be a healthier people and church. Some people participate in congregational life from a carnal basis rather than a spiritual one. Usually, they either have had bad role models in the church, they have not been discipled, or worse yet, they have not truly been converted. (Or, if they *had* been converted they are not allowing the Spirit to have control.)

Therefore, when a person is driven by, or acting upon, any of the above scenarios, it is very likely there will be conflict that may lead to disunity. If selfishness is the basis of a person's actions, that person will stop at nothing to fulfill those desires. Unity is based upon concern for others' opinions, as well as yours. If it does not go against the essentials, then there should never be a hint of disunity.

Personality conflicts are at the center of most conflicts. When we don't understand others, or even more basic, when we don't understand ourselves, we are on the precipice of disunity. An un-informed "D" will not understand why an uninformed "S" acts the way he does, and vice versa. Most often the difference is taken personally, and then the conflict begins. Ignorance is no excuse for this misunderstanding. Once each person knows himself and why others act the way they do, then the church will be on its way to more healthy relationships and less conflict. If the problem is personality then there is also hope. Learning about your personality is the first place to start. I suggest when a person becomes a Christian, a personality profile test be taken, and a year or two later, taken once again to measure personal growth. If we're aware of our personality type, we can work on any aspects that may be seen as negative. We will look at this further, later on.

How can you have unity? Galatians 3:28 and Phil 1:27. The church that is unified in its direction and in its love will not be able to keep people away. God works with people who are in unity with him and the rest of the church. If the church is going in different directions, then it cannot live up to its potential. God will not be able to bless and use each person as He would - and could - if there was unity in the body.

So what must a church do to promote and develop unity?

1. Agree to disagree! None of us are infallible, even though some of us may act like it. How many times in your life have you been proven wrong? If I feel I have all the facts, and am convinced of something, then I will usually disagree, but I'd better be sure before I make an argument. We all should seek peace first. We must be sure that, if we disagree, we don't make it personal or divisive. Be warned, the moment you think you stand in your opinion, you will find yourself falling in your ignorance. It isn't worth it to the kingdom, or to the relationships in the church, to have division over most of things on which we disagree.

2. Agree to work things out. That is, understand the other's view and honor other person's right to take a stand. Agree to disagree, with the stipulation that both will search for the truth in the other one's argument. In some things, it isn't even worth continuing the discussion if it might lead to controversy. If it isn't an *essential*, then it may be best to let it go and move on.

3. Understand others' personality bents, and try to work with each other on this basis. Most problems in the church usually stem from personality conflicts and misunderstandings. If we were to understand our personalities first, then we would learn our weaknesses and strengths. This would help us understand why we act and react as we do, why we get along with some people and not others, why others seem to tick us off and cause problems in our lives, and why we do the same to others. The more we know about ourselves and others, the more we will promote unity and harmony in the body.

4. Learn to honor, love, and respect one another. Most divisions and controversies begin when we don't respect others as we do ourselves. When we gossip and back bite, we accomplish no good. The fastest way to create disunity is to hear that someone has talked about you or someone else you care about. The sin of gossip can be so hurtful that it can cause someone to lose his or her faith, or at least his or her trust in the Church. You might object with: "Our trust must be in Christ." True, but if Christ is not seen in His followers, their faith (especially

that of new believers) may be shaken by the uncontrolled tongue of a gossiper. There is no difference between a gossiper and a murderer in God's eye, and gossip's results will breed spiritual murder.

5. Don't demand your way, unless in conflict of essentials. Be sure though, it is *Biblical* essentials, not your own pet peeves. The old saying still holds true in the Church today, "In essentials unity, in opinions liberty, in all things love." Deciding what are the essentials and what are not is the subject of another book. One of the essentials is that the church be unified - not at all costs, or at the cost of truth and absolutes, but in every other context.

6. Make decisions based upon consensus and direction of the Bible and Holy Spirit, not divisive voting. When decisions are based on voting, there's a 100% chance of division. *Why even go there?* Why put the church in the position to have divisions? Anything you can do to get away from voting, will be of benefit to the church, and likelihood of division can be greatly lessened. Voting can - and does - polarize, while consensus decision-making usually promotes unity and dialogue.

7. Don't let your agenda get in the way of God's! How many times have you seen or heard of a church splitting over the agendas of individuals in power? For example, the Bible is clear that we are to seek and save the lost. But, if a leader says "We like a small church and are going to do all we can to keep it that way", they're going against the wishes and direction of Jesus Himself. This kind of attitude breeds contempt for God and invites division from those who want to follow God's leading. When a man or woman wants control in the church, at the expense of growth, he or she is the one causing division, and needs to be removed from power or influence. Even more appalling is when someone's agenda is his/her own selfish desires. "I want blue carpet, I want this or that, and if I don't get it, I'll just quit or take my money someplace else." The response should be, "Be sure to close the door as you leave." The church should not pamper those who want to cause division. We should try to show them their error, <u>with love</u>, and hope they see it and repent. If it is a non-essential, compromise can be an option, but it should never become divisive.

What is the cost of disunity? Or, what is at stake? John 17:20-23.

There is a lot at stake when the church has disunity. In John, we see Jesus praying for those who would come. Two times Jesus said that unity is important so the world will be drawn to Christ. If the church has unity problems, this will affect those who are outside. The world is watching to see if there is anything worthwhile or different in the church. When the world sees selfishness and fighting, they don't want to be part of a group like that. Sometimes, the church seems more immature than the world. Why would people living in a dysfunctional world want to enter into a dysfunctional church?

> When a church fights and argues over minor, selfish things, the world watches and is turned off.

　　Let us be frank and honest. When a church fights and argues over minor, selfish things, the world watches and is turned off. What happens when the world is turned off? What happens when a person is turned off and runs away? The plain fact is that the person will go into eternity without Christ. In other words, they will go to hell. Be assured that the disunity over minor things will cause people to run away from Christ, and their blood will be on the hands of those causing disunity. This may sound harsh, but so are the results of our infighting and bickering.

Even those in the church will be affected. The mature, or those who know where they stand, will either try to solve the problem or they will pack up and go somewhere else. Those who are young or immature will not be able to handle it and will be turned off or away from the Church and, in some cases, from Christ all together. Is there more at stake than winning your way? If argument is selfish and opinionated, then it is an atrocity that people are turned away. We need to grow up and see the consequences of our actions.

Responsibility of the leadership and unity in the Church!

In Ephesians 4, the leadership is charged with keeping the unity in the faith. If not, then they will not be able to keep the work on track or the people intact. The Spiritual destiny and outcome of those turned away by church members and inept leaders will be on the hands of the leaders. Therefore, it is important that each leader and body of believers is under the understanding that what happens in the church is of importance to the survival of the souls of those who are put under their care.

Let us look closely at this passage. In this passage, those who have been given gifts of leadership have the responsibility to lead and care for those they are leading. In verse 11, we see the types of leaders. And then in verse 12, we see that the overall task is to equip the saints to do the work. This is where many leaders fail, including the elders, ministers, and teachers. That is, they do not see the importance of getting everyone trained and involved in some type of ministry. We've failed to train every member, nor do we expect them to do some type of work or service for God. Verse 13 goes even further and tells us that each leader's goal is to maintain unity, and see that every believer is on the road to maturity. How is this done? In later chapters, you'll see ways to bring this all to fruition. But, it is important to see here that unity will take place, in part, when each person understands and accepts his/her responsibility in God's body and service.

Jesus prayed to the Father that His followers would all be one. This is one of the most important prayers Jesus made while here. Without oneness, the whole health of the church or body is at stake. This is true for the Church as a whole, and for every congregation that makes up the whole. In accordance with the whole, when unity is not a priority, denominations result. For the local church, this is where splits can occur. In the majority of cases, unity is broken over selfish, non-doctrinal issues. Most denominations are usually centered on differences in doctrines. Whatever the case, it is how the leadership handles (or ignores) each problem that determines the outcome.

> REMEDIES: 1. Be sure that those who are in leadership are qualified. 2. Be sure they know what it truly means to be a leader in the church. 3. Be sure that all understand the importance of unity, coupled with love and truth.

How much faith does your Church have?
This faith will determine what kind of church you will be.

A growing church meets needs!

The difference in why one church grows and another doesn't is usually dependent on whether it meets people's needs. These needs are both within the church body and in the world. We see in the ministry of Jesus that he met people's needs.

> The difference why one church grows and another doesn't is usually dependent on whether it meets people's needs.

He met them where they were in life, even if they were not a part of His following. He saw the dignity and the need of mankind. Jesus was no respecter of persons; He only loved people with compassion.

The first church showed the world around it that it cared for those in the fellowship who were in need. This demonstrated to the community what true love and oneness were. This was a major factor in the growth of the church. What made it even more wonderful was, this wasn't something they decided to do as a church growth strategy, it was from their heart and their love for one another. The people on the outside could genuinely see what was taking place. If a church tries to just plan programs without truly doing it from the heart, oftentimes their efforts will fail.

How will the 21st century church meet needs? Let's look at some areas that need to be mentioned in order for a church to be healthy and growing.

Church member needs.

In Acts 2, we see the grand old example of how church members need to treat one another. Congregations many times end up just being a place for social action and/or gatherings, forgetting their need for community. In some cases, I have seen secular, community-based organizations developing and meeting needs of individuals and the community, rather than the church. Of course, the local body is not to take care of *everyone's* needs, but it must try to at least take care of its own. Would there have been a need for our current welfare system if the church worldwide had taken care of its own? I think not. A growing church will endeavor to meet the needs of its flock, both spiritually and physically. This should be obvious to most of the church; unfortunately I've found this is not the norm. People understand that meeting one another's needs is a part of their mission or work but fail to implement it. Let us look at this passage for more insight.

Why did the church have so much favor with the community around it? They took care of their own. They met each other's social and emotional needs. They met each other's physical needs. They truly loved, and had concern for, one another. This is inviting –even contagious! Normal people would want to be a part of a family like this. This is why they grew and grew.

Can the church today become like that of the first century? Of course, they had the Apostles, and many who had actually seen or been with (or knew someone firsthand) who had been with Jesus. Was this the difference? The truth is, people are, "All about now" people.

That is, what happened in the past is not as crucial as what is happening at this moment in time. All the children of Israel could think about was to complain about the lack of variety of food, but had forgotten how God provided for them to escape across the sea. The same is the case with the people in the first century. Had the first church only preached Jesus, without showing the love of Jesus, through taking caring for their immediate needs, there wouldn't have been nearly as much success. The world today is no different; people don't want to *hear* about Jesus' love, they want to *see* Jesus' love through us!

A church that wants to grow must not do things just to grow. There must be a genuine concern and love for others, otherwise people can see through it. The first church was spontaneous and genuine; there were no pretensions or programs. When people had needs, they were met. Community was the center of focus of church life.

Community needs.

This may seem obvious, but in most churches the needs of the many are overlooked for the needs of the few. When I say 'few', I mean those already in the church. Of course, the church <u>must</u> take care of the needs of its own, and focus on their needs, sometimes at the exclusion of those in the world. It's true that in Acts 2, those in the community were astounded by the love and care the church in Jerusalem had for each other. Every need was being met, and the world around them was attracted and converted. But, when does a church shift its focus onto the surrounding community? Or, should it see meeting community needs as its responsibility? How far and how much

> The world today is no different; people don't want to hear about Jesus' love, they want to see Jesus' love through us.

effort should be spent on meeting needs in the community? Each church must determine what its priority is and, if at all, what efforts will be made to help the community?

This may sound ridiculous to some who read this. You may say, "Of course, we must meet the community's needs", but actions and philosophy indicate otherwise. Most churches seem to be self- absorbed with their own buildings and programs. It's easy to spend most, if not all, of the time on the support and self-preservation of their own status quo. But you may say: "We are concerned about growth and are reaching out into the community!" In most of these cases, the effort targets *churched* people rather than *non-churched* people. It's easier (and much less costly) to encourage those who have some affinity to transfer membership to your church, than to reach out to those in need. It's easier to care for a 'non-infant' transfer, but much more time, cost, and effort will go into ministering to non-Christians, or babes in the faith. But, when the church begins making inroads into the community, the world will listen.

While working with a church in Poland, I suggested to one of the elders that, since a lot of people were in need of food or clothing, the church might open up a soup kitchen once a week to the public. His response was, "I really don't think that's a good idea. If we do, we'll have to deal with a lot of people's problems, and that would be too much work." *What are we here for*? To reach the world, help them in their time of need, and give them the answers through a relationship with Jesus, or to be *comfortable* in our little religious world?

Church paid staff or ministers' needs.

In general, those who minister full-time for the Lord are considered second-rate in many arenas. Even within their own congregations they may hear, "They're not really working, or if they do, it's only on Sunday." I have actually heard some say this. Some in the church who've seen bad examples, or who have ignorant viewpoints has perpetuated the belief that "ministry is not a real job". Some ministers made a bad name for themselves by their laziness, but that's the way it should be viewed - their laziness, not general chauvinism towards the whole ministry. Of course, there have been abuses by some high-profile TV preachers, but this again should not, in general, call into suspect the entire system.

The financial, social, spiritual, and physical health of the church's leader should be a concern of the body. The Bible says that those who serve full-time should be given a place of honor and respect. This is very rarely practiced in our churches. In many of our churches, the minister is seen as a hireling; this should not be. Are they better or more spiritual than non-full-time believers? No, but because they have decided to give of their time fully for the Lord's work, they should be respected for that decision. I've seen, and experienced, planting churches without adequate support. The pressure to survive, to put food on the table, takes a lot of time away from the ministry. I've heard people say, "If we pay them too much, they will get the big head, so we need to keep them humble." I know, in some cases, when the church is small or young, it can't meet all the financial needs, but that should only be temporary, if the church grows. Most churches don't grow because they don't pay a man enough to stay and help it grow.

> If a church, time after time, goes through a preacher every year and a half (average of the majority of our churches), then there may be a problem with those churches.

If 20 working adults tithe, they'll be able to pay the minister's salary, a salary that is in the middle range of those who are giving. Another 20 will be able to take care of all the other general expenses. Therefore, a church of 40 adults who tithe will be able to take care of both general needs and their minister's needs. If you have any say in providing for the minister and staff's needs, realize that if they are taken care of, the church will usually be taken care of as well. Unfortunately of course, some ministers, even if they're paid well, still don't live up to their obligations. This is another problem; this is their problem, but their needs are the church's problem, and should be taken care of by the congregation.

Not only are there financial needs of the paid leaders; there may also be personal needs in the ministry by the third or fourth year. In some cases, the man wasn't prepared for the job. In other cases, his area of giftedness didn't relate to that type of ministry, or he wasn't truly called. In many such cases, the man may be destroyed and discouraged by churches that hire him. Many small churches remain small for a reason; this isn't the place to discuss that issue. In many of them, they're dysfunctional. If a church "goes through" a preacher every year and a half (average of the majority of our churches), there's obviously a problem with the church! It simply can't be *the preacher* who has the problem in every situation! Many small churches can only afford a part-time man, a young preacher recently out of college. He is just "getting his feet wet", and they think they have to "keep him humble" and in line. In this scenario, both lose! The church never learns, and so continues the practice, the young minister gets discouraged and quits, and the story is repeated across our nation. If the church wants - and <u>wills</u> - to grow, it must nurture its own workforce with love and care.

> REMEDIES: 1. Treat the full-time workers with respect and honor; this is Biblical. 2. Pay them enough so they can minister without worrying; be fair to them. You would want your job to give you a raise and pay you enough to take care of your family. 3. Don't expect the ministers to do all the work, but do expect them to help all the others do their service. 4. Be honest and up front; do not play games and go behind their backs and play politics.

How are you to fulfill God's intention for this church? Of course, this "you" is plural, but at the same time singular. It mandates *the whole*, working together to make the changes necessary to go forward. This goal can only be met when each part is in unison, in mind, direction and Spirit. What responsibilities to which each of us need to yield? As we continue in our study, let us look at the attitudes and changes "you" need to make to help the church grow in your community, as well as around the world.

CONGREGATION'S RESPONSIBILITIES:

The church is not the only focus of our work. What is? The world is the main focus of our ministry. (Agree/Disagree).

Both of these views have become extremes in their own right. Some churches have placed more effort or emphasis on one or the other. Some churches place most of their effort or time on taking care of themselves, on nurturing and internal growth. The world is a concern, but not as much a priority as maintaining its own *status quo*. Most of their resources are spent on themselves. The result? Numerical growth may be diminished, by lack of outreach into the community.

The second group focuses on social aspects of the world at the expense of spiritual growth of their own. They also fail to grow numerically, and fail to prevent "church flight" because they aren't concerned about their own needs in the word.

What's needed is a combination of both. The Great Commission is thus balanced, giving half to the world and the other to the spiritual growth of those in the church. The healthy church will grow in both areas. No dichotomy, no 'wars', but rather a strategy to fulfill both obligations.

Why does "our church" become our main focus? This is a crucial question that many fail to ask. They fail to ask it because asking may mean admitting a need for change in their lives, and in the ways the church carries out its ministry.

First, it's all they know. They don't know any other way; it's what they've seen modeled for the past few generations. Sadly, few people will take the initiative or 'go out on a limb' to seek out what is the truth or to seek alternatives to the present structure. This is what makes the difference between a leader and a non-leader. But some leaders can only lead by direction, while others lead by intuition and creativity. The latter are pioneers, the former conformists. Both are needed in the church, but the pioneer is hard to find. Pioneers seldom need outside motivation, merely outside help and confirmation.

Second, it's more comfortable to focus on self than on others. This is obvious in most people's lives, and it bleeds over into the church. Change is hard and complacency easy. People are people, and the tendency in the world is to 'take care of *number one*'. But it should not be this way in the church. Churches can be selfish as a whole. That is, they can become concerned and wrapped up in their own agendas. This may include a new building, a new sound system - anything that may enhance their situation. This is not wrong in and of itself, but if it gets in the way of saving souls or sending others out with the gospel, the congregation may have priority problems.

Two ways of going forward!

First is being sure the basics are covered. These are the areas that are not optional and must be done. These are the things the church must provide. This is *scriptural*.

Certain things must be included in the normal function of a healthy church. The church is obligated to provide doctrinal teaching that leads to spiritual disciplines in each believer's life. It is here that many churches fail to meet personal spiritual needs. Most churches provide times for group and corporate meetings, but fail to spend time in personally discipling members. Therefore, in some cases, individuals may be lost in the shuffle. The church is also obligated to provide times of gathering, both corporately and in small groups. Things like teaching, communion, worship, and fellow-ship are basics that must be offered.

> **REMEDIES: If every person is individually assigned a mentor or discipler, especially in his first two years of new birth, then this nurturing will help in developing his needed spiritual foundations.**

Second is ministry and gift-based ministries determined by the gift mix and the needs of the congregation and community.

This is contextual and Spirit-led. Excluding the basics mentioned above, no ministry should be done if there are no spiritually gifted people desiring to carry out the ministry. It is better to wait, than to begin without trained gifted people, because if no gifted people desire to serve, then there may be no Spirit guidance in this area. This will only provide an opportunity for frustration and mediocrity because people are doing things on their own, without desire or spiritual power. Frank Tillapaugh's book "*Unleashing the laity*" is a great source in this area.

> REMEDIES: The place to start is by not asking for volunteers for ministry. Rather, deploy people by their gifts. First, find out what each person's gift is. Secondly, either add them to existing ministries, or create one that will use these gifts.

Of course, both the basics and the contextual ministries are to be guided by the Spirit, and both are to be Biblically based in guidelines and practice. But the first has already been written down, and the second is yet to be written. The first is for every Christian to be involved, and the second is based upon the needs of the moment and the individual.

After the basics, the ministries should be initiated when a need exists and there are enough gifted people desiring to take on the ministry. If there is a perceived need, but not enough gifted or desiring people, then it should not be done until both are in place. To do so before everything is in place runs the risk of putting people in the wrong area of service, and that will end in frustration and 'burnout' as well as put a bad taste in people's mouths. Then, the next time something is tried, you will hear the old cliché, "We tried it, but it didn't work."

We need to have a framework to work from. **Develop a sense of who we are as God's people. Know where God wants us to go, and get to know who He has put in our path to minister to. How do we do this? We need to have a ministry that is:**

1. Evangelistically based! Many churches, typically small churches, have no sense of evangelism. Usually a church stays small by choice. If they have an attitude that 'small is what they want', then evangelism is a threat to that smallness. What they hold dear emotionally and traditionally is also that which leads to inertia in evangelism. The Great Commission must become their battle cry, not inertia.

> You don't use this as a ploy to attract new people, but you do it because you have compassion for others and are lovingly meeting each other's needs.

2. Need based! The church of today can see the best example of church growth that we've already seen in Acts 2. The reason is that each individual in the first church was concerned about the needs of others. The result wasn't just talking about needs, or teaching about needs, but actually doing something about people's needs. The world then saw how the church took care of its flock and, therefore, the world was attracted to the fellowship. Don't use this as a ploy to attract new people, do it because you have compassion for others and are lovingly meeting each other's needs. Meeting one another's needs will grow a church faster than anything - unselfish love that meets needs.

3. Gift based! A church can fulfill the first two things, and still fail in this area. What will that matter in the success of evangelism and meeting needs in the local church? We can see, in many churches, one or two are done well - at the expense of the other. But in some cases, both are successful in these two areas, but lacking in workforce. When a church doesn't have their people ministering within their giftedness, then the success and the health of the church will suffer. All three parts must be evident in order for healthy, successful growth. Without this third aspect, the church may have workers or servants who end up frustrated and ineffective, because they're trying to fulfill the first two things we mentioned above, outside of their giftedness, as we have touched on before.

REMEDIES: The established church should make an effort to equip and find the gifts of every member, and then there should be places for them to serve based upon their gifts. If there is no place, create a ministry, when there are enough gifted people ready to start it.

REMEDIES: A new church plant should target the end of its second or third year to have its believers *officially* identify their gifts through the gift's questionare. I am not saying they wait two years to let people find and use their gifts, but using this tool to soon will run the risk of a false result when there is no evidence of the gift in experience.

We can invite, and have evangelism campaigns, but if we do not take care of people, then they will not come back. Seventy-five percent of people surveyed usually stay in a church in which they have at least two to three good relationships within the first two months. If there is no plan in the church to provide this or no encouragement to make it happen, it will not happen by chance. So a church must make an effort to get people together. In the chapter on shepherding, you will learn about family groups and how they naturally make this happen and therefore close a lot of the back doors.

> When you have a church that is bearing the Fruit of the Spirit, especially that of love, it will attract others to your body.

Some say I want quality, not quantity, but true quality results in quantity. It is a copout to excuse lack of growth for the pursuit of quality. Usually, those who are small are that way because they do not want to commit to doing what it takes to help the church grow. Again, growth will be a by-product of genuine, healthy, quality growth.

God will not send people to churches that will not take care of them. He will, though, send them to churches that win, nurture, equip, and send its believers into the world and community.

The more you do with your talents or gifts, the more He will give you or bless you in regards to your gift and ministry. Look at Exodus 31:1-6. God gifted these men not only with abilities but also with wisdom and understanding to use them. God will do the same today for each child in the church. Believe it, pray for it, and allow God to use you.

God expects faithfulness and fruitfulness (John 15:8, 16; Colossians 1:10). Not only does God want a church to fulfill their basic obligations of preaching, teaching, and worship, but also to be fruitful. What does it mean to be fruitful? There are two basic answers: the fruit of the Spirit, and the fruit of your labor. This will include both a changed life and the result of evangelism. If you have a church that is bearing the fruit of the Spirit, especially that of love, it will most likely attract others to your body. Again, remember the first church and their love, and see that the result was favor with people in and out of the church.

Churches grow <u>Warmer</u> through <u>Fellowship</u>
"   "   "Deeper"   "Discipleship"
    "   "   "Stronger"   "Worship"
    "   "   "Broader"   "Ministry"
    "   "   "Larger"   "Evangelism"

Churches grow <u>Warmer</u> through <u>Fellowship.</u> If a church fails to provide fellowship and times for community the usual result is coldness. Ask yourself as a congregation, "How do we come across to visitors?" Is the answer cold or friendly? Make an effort to visit with your visitors; ask them, and if you don't like the answer, search yourselves as a congregation for the reason why. Do not assume you're friendly, don't try to ascertain without asking those who don't come back. Make the effort to see what others think about you.

Churches grow <u>Deeper</u> through <u>Discipleship</u>. Discipleship, as you will learn more in depth in section two, is the place where believers are challenged to grow - not by hearing alone, but by change of attitude and lifestyle.

Churches grow <u>Stronger</u> through <u>Worship</u>. In Hebrews 10:23-25, we see that in assembling together we encourage and strengthen one another to grow and do good deeds. The individual and congregation both grow stronger when we grow together. You will learn more about true worship in section two.

Churches grow <u>Broader</u> through <u>Ministry</u>. As a church adds to its outreach and ministers more to the community, it grows wider as well as deeper. It is in your outreach that ministry is truly realized, and people are brought into the kingdom. Now as the Congregation expands its ministries, it also expands its responsibilities, and increases a need for more workers. But if you are mobilizing the flock by finding and using each member's giftedness, then both will expand at the same time.

Churches grow <u>Larger</u> through <u>Evangelism</u>. Now, of course, you can grow larger without any evangelism. As we have referred to it before, that's called "sheep shifting", not true kingdom growth. The local church grows, but not the kingdom. It is only through evangelism ("birthing" new members) that you produce genuine growth.

Practical Challenges:

1. Repent over disunity, over apathy, and over thoughtless routine, but unite in prayer and common work.

2. Develop Christ's vision to saturate your territory. (Try to see through Jesus' eyes.)

3. Develop evangelism and discipleship goals.

4. Know your territory, people's needs, and the community's needs.

5. Focus on spiritual growth and commitments to find your gift; your place in the body. Have "everybody do something so that some don't do everything!"

6. In the next 12 months, if each baptized believer will win one and keep one, then you will grow.

7. Are you willing to do the things necessary to take care of the new babes in Christ?

Realize there are changes when a new baby arrives. Are you willing to do the work?
   What changes will you have to make, to make room for new people?
   Are you willing to make them feel welcome and a part of the fabric of the fellowship, or body? If not, then why not? Be honest!

IMPORTANT TEST: Compare attendance figures from two years ago to now. How many additions have you had? Does your attendance reflect the additions? If not, then you're probably not retaining those you're adding. Also, of those who have left, are a bigger percentage recent converts? If they are, then your church is subconsciously running them off for some reason.

Preaching for Growth

Growing the church is a long process that does not happen overnight. One way a preacher can help in the growth of the people is to plan his preaching for growth. I first learned of the importance of planning your preaching in a seminary class under Dr. Wayne Shaw at Lincoln Christian Seminary.

It is important that a preacher knows where his people are and where they need to be in both knowledge and change of life. To promote growth, the minister must plan his sermons in a way that will meet the needs of the people. He must be insightful about what their needs are and about how to get people there through teaching and preaching. The goal must be to change character as well as to impart new information. To do this, you have to have a plan that will make wise use of preaching and teaching to systematically take the people from where they are to where they need to be.

To fulfill this task, the leader must have the gift of prophecy. Not that of foretelling new revealed information, or a word of knowledge about a person, but an ability to have insight into how to lead the people. One way to lead people is through preaching and teaching. A person who has this gift can see where his people are, where they need to be, and how to apply the Scripture to their lives to get them where they need to be. He must be able to share what will happen if people don't make a decision to follow Jesus or follow His plan for each congregation. This is New Testament prophecy.

> The goal must be to change character as well as to impart new information.

Some ministers have the idea that planning your preaching handicaps the Holy Spirit in the process of preaching. This is ridiculous because the Spirit, being God, has the power of knowing all. So He knows what a church needs now, as well as in the future, and has the foresight to reveal this to a preacher a year or more in advance.

The Bible is so rich and full of information that a lifetime only allows one to begin to master it. But as humans, we need to be reminded and prodded to change and do as the Word commands. So this means that a preacher (or an educational program) needs an overall plan to help the people reach maturity.

REMEDIES: 1. Make time to make a plan. 2. Take time to listen, and write down the concerns and needs of the people, both in and outside the church. 3. Pray for the Holy Spirit to be a partner in it all.

One of the major problems in preaching is that what is preached is never seen in the lives of the hearers. Every preacher prays that what he preaches makes a difference in the people's lives. So what is the problem with today's methods in the pulpit? Let me give some reasons and possible solutions to the problems.

In many churches there are, at times, four to five different services with the same number of different themes of study. That would mean that in a year, the people in any given church hear 208 different themes. With this number of themes, the people are being overloaded with subject matter without any true method of application. Most people think that if we merely give information we have taught. This is not Christ's goal. His goal is that people are to be changed when they are taught. The Western way of teaching is very inadequate when it comes to true learning and application of what is learned. If all you're concerned about is giving out information, then you're short-circuiting any long lasting change or transformation. Transformation and change of lifestyle should be the goal in Christian teaching.

Remember when Jesus said, "Go and make disciples"? He meant to take a person where they are and help them become someone different than when they began following Jesus. To do this, the church must change the way its people are taught, and that must start with coordinating sermons (and other teaching opportunities) in a way that people will be helped to change, without overloading them.

REMEDIES: 1. Reduce the number of themes, not services. 2. Try to apply what you preach in another service. For example, elaborate on the themes you have in Sunday school in the sermon. 3. Apply what you preach in the morning in a discussion during the evening service or during your cell growth groups during the week.

A Growing church tithes! How does tithing help a church grow? When the people grow so does the church. One of the ways that people grow is in their tithing. This helps in spiritual growth as well as physical. How do you expand the gospel except through the funds that makes it happen? You cannot meet needs and run the day-to-day task and expect the church to grow. Plus, tithing is a barometer of the health of the church People. If their not tithing then what does that say about their faith and growth?

Finally, a healthy growing church will grow to the level of their dysfunction. Churches that do not grow are usually dysfunctional in some way. Now most churches have some dysfunction, but those that do not grow have more dysfunctional tendencies than those who are growing. How can a church become healthy in their dysfunction? What is any congregation made up of? People, people who are in dysfunctional relationships cause their congregation to be dysfunctional. Any congregation is the sum of its people parts. If the leadership is in any way dysfunctional then it has to deal with the problems. But like most of us who have dysfunctional tendencies we cannot see them. Therefore we all need help to identify our dysfunctions. The Bible, Spirit, and other believers can help us in this process. But if there is an unwillingness to be honest and open then no change will happen.

What needs to happen? The leadership, including its individual parts, must look inward to see what kind of leaders they are. We will look more deeply later in the chapters on leadership.

Each person in the congregation must evaluate where they are in their relationship with God and each other. Each person must look at himself or herself to see what God has gifted him or her with. When a person refuses not to be used there is a problem. But in most cases I have found that most people have not been led. They are not dysfunctional, but the leadership that fails to help them get involved is usually dysfunctional. But again in most cases they too do not know how. So at some point the cycle must stop. If there is a will and a desire to be what God wants then dysfunction will be eradicated within the body. Again more of this will be discussed later in the chapter on 'Healthy Growing Person.

�֎ The Growing Challenge!

Let me leave with a challenge for those who want to be a healthy growing person or church.

◆Check your own growth. How can we truly know our shortcomings and needs if we are not truly honest and open with ourselves? A periodic check is just as important in your spiritual health as it is in you physical.

◆Help others grow. It is when I am helping others grow that I also grow. When I think I cannot learn and grow from others then I am beginning my death march.

◆Always have faith in the One who can help you grow. When we know from where our growth comes from then we will go to that source to grow. Never loose sight of our need for faith in the one who can give us our growth.

◆Learn how to grow. We must take the time to continue to learn how to grow. We do not have all the answers. Sadly, most do not learn how to grow. Those who come before us may have never as well, and that inability is passed on. It is best to seek out how to grow than to just accept where you are. You are more interested in yourself than any one else. So just go do it.

◆Love as you and others grow together. It is love that encourages one another to be concerned about other's growth. Those you love by helping them grow will then often return that favor and help you grow. Just loving is growth in itself.

◆Eliminate the obstacles to growth. It is getting rid of old habits or attitudes that stand in the way of growth that frees you to grow. Someone told you you're to stupid to grow, or you have fed yourself the lie that you can't learn or change. These attitudes must be eliminated before you can allow yourself to do the things it will take to grow.

◆Never quit growing. It is when we become satisfied with whom we are, and what we know that we fail. We must always be open to learning till the day the Lord decides to take us home.

◆Get up and get growing in God's way. As with anything worthwhile you just have to make the effort to see the benefit. But not any effort, it must be in God's way that we walk. You can walk a mile in the wrong direction. You get somewhere, but your still lost.

◆Endure when growing gets tough! It takes effort and change to grow. It also takes habitual non-stop dedication when the growing becomes difficult. Growth is hard to take, for it is change of mind and lifestyle, and that is never easy. But the greatest obstacle is complacency and apathy. Both will take away the will to continue growing to the end.

The Healthy Growing Person

Chapter Three

A healthy, growing church must begin with healthy, growing individuals, each brick, each piece of the body in its place, at the right time. In Ephesians 2, we see the mention of the body and the building of Christ's church. The foundation is built on the teachings of the Apostles and the Prophets. These were those men whom God spoke to through the Holy Spirit. The word of God is the result of that foundational revelation. The cornerstone then is Jesus-laid by His deity and work. The cornerstone is the key piece that determines the trueness of the rest of the blocks and the finished wall. But, any building is incomplete with only a foundation and cornerstone. There must be the added bricks to make it a complete structure. People feel sad for or laugh at a person who cannot finish their building. God's building is in progress and someday will be finished.

As you have already read in Chapter One, the purpose of the church is to make disciples. In the world, there are the ingredients or materials to make bricks. When one wants to make bricks, they have to go and gather the material. Clay, straw, and water are primary elements in making bricks. To make them, you have to go and get these elements. But, you have to put them all together to make the brick. Once the brick is made, then it needs to be used for its intended purpose. The non-Christians are those elements in the world. Bringing the elements together is the first step of the process. Evangelism is that spiritual step. But, is that all? No, a lone brick is useless if it sits around. It must be put to use. It must be lined to other bricks to make it useful. Lying around, the bricks can become damaged and then useless but put together with other bricks, they become strong and useful. You may also have bricks lying side-by-side to make a walkway, or you may also have them for building walls. Side-by-side and placed together they are strong and can stand together. There is another element that must be used in the process that gives them strength, the mortar that binds them all together. In the spiritual building, that mortar is the Holy Spirit. Without the Spirit, the walls will not be able to stand. The bricks will become just a stack of bricks, easy to push over, because they are not stabilized by any mortar the mortar of the Holy Spirit.

> **In the making of disciples, each individual brick is important to the health and stability of the structure.**

Ephesians tells us that each person following Jesus makes up those bricks. Each church has its holes due to missing bricks. The bricks may be lying around, but they are not of any use to the building. In the making of disciples, each individual brick is important to the health and stability of the structure.

As long as there are materials out there to make bricks, then the building is not complete. Also, there may also be bricks that have been left out or discarded. These bricks must be gathered and used in God's building. The twist is that each brick must choose to be used. Some know how, but some do not know how and need to be instructed.

Any part that is neglected will grow weak, and could be a liability for the health of the whole Church. If a brick gets damaged or deteriorates, it is good maintenance to repair it. In other ways, just think about how important maintenance is for the health of your teeth. Just one tooth unattended can get infection and poison and even cause a person to have heart trouble. Any neglect of any part is important to overall health. Therefore, let us look at the responsibilities of the individual and at how to keep up the health of each individual.

PERSONAL RESPONSIBILITIES

Three attitudes of a church growth person!

First attitude is Obedience:

To Jesus as Lord. I John 2:3,4. On various occasions, I have asked groups to share what they thought of Jesus or what He meant to them. In most cases, no one referred to Him as their Lord, but rather as Savior, or in terms of what he has done for them. The church will not usually grow when the members believe in Jesus more for what He does for them rather than serving and loving Him because of His Lordship. When the focus is on what we get rather than what we give, then we will become selfish in all facets of the church life. Obedience will not be a priority, but rather personal fulfillment becomes most important. Therefore, if a person feels they are not getting all they think they should, they get discouraged. This is self-focused worship or relationship, but, if a person's worship or walk is Lord-centered, then obedience becomes the focus of the relationship.

To His commands, especially His Great Commission - Matthew 28:19-20. When Jesus gives commands in the Bible, it is as He is standing in front of you in person. When you think of it in this way, you find yourself more obedient. But, we usually choose to rationalize or put it out of our mind, for it's easier that way.

> **Methods are just that, a means to fulfill the principles of God. If they fail to meet their means then the methods loose their usefulness.**

Any and every command is not an option for the Christian individually, or the church as a whole. Especially important are the commands to love one another, and to fulfill the Great Commission.

The reason that Biblical commands are not options is that it is God who gives them. But, there are reasons and results for and of His commands. The reasons are that God knows best, and they are not arbitrary commands, but from the wisdom of God. Any command that it is given is for the good of both the individual and the whole. God knows that, if they are not followed, then dire consequences will occur, or good results will not happen. In a perfect world, there are few, if any "no" commands. Adam and Eve only had one, and they couldn't follow it. For the Christian, it is imperative that we follow every command. But praise God, if we yield, He gives us the power to follow through; the power of the Spirit that lives within us.

Second attitude is Pragmatism

Doctrine and ethics are sacred, not methods. "To the weak I became weak, that I might win the weak; I have become all things to all men, so that I may by all means save some." I Corinthians 9:22 Certain Biblical principles are non-negotiable, but methods may be. Methods are just that, a means to fulfill the principles of God. If they fail to meet their means then the methods lose their usefulness. In this passage Paul's method is to become weak. What does that mean? In another passage, Paul speaks of a weak brother who had a problem with eating meat. He called him "the weaker brother". The method is, if it isn't a matter of saving faith for you and the scripture, then be willing to bend and change your methods of approach. The methods are not to become the focus, only the application. Another example might be that of head covering for women. The principle there was, "Who's in authority?"

The principle still is important, but the application, in my opinion, isn't. In New Testament times, the culture dictated how authority was demonstrated; wives and unmarried daughters wore head coverings to show their submission to authority. In our culture today, wearing (or not wearing) a head covering means nothing. However, a modern parallel might be joining the Women's Lib Movement. Therefore, Paul might say to a Christian woman today that she should not be a part of this group, the reason being that organizations like these sometimes promote rebellion and usurping of authority. Now, I'm in favor of every individual, male or female, using his/her gifts, and I don't believe that women are slaves underneath the man's thumb. But, this illustrated how principle stands, while methods may change. Needs of man overrule traditions. Whose tradition? Most people think of the Pharisees and scorn their traditions, but there's no difference when a leader in a local church feels the same way about certain programs he or his friends started, or about the building in which he worships, or the style of music that is sung. If a change does not involve manipulating or changing Biblically essential doctrine or ethics, then be willing to change something if it will mean you will be able to meet the needs of others in your ever-changing world.

I Corinthians 10:23-33. What is important, your wishes and wants, or the needs of others? A "church growth" person will sacrifice some of his/her wants to help someone else's needs. If my wishes or wants deprive others of their needs, then I may be guilty of lack of compassion and/or selfishness.

Third attitude is Optimism

Power over Satan! Powers of Satan have no power over us now. (Matthew 16:18) The gates of hell will not prevail if we are living in the faith. In James 4:7 we even see a more personal promise. A believer can do two things that will assure Satan has no power, and that is to submit to God and resist the Devil. Why should this give us hope in our seeking for growth, both individually, and within the church? Whatever we hope to be or accomplish, Satan wants to thwart or sidetrack us, but we can have assurance that we have power to overcome the powers of Satan. Often, however, we fail to rely on the power of the Spirit to give us strength and wisdom. When we do, then God can work in and through us. Jesus could do little in the city of Capernaum because of their lack of faith. That is still the case today. Their pessimism thwarted God's work, and this can still happen today in each individual and church. If the congregation will submit to God, it will be protected. This, though, must start with each individual, and be carried out through the leadership and the congregation as a whole.

> **Whatever we hope to be or accomplish, Satan wants to thwart or sidetrack us, but we can have assurance that we have power to overcome the powers of Satan.**

Triumphalist (The back of the Book tells us we win). The church growth person or church will go forward with the idea that we can succeed in the work of the Lord. Therefore, if we are backed and supported by the Lord of the universe, who can be against our plan, or against us, assuming our plan is God's? God is our support, and we can have confidence that God wants men and women everywhere to be saved, and that He will give His people, the church, and us, His means and the power to accomplish the task. But, it is up to each of us to believe this and allow Him to move in each of our lives and congregations. _He will win._ But will we be a part of the victory and its celebration?

Some people, however, come to the table with a defeatist or negative attitude. Even if they affirm that what's happening is Biblical, they will not support it, and they usually sabotage most anything that comes their way. These people are hard to deal with, and sadly, may not be happy or cooperative with anything that goes on, especially if they are not in control.

> **REMEDIES**: **1. Enthusiasm and motivation are important to keep the atmosphere positive. 2. In some cases, a negative person must be approached and sometimes asked not to be a problem, or not even to be involved, if he is always to be a negative. There is no easy way of doing it, but do it - and do it with love.**

What are you capable of?

Moses said, "I can't speak." Elijah said, "I can't speak. I am a man of unclean lips." Is God big enough to do anything? Is He big enough in your life to do anything? The place to start in any type of growth is to have the faith that it can, and will, grow. Without this in your life, and in the life of the church, there is no reason to go any further. All else will be doomed to fail.

> **When you allow God to work and help you reach your potential, then you will see the change and feel the joy of God's blessings.**

Recall the story of Esther. Esther was told by her uncle, "God has placed you in this place and time for such a time as this. Now he will either use you or raise up someone else to do the job."(Esther 4:14) Have there been times that God has wanted to use you and you didn't let him and, therefore, gave up the blessing?

What is your excuse for God not working in your life and using you? Is God big enough to change you and give you strength to do the task? Maybe this is not the case for anyone reading this book, or any members in your church. I don't know you; maybe you _are_ allowing the Lord to lead, teach, and use you. Praise the Lord! But even if this is the case, there is always room for more. If you are not allowing Him to use and move you, then both you and the body will be losing in the process. God wants all church members to be participating and growing. When you allow God to work and help you reach your potential, then you will see the change and feel the joy of God's blessings. This is not a call to sensationalism, but to fulfillment in what you were intended to be.

Resistance to Change

Some of the things I am going to say may offend you, but I hope they make you think and pray. Hopefully, what I say will challenge you to change and allow God to use you more and more.

Many people fail to let God work in their lives because they resist change. It is easier to stay where you are than to make the effort to change. But with God, the change results in wonderful, eternal, and temporal benefits. Of course, God promises to give us eternal rewards for our willingness to change and follow Him, but there are also benefits now. God wants to bless us now. As you read in Proverbs, our actions and choices will affect our everyday existence. So if we change under the direction of God, then we will reap the benefits now, as well as in the next life.

> **So if we change under the direction of God, then we will reap the benefits now, as well as in the next life.**

The refusal to change may be for three reasons. First, you do not see the change as more beneficial than what you have now, so there is no motivation to change. Second, one's pride is more important than submitting to change, even if change is right and beneficial. The first may be wisdom or lack of explaining, but the second is mere foolishness and is harmful. The third was alluded to above. Some people just want to have control at any cost. They choose to resist change because it may mean a loss of control, and they will resist until death or conversion.

Most people are often resistant to change or unwilling to accept new thinking or methods. In Poland, where I served as a missionary from 1995 to 2000, I heard from some people and preachers, "We do not want the Western way of thinking." In some cases, I understand and agree. There are a lot of negative things and ideas coming from the West, but there are a lot of good things as well. Each person, as well as each church, must decide what is good, and what to reject. This is also the case, no matter where you live. But, how do you determine this for your life and for the life of your church? The mark of standard is not that America or any country is doing a certain thing, but whether or not they doing things based in the Bible. If they are, then it does not matter what country the example is coming from if they are being Biblical in their teachings and practices.

Another opinion I heard was, "What works in America won't work here and vice versa." Maybe it worked in America because it was a result of Biblical principle and commands. If so, then it will work in other situations. Even in America's big cities, there are pockets of other countries. You step into their little community and you step into their country. It is like crossing the border, culturally speaking. The basic task of the church is universal. How we package it may be different. What works in California doesn't always work in the South, at least at first. Californians are risk takers; Southerners usually are not at first. They must look, analyze, and digest a new idea before they accept it. They may have to see the principle work in a number of situations before accepting it.

The Apostle Paul went from country to country, and in each country they had their own traditions, but the church was and is universal and catholic.

Americans have a lot of attitudes that are distinctly American but go against the Bible, and they need to be changed. American individualism can be taken too far. The church is a body, not renegade individuals. The church is not a democracy, but many people run their churches like one. The church is an oligarchy with one leader, being Jesus Christ, and with one constitution, the Bible.

Remember, just because Americans do it does not make it good or bad. Regardless of origin or ethnicity, if someone follows the Bible, then do not dismiss their conviction or beliefs. Biblical principles did not start in America, but in the East.

> **Note: It is a good time to look at my Be-attitudes of Change found in Appendix 1 of my book, "_A Walk in Discipleship_". Read them, and then pray over these ideas, asking God to help you in these attitudes of change.**

What does a teachable person look like?

He/she is Humble! Willing to accept; open to change, knowing we do not know everything. Being humble is the first step in the process of learning and growing. If you think you know it all, or have everything in control, then you will find it hard to learn from others. It is the prideful or non-humble person who refuses to admit they are not all-knowing. The reason that pride comes before a fall is that you don't see the pitfalls because of your big head that is in the way. Perspective changes when we realize we should be teachable because we are not all-knowing.

> **Being humble is the first step in the process of learning and growing.**

He/she is a Listener! Willing to hear; open to new ideas. Although we joke about teaching dogs new tricks, the problem again is an attitude problem, not a spiritual senility. There are so many factors that arise when we talk about the problem of listening and truly hearing what needs to be heard in any situation.

Many do not want to listen because they have something at stake that they may lose. There may be a number of reasons that might cause this to happen. One is pride of losing face. They might not want to admit they have bought into some idea or theory and were wrong. People may be embarrassed in front of their peers. They may have to change directions and lose the friendships around them. Therefore, they will do anything to not listen to or to explain away any evidence, no matter how compelling and true. Truth is not always as powerful as self-preservation or self-interest. This being the case, truth will be sacrificed.

He/she is Guidable! Willing to follow; open to suggestions, constructive criticism, and directives. A person who wants to listen with the intent of changing will naturally be open to the tenants being proposed. A wise person will not want to re-invent the wheel each time but will be willing to bask in the experience and wisdom of those who have gone before. Now, it is important to choose those who will guide you. A blind or corrupt guide is worse than no guide at all. Look at Psalm One. In the first part, it talks about those who sit, walk, or stand in the counsel or under the guidance of the wicked; not a wise choice. But, it ends with those who are guideable under the leadership of the wise. It is in true discipleship in the Word that one finds the wisdom. It is also important to be taught by those who are guiding you and the flock under the guidance of the Holy Spirit and His Word.

What do church growth eyes see?

The world from God's perspective! (Luke 19:10) "For the Son of man has come to seek and to save that which was lost."

They see the lost and their need of a Savior. How often does the church lose sight of the people of the world's need for a Savior? Everyone who is evangelized has a chance to escape from eternal punishment because they have the opportunity to hear about the one and only Savior.

Church growth eyes see the flock's need for guidance and protection. The church that will grow will be sure that those in their fold are taken care of. This will, in turn, keep them from danger, as well as close the back door's attrition.

Church growth eyes see their need for fellowship. The world is a place where mankind is floundering in its own loneliness and lack of love and community. The church that will grow will be one that meets basic human needs of fellowship. The church in Acts was so noted for its love and fellowship that they drew the attention of the world and local community around them. There is no difference today in our communities. Try meeting people's needs, help them feel protected, and show them a loving Savior, and your church cannot help but grow.

Your place in God's plan!

God will not do it alone. (2 Corinthians 5:18-21) "Therefore we are ambassadors for Christ...." He will have His way fulfilled with or without you or me, but He will not do it alone; that is not His will. He wants us to fulfill the ministry of reconciliation through each of us who have decided to follow. We are His ambassadors, His representatives. We are God's choice to reconcile the world to Him by sharing Christ with the world. Will God use any means other than the church? The answer is NO. There is no other plan or vehicle but the church. Now each of us, corporately and individually, must decide if we are going to be part of this ministry. Notice the last part of verse 20. Paul is begging the church to be reconciled first. If you are not ambassadors and reconciling others, then you must first start by being reconciled yourselves.

It is through the Church that the mystery is revealed (Ephesians 3:10-13). It is through His body of believers that Satan realizes God has victory in an individual's life and that Christ's sacrifice and resurrection did make a difference. He has no other plan; we are it.

God has given you the resources you need. Before anyone should expect someone else to carry out a task, they should expect that person to have the abilities and resources to do the job. If a person has to blow up a bridge, he must possess the knowledge and the material to do the job. If they are not equipped with these two resources, the mind and the material, then they cannot get the job done. So it is within the bride of Christ. He does not expect each of us to do anything before we are equipped to do so. It takes His resources and our willingness to learn and do to make the church healthy and growing. Let us look at some of these resources.

The Word of God is each person's source of strength and wisdom to carry out God's calling in his or her life. It is primarily through the Word that God's Spirit will speak and teach. The Word and Spirit will agree. When you see anything that goes against the practices and principles of the Word, then you know the experience or teaching is not from God. This is the best way to "test the Spirit to see if it is from God."

> It is only when we are filled by the Spirit that we can be victorious over our will and attitudes, and over the powers of Satan and the world.

Himself! Himself in the person of the Holy Spirit. It is only the living presence of God in us that gives us the ability and will to be who we should be. It is only when we are filled by the Spirit that we can be victorious over our will and attitudes and over the powers of Satan and the world. One can see in Ephesians 3 that the whole of the Godhead lives within us. That is mind boggling to me. It sounds impossible, but with God, all things are possible. What is mind-boggling is that many Christians fail to realize or believe that this is true. In most cases, it is because they have never been taught. Believe that God is in us, begin living and acting like it is so, and God will prove many things to you. Yielding to that presence will also be the major key to your growth in Christ.

Other Christians! No person is an island. There is no army of one. In 2003, the Army ran a commercial with the slogan, "Be an army of one." I saw a commercial recently with this theme. As two Army men walk up a hill, the words "Be an army of one." Flash on the screen. Never has an army of one won a battle, except if you consider when God's death angel punished or killed the Egyptians. But, God does not expect or want us to go at it alone. God has made it that we depend on each other as a team, as a family, as a community. Where there are two or more gathered in His name, He is there. We must depend on others for strength, encouragement, guidance, and growth.

Spiritual Gifts! Besides the actual indwelling of the Spirit, the gifts He brings are very crucial resources to help each person, as well as the whole body, to grow. Spiritual gifts are just that; they are supernatural, and they are gifts. They are given for the building up of the body and for each person to have a place to minister. It would be sad to see a bunch of children around the Christmas tree and for one to not receive a gift. God does not work that way; He has promised through His Spirit to give each Spirit- indwelled person at least one gift. When you find this gift or these gifts, then it is your duty and responsibility to use them for the glory of God and for the sake of fellow believers.

Emotional Experience! Emotions can be a great indicator that something is moving in one's life. While in the Grand Caymans, I was teaching a seminar on the Holy Spirit. One of the main conversations was over the emotional experience people have in church life. I mentioned that the Bible is the guide and partner with the Holy Spirit, and that one could not always depend on their emotions or experiences alone to validate their experience. Truth is not swayed by emotions. One must be careful not to confuse an emotional experience with it being from God.

Although God gave us emotions to express ourselves, He did not intend for them to control us, or to be the means of revelation of truth. I can actually feel that something is really real and happening when it actually is not. People can create false situations that drive and mislead people by emotional manipulation. The emotional feelings are genuine, but the basis of the reaction is not founded on reality. Emotions can be a false indicator of what is truly happening.

On the other hand, emotions can be an internal indicator that what you are feeling is driven and authentic. Your feelings can be genuine, but the actual reason for those feelings could be false. A person can tell you that you have won a million dollars. You get all excited and emotional, but you then look at the date and see that the truth is it's April 1st. Your feelings were true, but they were based on false hopes. Even in church situations, you may be led to believe certain things are true and you emotionally react, but if your feelings are not based on a true foundation then you stand on false assumptions. That is why you must rationally temper your emotions with the objective truth.

> **Although God gave us emotions to express ourselves, He did not intend for them to control us, or to be the means of revelation of truth.**

God will hold you responsible! 2 Corinthians 6: 1-4 Usually, this passage is used to encourage a person that today is the day for their salvation, but in fact, it is a message to those who have already accepted Christ to be faithful as a minister of grace and reconciliation. We are responsible not to receive grace in vain, or not to discredit the ministry we have been given by offending others. Of course, there are those who will be offended, no matter what you do, but it is the Christian's responsibility to do nothing that will outright offend someone because we have acted inappropriately. But the biggest problem is not the wrong acts, but the lack of action; the lack of any remorse or wrong doing when we are at fault.

You have been given the resources, and God does not look kindly on those who do not use them wisely, or do not use them at all. So be confident that God has begun a good work in you, and wants to continue it throughout your life on earth.

Personality and growth!

Have you ever been in a meeting in the church and witnessed personality conflicts take over? "We need to do it because it is the right thing to do, and it is all planned out." The next one is excited, ready to do it right now, and sees no need for more talk or facts: "Let's just do it." A third person seems hardheaded about the need for more facts: "Let's wait to do it, we do not have all the facts. The last one says, "If we are going to have conflict about it, then I won't have any part of it." In most cases, this situation would end in hard feelings, misunderstandings, division, and nothing would get accomplished.

But each man's reaction is predictable. In Mels Carbonell's book, *What Makes You Tick?* The four DISC personality types are defined. The first guy is a "D" personality, the driving force, the visionary, and this was probably his plan to begin with. He sees that it needs to get done, and is willing to plow ahead, no matter the cost. The second person has a high "I" personality, and once he sees the benefits, he is ready to do it. Don't bother him with all the facts; "I am motivated and excited. Let's just do it." The person that seems hardheaded and wants all the facts has a "C" personality. He just needs all the facts, and if he does not get the facts, he will feel strongly about not proceeding with the plan. It is not that he is against it; his personality needs this for him to accept the proposal. The last fellow has an "S" personality, and is more driven by harmony and unity, so he will have a tendency to resist anything that will cause hurt feelings or disruption.

One's personality and how a person reacts with others is very crucial in the growth of the person and the church. The church is made up of personalities. If those personalities do not get along, then the church is in danger of having problems, and problems will hinder the growth and health of the church. I estimate that 90% of problems in the church are the result of personality and not doctrine. I have no hard facts or data, but I have done a lot of observation, and personality conflicts are at the source of most problems.

So, it is important

> **When we know why people act the way they do, then we can learn how to work with them, and at times, tolerate them.**

that each individual understands and has a handle on their personality and how they interact with each other. It is just as important that we learn how to understand and identify the personalities of others. When we know why people act the way they do, then we can learn how to work with them, and at times, tolerate them. This does not mean that, in every case, we should wholesale accept their bad behavior or bad personality, but it is the first step in helping ourselves and others identify and change the bad behavior we do have.

If you knew how to understand why each person, including yourself, acts and reacts to certain things, then you would be on your way to working together in harmony. If the "D" person understood the "C" person, then he would understand that he needs to have all the facts and, if there are some missing, not to feel threatened by this person but to give him the added facts needed to answer his objections. You would also be able to see that the "I" person is excited and to encourage that, but assure him that, when it is right, we will do it. The "S" person will not have any hindrance if the other three can get along, and the "D" person must step back and work with each one differently, not giving up the vision, but rather leading in a wise and calculated way. This is in no way manipulative, but wise, in knowing how to meet other people where they are and to meet their personality's need. But how do we do this? How is this done in the fellowship of believers?

Realize that personality has both learned and hereditary tendencies. It is without a doubt that personality is a learned aspect of our behavior. Some, people however, believe a person's personality is also affected or determined in the genes. This is harder to determine. You may have a family that has four children, and you have four different personalities. Have all learned their distinct personality, or is there some tendency from heredity? One of the answers lies in the birth order. Again, this is probably more learned than inherited. The firstborn is under far different expectations than the second and subsequent siblings. Usually, each is treated differently, and therefore responds differently and develops different personalities. Some though have a distinct personality from birth. But again, it is easy to see that anyone can develop in his or her distinct environment. If not, then it will be unlikely a person will change. But if the Bible is correct, then change is the common thread that makes Disciples of Christ different from those in the world. If a person's personality and life style cannot be changed then no one can become a new creature. Being willing and able to change is at the center of one's walk and salvation. How do we go about this change?

Realize we do not have to accept bad behavior. The goal in learning your and others' personalities is not that you can manipulate but that you can increase the positive parts of your personality and decrease the negative. If the majority of our personality is learned, then it can be unlearned or altered with time and effort. Therefore, no one has the excuse, "I am the way I am because of my past and upbringing, and therefore I can't change." The first statement does have truth. We are what our past has made us, but we are not forced or trapped in it so that our future cannot change it.

Realize bad behavior or personality can be changed. It is in our Spiritual walk with Christ and His Spirit that we can begin to realize and be motivated to change. This is possible when we yield to Him and will to change. In discipleship, we help each other in this change. There is no excuse for bad behavior or personalities once they are learned. "That's just who I am." Know it does not have to be that way. Everyone can and should change. If there is a refusal to change, then it is a good indication that conversion has never taken place. Personality is learned and can be re-learned.

Participate in a personality discovery course like DISC. The first step is awareness of your personality. This is frightening to some. Those who are afraid or who do not have a converted heart or disciplining lifestyle may resist, but it is important to encourage everyone in the church to go through this process of discovering their personality through Mels Carbonell's questionnaires available through Global Church Growth.

Be willing to find out what personality you have, and be willing to strengthen the

> **Being willing and able to change is at the center of one's walk and salvation.**

positive part and decrease or eliminate the negative. One sister-in-law of a disciple of mine completed a questionnaire. At the end of it, she just insisted this was nothing like her, and the questionnaire is wrong, but everyone sitting around her confirmed, at least to each other, that it was an exact picture of who she was. In cases like this, the person must convince themselves that it is not true or face the reality and deal with the need to change. Some people just are not ready to face the music.

It is important to stress that, on the other side, you are not doomed to the personality you have now. It can be changed and strengthened. It is not that your personality is wrong, but that certain tendencies may be less desirable and can be changed in order to become a better saint in God's kingdom.

Learn how to truly admonish one another in love concerning their personalities and behavior, and be willing to receive the same admonition in return. The goal is that each disciple, has the will to look at themselves honestly. I have seen, time after time, where a person is blind to his or her own shortcomings. The reason I have seen it time after time is that I am looking in the mirror at my own flaws of misinformation, of my own personality. This is where maturity in each of us is either developed or left dormant in immaturity. When each individual, and the body as a whole, is able to admonish one another and accept one another's admonishing or encouragement, then the individual, and the church as a whole will be on their way to health and maturity.

Do not use this information about personalities for selfish reasons. This can easily be done. Knowledge is powerful, and God wants us to know Him, others, and ourselves so that we can be the best disciples in His kingdom, not for our own gain alone but for others. With this positive attitude and the right motive, the church and each member of the church will reach their intended goal of maturity and growth.

If there is a person who mistreats this trust, then that person must be approached and dealt with, or the destruction and health of the body might be in jeopardy. This is to be done in love and with the hope that there will be change and sensitivity, but if not, there must be tough Christian love that does not allow this type of manipulation, for the sake of the whole body and the individual himself. The hope is that he will realize and change his tactics and manipulation. If not, the eldership/leaders must step in and remove the person until such time he changes.

The Woman's place in Growth!

As I travel all over this world, the question keeps ringing loud and clear, "What about the role of women in the church?" Some churches have easily answered it by just giving "Carte Blanche." Anything and everything is open for the women of the church. No

> **Jesus was and is the greatest women's liberator, and men should not take that away.**

restrictions and no holds barred. At the outset, all this sounds great and liberating, but is it practical, and is it in God's will? This is what we want to explore in this section. You may not get all the answers you want or like, but I hope they are in accordance with God's will for the growth of the church and each individual, and that includes women.

Jesus was and is the greatest women's liberator, and men should not take that away. In my estimation, Jesus was the greatest women's libber who has ever existed. He came along at a time when women were less than dogs, even in religious circles, but Jesus went against all discriminations in His culture, even including religion. Jesus saw through the facades and even the curse of Eve to see the precious soul of women. He allowed them a place at his side and in His confidence. Just acknowledging them in public was a quantum leap. He made them equal as persons, and that was the place to start with their liberation. What function or place a person holds in society does not, in God's eye, diminish the person's ultimate worth, but then, and even today, our place in life determines our worth. Jesus, however, knew that position does not equate with personal worth. He is no respecter of persons as regards to being persons. So no person should tie their worth in God's eye to their position in life. Our God is the God who wants to take each person where they are and make them into who they should be. He wants to restore each person in His creation to their rightful place as children in His kingdom, regardless of sex or status, equal in desire, worth, and soul. There is no debate, in God's view, that men and women are equally created and endowed with the Creator's image. Are men and women the same or equal in every way? This, of course, is a logical absurdity. In the spiritual world and the world to come, sex is a non-issue, but here and now it is usually a situation of contention. It is important to see that a persons function in life and job status do not equate the true worth of a person's soul in God's eye. As does God, each believer should have the same perspective towards each fellow human being. Although the world will continue to have different standards the church cannot afford to ignore the world's view but it does not have to make our rules. The truth is that man and woman came from the same source, God's creation. God created man and woman from almost nothing, one from dust, and one from bone of the first dust ball. God must have also breathed life into both Adam and Eve. They were not born; they were both created, bringing about an equality of worthiness. Even though Adam was given a different responsibility than Eve, they both were equal in worth of soul and desire. Therefore, give the women their due. The important thing for most people is to know they're equal in worth, and are a contributor to the great scheme of things. Their self-esteem is important to their health and growth. Women are not second rate or inferior to any man. All in the eyes of God are precious, no matter what sex.

Equal in ability and responsibility! This is where the major disagreement begins. There are differences, just as there is a difference between a bolt and a nut, but one without the other is useless. When we think of the bolts intended use we cannot also but think of the nut. For without the nut and it's threads the bolt must become useless, or look for another reason to exist. You may use it as weight on a fishing line, or as decoration on a craft, but not as a nut and bolt combo. Is the nut any more important than the bolt? Of course not; they are equal in worth, but not in function or responsibility, just as it is between man and woman. Both have God-given gifts and responsibilities but at times different functions, and the worth of each is equal in every way.

As I write this paragraph, a female golfer is making history. Today she is playing in a men's PGA tournament. If she makes the cut, she will be the first woman to accomplish such a feat. She is one of the greatest women golfers ever, but can she match and beat the greatest men golfers? I know she can beat this man, or most other male duffers on the links, but can she ever match or play some men like Tiger Woods? Can the best of the women ever compete with the best of the men? Does she have ability? The question and fear most of the men golfers on the tour have are, "Can she beat me?" In certain things, women and men don't have the same abilities or capabilities, but in most things each person, if they strive hard and long enough, has great potential to do great things.

> **It is important to see that a person's function in life and job status do not equate the true worth of a person's soul in God's eye.**

Women are just as responsible for their God-given gifts and duties as are men. I am afraid that, in the past, most women have been pushed aside in many areas of the church so that the full extent of their contribution has been thwarted and lessened in the advancement of the Kingdom. In other situations, if it were not for the dedication, gifts, and prayers of the women, many churches would have died long ago. This is a bigger problem because it is the lack of responsibility of the men, or lack of, men in many situations. The church should not ask less of the women, but more of the men in these situations. In many cases, there were no responsible men who fulfilled their God-given responsibility. There is no excuse for the men to not take their responsibility, nor for women to not take their responsibility. In God's eyes, he gives gifts both to the women and the men, and he expects both to use them in His service.

Women as shepherd leaders!

Men can't and shouldn't go it alone. Over 50% of any given church is usually made of dedicated women. Who is best to shepherd other women but other mature women? That is what they are asked to do in Timothy, to teach and disciple other women and children. In the shepherding family system that is suggested in Section Two, Chapter Four, the wives are qualified women to be co-shepherds with the elders and family leaders. In some cases, the shepherdess will be any qualified woman as we see in Timothy, not just wives of the elders. The hope is that a wife of an Elder could be a co-shepherd as a team, but this should not be expected if the wife is not qualified or especially not desiring this ministry.

Women as deaconesses! What is the work or responsibility of the ministry of deacons? It is nothing more or less than service. Who can serve? Everyone can and should. The problem with some churches' objection to women being official deacons is that they have a wrong view or system of polity in their church. If a church has a deacon/elder board, where both groups gather together each month to decide and vote on the direction of the church, then they may object because the deacons have authority in the decisions/policies of the church. Is this Biblical? No, but many of our churches have this system and, therefore, in their eyes, it would not be right to have women as deacons. The problem is that this system is not Biblical, but is based incorrectly on an American democratic platform. Deacons, whether men or women, are not equal in authority with the elders of the Church, but when they are placed on a deacon/elder board, they become as authoritative as the elders, and this should not be. This subject will be discussed more in depth later in Section Two on leadership.

What does it mean, "Do not usurp authority?" It means not to overtake or go over the head of someone to take their place of authority out of their hands. Paul told the women not to do this. How is this done today? In some cultures that I have ministered in, there was a matriarchal society. This is problematic to their culture, but the church should transcend any culture. Although the missionary should be sensitive and patient with the culture, he or she should not excuse it and overlook the principles of the New Testament. In many of these cases, the men are not responsible in the home and, therefore, this lack of responsibility to lead transfers to the church. In this case, some of the women leaders need to step back in some cases, and let the men take on their responsibility. To do this, some of the work may not get done until they really see the need and their God-given responsibility. Unfortunately, I have seen it in almost every culture, if the woman wants to take the lead in leadership, then the tendency of the immature men is to let them take on the responsibility of the leadership. But if the men of the church are equipped, challenged, taught and forced by necessity, then they generally will step forward and become leaders. But again if the men do not stand up then the best thing may be to let it go until they step up.

> **Although the missionary should be sensitive and patient with the culture, he or she should not excuse it and overlook the principles of the New Testament.**

Does separation of roles matter today in reference to some places of service in the church? It seems to in both the case of culture and maybe in God's plan. Why or why not? What are the implications of both? Let us look at this below.

Biblical Mandate: Genesis 3! This was not the way it was supposed to be. The old saying that woman came from the side of man, not from his feet, is true. There seemed to be a sense of equality between Adam and Eve, even though Adam was created first, but this was all shattered when Eve decided to step out on her own and go against what God had wished for His children. Because of this choice, God gave a curse that came with a prediction. The curse was that woman would be under the influence, or in some cases domination, of man. This was not just for Eve in relation to Adam, but also for all women of all time. God could see and predict the future, and therefore, knew what was to happen.

Cultural Mandate: Nature and culture demands that in the church a woman is not to be an elder. For unity, and for the most effective way of ministering to the lost in and out of the church, women should not be in the eldership of the church. Because of the curse from God, the future was inevitable. The result was that the curse has played out in history. In a perfect world, there are no inequalities, but history to this point shows us that, in some cases, there is a liability for a woman to be in certain positions. I know this is controversial, but it is important to study history.

Since there are a number of denominations that are ordaining women into the pastorate ministry and as elders, let me ask a question. If a man who is qualified to be in leadership leads, will any man or woman object and refuse to follow this man as long as he follows God's ways? The answer is absolutely no. But if there is a woman in this position, there will be a greater chance that most men will not follow. God knows this and does not want there to be any reason for a man not to follow. Some may say, "Well that is the problem of the man and his ignorance." May be, but we are dealing with reality here, and each person is precious to God. This is the practical reason. The theological reason, as was stated above, is that God chose this way because of woman's rebellion and curse.

In my opinion, the only prohibitions for women today are that they are not to be in authority as an elder, or as the head minister or preacher. Why? Because the position of the preacher or pastor naturally operates as an equal authority, or at least leads by his position a place of authority. Again, some will disagree. If so, then you and the Spirit will have to deal with the Bible and God's revelation. The thing to realize is that, except for these prohibitions, there should be no limit to where or what the women should do or be in the church.

> **But if the men of the church are equipped, challenged, taught and forced by necessity, then they generally will step forward and become leaders.**

Conclusion

The church or congregation is only the sum of its parts and if those parts are unhealthy or unholy then that whole congregation will be unhealthy in turn. The churches in revelation were such churches, and one can see what Jesus thought about that part of His bride. He wants a holy and healthy bride, and he has given the leaders of each congregation the responsibility to help make it so. Now, of course, that does not relieve each person's responsibility from striving to be holy and healthy. Therefore, to be a healthy church (or person) then is synonymous with being a holy church or individual.

Revitalizing the Church for Growth
Chapter Four

Why do churches need to be revitalized?

First, Loss or lack of focus or vision! What are the reasons for impaired or lost vision for growth in the body? There may be many causes.

Some are born blind. Sometimes congregations, even from the beginning, fail to have a vision of what the church should be. The congregation starts off with no real direction, except only to exist and "be a church," or a people meeting together. At first the members reach out to bring people in, but after the initial gathering, there is no real long-term vision or concept of what their task is, or who they should be. In most cases, this is the fault of the ones planting or delivering ("birthing") this church into the world. It may be done by a team or an individual. In some cases, it may be a mother church planting a daughter church. If the mother is not healthy and visionary, then in all probability, the baby won't be, either.

Some are diseased, or suffer from malnutrition! Sometimes over a period of time, congregations are simply not fed (taught) about the church's purpose, and lose sight of priorities. Men who stay on a ship for weeks and months become sick if they don't have the right kinds of vitamins and nutrition. Long ago, voyages lasted for months, and sailors would get scurvy while onboard. In the beginning of travel, the captain or leaders did not know what would happen on long trips, nor the needs that would arise. After a while, the oranges or fruits would run out, (in some cases, they weren't even included on the menu). After some time, the men would become sick, and many would die. Simply, many churches today have run out of nutrition, or have even failed to provide it from the beginning. Their teaching and sermons are shallow, failing to give the right motivation and foundation that is needed in order to have a healthy church.

> Unless the leadership is comprised of men who are spiritually healthy and gifted, there will be spiritual blindness.

Some are sinful! In some cases, it's blindness due to sin. When people live in sin, it's hard, almost impossible, to see the light or truth. Their minds and hearts are conditioned not to see, and will become blind to the truth. Satan, who helps spread the disease, is an agent of blindness. We give him that opportunity by our sinning. There are a lot of selfish, blind, sinning people in our churches. Unless the leadership is comprised of men who are spiritually healthy and gifted, there will be spiritual blindness. Therefore, when someone comes along who can see, those who are blind will suppress them. If there is blatant sin in the church, it must be eradicated, or eventually blindness will occur.

Some are negligent! Sometimes people are just lazy or fearful, and don't take care of themselves, or in most cases, just don't know how. My great-grandmother developed a cataract on one of her eyes when I was very young. She didn't think it was serious, and just didn't make the effort to take care of the problem. After some time, it deteriorated until she had to have the eye removed and replaced with an artificial one. Often, many churches and their leaders are fearful of what it might take to take care of themselves, and therefore, neglect their health.

Second, is inadequate ingredients! Nothing is as disappointing as omitting the right ingredients, or mixing in the wrong ingredients in a recipe.

Wrong ingredients! When a good chef prepares a dish, he knows just how it should taste. He also can immediately tell what ingredients are correct in the mix. In many of our churches today, many things are improperly mixed. Sometimes just one thing done wrong can affect and destroy the pie. Sugar and salt look a lot alike. There have been times in my culinary experiences that I have put salt where sugar should have gone. Let me tell you, the first and last taste was unbearable. Sometimes it is very easy to correct and teach with a hard hand of the Lord, but most times the love of the Lord is the best ingredient. The love shown may be the difference between telling and showing.

> Each church must ask the question, "What's missing that will make our church what it should be?"

Missing ingredients! I love to cook and watch the product evolve. When making soups or chili, one can see it evolve as you add each ingredient. It can be difficult. You taste it, but you can't just tell what is missing. Sometimes, you call on someone else to taste. Maybe they can tell what is missing. A little salt? A little cumin? When it is right, you know it! **Each church must ask the question, "What's missing that will make our church what it should be?"** Just suppose the cook doesn't know what the recipe is supposed to taste like. In that case, it would be hard to know what to do to make it turn out the way it should. Often, the missing ingredients make the product edible, but at the same time bland and boring. If we don't know what the final product should look or taste like, we'll have no idea how to make it right.

> REMEDIES: First, study Scripture to see what God requires. Second, you may have to bring in someone who can see what is needed. This may be a new staff member, or an outside expert.

Spoiled ingredients! In a "worst-case scenario", imagine what would happen if bad ingredients were added. Have you ever cracked an egg or poured in milk or cream, only to find out too late, it was bad? What do you do? You have to throw the mixture away and start over again. In some extreme cases, people have become ill, or even died, from tainted ingredients. Sometimes the spoiled ingredient is there from the beginning or the mixture is ruined as a result of something being left out.

The church, too, can have bad teachings or bad foundations from the beginning, and the product will never be good. If the people are taught that "truth is relative" and that "we all can get there by our own way", the church will be tainted from the very outset, with spoiled doctrines. The church may have been started properly, but it may go astray if it isn't watched over and cared for by qualified leaders.

Third, is Lack of power! Have you ever been preparing a meal - have everything ready - all the ingredients, everything in place, everything mixed and ready to cook, only to find out there is no power or gas to finish the task? There's nothing you can do but wait - or give up the project entirely, for without the power, you cannot finish your recipe. The church may have all the right teachings, all the right leaders, all the right stuff, but still fail to produce if there is no power. Without the power of the transforming Spirit, the church is destined not to finish or to become what it can be. Usually what happens is, people give up and discontinue or wait around without any results.

> REMEDIES: Prayer, faith, and work. Sometimes, you have to take the time to pray and wait. It is also important to have the faith that God will act and move.

What needs to change before a church can grow?

First is Attitude (Negative to positive - Faithlessness to faithfulness). Nothing can change in the church unless the members' attitudes change first. If a person doesn't want to change attitudes and habits, or doesn't see the need to change, then he won't. Over time, a person may develop a negative attitude – i.e., "nothing is good; nothing is worth doing." In many cases, people are blinded by their own negative attitude, not even realizing *they* are hard to get along with - a "pain" to be around! Individuals - even entire churches - can become negative and non-productive. In most cases, the problems begin with a few powerful personalities who control by negative attitudes. "We can't do this. We tried it years ago and it didn't work." Or, "That's just not the way we do it here." In these cases, the person is in control, and not the Spirit of God.

> REMEDIES: In some cases, the person may change, if shown how he is negatively affecting others. In other situations, it will take a change of will and repentance, maybe even being converted. In other severe cases, the person or persons who will not change their attitude or disruptive actions, should be removed from the leadership, or the body, until they repent. This may be drastic, but the whole church will be destroyed if a negative attitude is allowed to control.

Instead, we should develop a new set of attitudes that will promote growth and the influence of God's Spirit. We should each change our negative thoughts to positive and become faithful to God instead of being faithless. Therefore, please look at the "Be-attitudes for Change" and for church growth found in the appendix of Dr. Householder's book, *A Walk in Discipleship*. If each of us can begin to live and think with new attitudes then the church will be healthy, both inwardly and outwardly.

Be-attitudes of Change

1. Be open to new ideas!
(Change will not happen if you're stuck in the past
and unable to see the possibilities.)

2. Be individual-sensitive!
(To "pigeonhole" someone will lead to your prejudice,
and hamper the possibility of their change.)

3. Be people-positive!
(Look for the best in yourself and others, change can happen.)

4. Be among your people!
(Otherwise, you can't help them see the need for change,
nor can they see how you've changed.)

5. Be a person of Bible ways and means!
(Even if others are not, be their example first.)

6. Be culture-sensitive!
(What may be evident to you may not be evident to others;
furthermore, others may not be wrong in what they are doing.)

7. Be patient!
(Others are not where you are, at this time,
therefore allow time for them to see.)

8. Be persistent!
(Even when others are not and things seem to be going too slow.)

9. Be visionaries!
(For those who need a vision)

10. Be challengers!
(For those who need a challenge to get out of their comfort zone)

Second is Leadership! Spiritually gifted, full of desire, and well trained are the three right ingredients for a successful and faithful leadership. When any one of these ingredients is missing, the church will not be a healthy, growing church.

> God will not give us a gift without giving a desire. Of course, we can suppress that desire and it will die, but God will be faithful.

Spiritually gifted! The saddest thing in most of our churches is that few people are doing things in their areas of giftedness. The healthy, growing church is one that has members serving within their gifted area. This is also the case for the leadership. If anyone in the leadership is not gifted to lead, or gifted to teach and discern, then he should not be in leadership. Seniority or secular occupation does not qualify a person to lead. Just because a person has been in the church for 30 years does not automatically qualify him or her for leadership positions, either; only Spiritually-gifted and guided men and women of God should lead. Those who work in areas without the required gifts, who have power or authority in that area, will not make decisions based upon spiritual giftedness. The result can often be destruction or impotence.

Full of desire! Nothing is more satisfying than to do something you desire. When I was younger, my Dad suggested I be an accountant like him. Well, I didn't have that desire. I didn't like math, and I didn't like a desk job - two important qualifications. There was no joy or desire to be an accountant. Many people, out of need, guilt, or ignorance, do something they don't desire. God will not give us a gift without giving a desire. Of course, we can suppress that desire and it will die, but God will be faithful. Many leaders or workers in the church do things in the Church because they had to, (or they would feel guilty about doing nothing). A leader who has no desire may become bitter, resentful, negative, and controlling in his position.

> REMEDIES: If a person seems to have a gift but does desire to use it, then it is important to figure out why. Maybe the person had a bad experience while serving in the past, or maybe he/she just has not yielded his/her life to the Lord. If the lack of desire comes from the former, then he needs to be encouraged to rely on the Lord in faith, if from the later, then she needs to be challenged to repent and ask God to give her the desire.

Well Trained! If the leaders are Spiritually gifted and have a desire to serve, then the matter of training is easy. If they are not Spiritually gifted, or do not have a true righteous desire, no type or amount of training will be enough to move them in the right direction. Only redirection of placement or removal will be the answer. This, in some cases, may prove drastic and divisive. The alternative is a non-growing, faithless, and dying church. But those who are willing to be trained and mentored will prove to be leaders - or they will prove they are not in the process - thus providing an out for both parties. But if they have not had the opportunity to be mentored then they will have a harder time in their leadership ministry. Training/mentoring is a precursor to success. Being teachable will make the training profitable and the person more whole in his/her development.

REMEDIES: If those in leadership are always negative or resistant to change, a change is surely needed. The difficult thing is that such a person in leadership will fight being replaced or changed. Until someone or some change agent or event shakes up the mix, the change won't happen. Right training in the beginning, and the right way of creating leaders will, in most cases, avoid such negative situations.

Third is Methods (worship, evangelism, greeters, ministries, and small groups). As in any worthwhile endeavor, it is important to have everything in fine working order. Many churches and their leaders fail to think through what they do in their activities. The result may be "making no waves", but also "making no leap forward" in terms of growth. It's important to always be examining what you're doing in every area of activity to see if the church is vital and is meeting people's needs and fulfilling its purposes. The leader should always be aware of what is going on, and be sure the methods used are fulfilling the mandates of the church, as well.

REMEDIES: Do not confuse methods with mandates that must be fulfilled in each church's life. Evangelism, worship, and shepherding are mandates. How one fulfills these mandates may be different in different situations. The mandate must be accomplished, but the methods may change. The method must not be sacred. If the methods are not working, or are wrong for the time and situation, then they should be re-evaluated or changed.

Fourth is Location (inadequate facility). Many churches have it all together, and have all the right ingredients for success in God's work but still aren't growing. If you want a big fish, you must have a big pond. A goldfish put into a two-gallon bowl will grow very little. He may be very happy, but he'll never grow to what he could be. The same goldfish, if put in a big pond, may grow to enormous proportions. Both can be healthy "fish", and both can be fulfilling God's will in their group. One may be limited in its outreach and in its evangelizing a larger number of people in the world.

> REMEDIES: If you want to have more children, you will have to have the space to take care of them. If you want to stay a small family, then don't bother. You might have to expand, or you might have to relocate if you do want to grow larger. You may divide and make smaller congregations, still accommodating many more fish or people.

Why do humans resist change?

Fear! Most people at first fear the unknown or what lies ahead. Change is threatening to the *status quo* and to those who at first see no need for change. Most people feel: "Why bother it, if it's working, or if it's not harming anything?" In many fellowships, things don't work efficiently or productively but the church functions, and that's enough - for some people. Also, people fear rejection. When someone moves toward change, it usually entails moving away from something or someone. When that happens, there may be rejection by friends or fellow associates. This rejection, or fear of it, is enough to persuade a person not to change. "What will they think?" has stopped many a person from changing.

Selfishness! In some cases, change will mean that a few people will lose their status or place of authority. Some people may think they'll lose benefits if there is a change and, therefore, they'll resist. Each one in the body must have the attitude of John the Baptist towards our duties or work: "I must decrease so that He must increase." If we trust in the Lord, then we can trust that whatever is in the future can be exciting and beneficial. Sometimes, an individual must give up or change something for the benefit of the whole. This, of course, is not about doctrine or scriptural mandates. They must never be sacrificed. Our methods and duties in the fellowship may need re-evaluated and changed to meet the needs of others.

> Sometimes, an individual must give up or change something for the benefit of the whole.

Ignorance! In most cases, the person does not know of any other way, therefore, they do not truly understand there is a need for a change. Many people and churches are not aware that there is a problem, or a better and more efficient way of doing things. Their hearts are right, their faith is right, but they are not able to see their situation objectively. Saul thought he was doing God's will by persecuting the Christians, but he found out that he was ignorant of the truth. When he did know the truth, he changed and was blessed in his work and ministry.

Complacency! To some people, being comfortable is more important than being right. Many people just find security in doing things the same way. Staying in the same way is safe and effortless. But in some cases it can become a rut without any worthwhile direction. Growth and progression takes getting out of your comfort zone to make a change, and many people do not want to make that sacrifice. The person who usually falls into this rut usually has a S personality.[*] I am not saying that things in the church has to be this way or people with S personalities have to be resistant to change, but their tendencies can lead to this dilemma. Most churches that do have a problem in growing and who wish to stay small by

---

[*] **This is in reference to the S found in the DISC personality test by Mels Carbonell.**

choice seem to have an overwhelming amount of people with a S personality. To counter act these tendencies there must be two things to help motivate these personality types. There must be a D person that is in leadership, and any change must be slow so that each person can feel secure in the move and change.

Traditions! The biggest enemy to change is traditions. It is true that some traditions should not be changed, although any tradition that becomes a mere shell of the real thing should have a change of heart and commitment. But, some traditions were wrong in the first place. Somewhere back in the past, someone began a tradition based upon faulty assumptions or information, that should have never been started. In some cases, the traditions were started out of evil intentions and also should be stopped. Some traditions have lost their meaning and usefulness and also need to be changed or dropped altogether. In

> Some traditions have lost their meaning and usefulness and also need to be changed or dropped altogether.

their inception, they met a need, but that need is no longer valid. The traditions just keep going without true purpose or need, therefore, calling for a change. But, tradition is a big cause of complacency and refusal to change. In some cases, the reason the change is hard is that the traditions have a lot of emotional baggage from the past. There is either a strong tie to the tradition's founder, or some personal tie to the past, again making it hard to change for some people.

Prejudice! Some people will not change because of some deep-seated prejudice towards someone. This causes them to have an excuse to place their lack of change on someone else.

REMEDIES: 1. Knowing His love and His will should help in overcoming fear. 2. Knowing your motive and heart and being honest with yourself, should help you in your selfishness. Here is a need for repentance. 3. Being willing to know the need and His will or plan. Ignorance can be bliss but also can be deadly. 4. Not being complacent. One must truly see what is priority and what is important. A person with complacency or Luke warmness is in need of repentance. 5. Traditions without substance are based on mindlessness. Think about what is important, and whether or not the tradition still fulfills a purpose that is progressive and right.

How can we facilitate change?

**Take it slow!** The older the congregation, and the younger the Christian, the slower you must go. Old ways are hard to change. If someone is left behind, or is not on the same page, they will later either quit, or cause problems through resistance and rebellion. It takes time to overcome the things mentioned above. It sometimes took years to develop the habits, and it will take some time in changing.

Explain the need for the change thoroughly! Misinformation or misunderstanding causes resistance. Being fully informed takes away anxiety and fear. With traditions, there has to be a lot of research and understanding on why it was started, where it went off track, or how it lost its usefulness. Also, there needs to be time to handle the emotional detachment from the tradition.

Know why there is a need for a change. If it is explained thoroughly, then people will know why there is a need for change. Leadership must first know and agree in consensus, then others in the church will understand and be motivated. If the leaders own it, so will the people.

> Matters of faith and Biblical principles must override our selfish wants and traditions.

Follow Biblical principles. Matters of faith and Biblical principles must override our selfish wants and traditions. I have mentioned this before, but let me say one more time that if there is going to be positive change for the growth and health of the church and the congregation, then the church must be on the same page with God. If you or your leadership or even congregation is standing on man's tradition at the expense of God's Word, then you will not be healthy and God will not bless you and your efforts as He wants.

Understanding what the church is and is not will help it grow.

The church is an organism, not an organization! The church is a body made of human flesh. It is not some organization, although it is organized. The organism is also made up of spirit, including each person, and the Spirit of God. The church is living and growing as far as it allows the Spirit to guide and partake in its functions.

The Church is the bride of Christ, not our possession or club! The church is not the possession of its leaders, founding ancestors, or any person or persons currently involved. It is not a social club for fellowship and joint interests, although fellowship is important. It is a relational entity that ties itself to Jesus Christ in its allegiance. Jesus paid the dowry, the price for His bride, the church. Our responsibility is to be faithful to Him, not anyone else's whims or control.

The Church is a light for the world not a private treasure! When the local church becomes closed to the world, then it is in danger of burying its talent and receiving God's impending judgment. The churches in Revelation 1-3 were New Testament churches that lost their focus and love for the Lord and the world. Many churches stay small by their choice. Once they get to a comfortable point, they close down their openness to the outside. In most cases, this is not their plan, but there seems to be a comfort zone, and when they reach it, a church will not be open to new people. They will unknowingly, and in some cases knowingly, do things that will discourage people from coming. In some cases there are times that a person or individuals in the satisfied congregation push people away because, in their opinion, the church is just the right size. When you hear people say, "I like a small church," look around and you will see a small church. In some of those cases, the church will not welcome or be friendly to anymore who does not share their view of what a small church is to them. If this is the case, and if you have ever had this attitude, or see it in your tendencies, then repent, for you are not thinking as God does or wills.

You're standing in His way of blessing you and others who need salvation. Remember it is not your father's church or your church, but God's. And He can be a jealous God.

Whoever is in control determines the growth

World or flesh driven! By world, I refer to the use of methods that are used in the book *Robert's Rules of Order*, or running the church as a business or democracy. After World War II, many American churches started running the church like a business. Many leaders in the church were at the same time involved in the growing world of business. The thought was that, if an organization runs well in the world, then it should also within the church. So joint (Elders, deacons, and non-ordained officers) boards and chairpersons of the board became the norm, and the Biblical guidance of the Elders was replaced. In many cases, parliamentary procedures overrode Biblical principles and Spirit led decisions.

> In many cases, parliamentary procedures overrode Biblical principles and Spirit led decisions.

Another factor and contributor to this rise in democracy in the church was the requirement to provide by-laws and trustees by State governments. To fulfill this requirement, the church adopted or searched for the right procedures to fulfill this demand. The common authority was the book, *Robert's Rules of Order*. The fallacy was that the church should follow all the procedures in the book to run their meetings and make decisions. The book does not have to be studied in most churches or new starts, for it has become a standard way of doing things in most churches.

This then put in place a system that, in some cases, provided a breeding ground for control and abuse by its leaders, especially the powerful position of Chairman of the Board. The problem was not only the system of carrying out business or making of decisions, but rather the maturity and spirituality of the leaders. If the leader is selfish, power hungry, or merely a human traditionalist, then the church will usually not grow. The means that were adopted due to this democratic/secular system gave rise to putting men into these positions that were not necessarily spiritual, but more than not, political.

Spirit-driven Church! Because many churches make their decisions based upon democratic procedures, the Spirit is voted out of the process. The church is to be powered and run by the power of the Spirit, not by our whims and will.

The spirit will guide the leadership and the church if the church will let it. Don't be afraid of Pentecostalism when you are true to the Spirit's guidance. He will guide you in spirit and truth. Your Spirit will be in tune, if your truth is in tune with the Word. That is, if you know the truth, and let it be the last say and guide, then you will have the peace and witness in your Spirit.

> **REMEDIES: If the church uses *Robert's Rules of Order,* or has a joint board with a chairman, then it may be wise to disband and create a new form of leadership. An eldership that jointly decides, through consensus, how to guide the church, will more likely deter problems by using the directives of the Bible as their guidebook, and not American business.**

CHANGING FROM DEMOCRACY TO BIBLOCRACY

One of the hindrances to growth is that the church is set up in many situations as a democracy. The church is not a democracy, nor is it to be run like a mere business. In many cases, the church has ceased being a community and a living spiritual organism, and has evolved into a political, organizational nightmare. How did this happen, and how can it be corrected and prevented in the future? The first step is to understand the purpose of the church. I hope we have introduced this subject in chapter one. The second step is to realize that our pattern should come from the Bible, not man's creeds or philosophies. The third step is to realize in whom and from where our power and direction comes.

So how do we change from the world's way to God's way?

Start Slow! It is very obvious that too swift a change may produce some of the problems and backlashes causing many of our splits today. If you are the change agent, you can see the end result, and maybe what needs to change to get there. But, those who have spent time in the old system and have not had a chance to morph into the new paradigm will resist at first, until they have time to digest and go through the changes. Help them see the whole picture before you make the changes, and be patient but determined and consistent. Now there may be some people who will resist to the end. Here it takes wisdom to see if they have a legitimate concern or are just trying to filibuster for their own agenda. If it is the latter then you will have to deal with that person and not let the conflict derail the needed change. In a new church as we will see in our next chapter the New Testament methods of apprentice and discipleship, or may I say, "Biblocracy" is easy to follow for there are no old ways to change.

Teach the leadership! Paradigms must be changed, and that takes a lot of teaching about what is wrong with the old one, and why the new one is more Biblical and workable. Sometimes, there will be problems with some who are in leadership positions. Those who may lose a position in the changeover may fight the change of models if they are not in tune with the Spirit. If they see it as losing control, instead of changing their function due to giftedness or the lack of it, they will fight the change. If they have a servant heart, they will recognize that new way is the best for all concerned. We will discuss more of this in the chapter on Leadership.

Get everyone on the same page, and teach the whole body. One of the main problems to changing something major in the church is people who want to make decisions but are consistently absent from the preliminary discussions. They miss this meeting, that sermon, or that teaching, but show up at the time of making decisions. Everyone else has made the mental and Spiritual change, but the person(s) who do not participate in the process still want to make their vote count. It is important that, if people in power fail to consistently meet, they should be relieved from making dissenting decisions, especially if they refuse to listen. Power corrupts, and sometimes people stay away so they will have an easier time refusing to cooperate and change along with the rest of the people. That is why it is important to try and get people there, or the information to them, so they do not have an excuse.

Having voting promotes this type of behavior. If there is no voting, it eliminates this problem. In consensus, the problem will be made in the process of working towards an unanimous decision with the foundation of the Bible and not in a vote. If you are not in the process, then you should not have a say without having the information. Just to object is not right unless it does not go adjacent to the Bible.

So, it is important that everyone is on the same page; that means the body, as well. This is true in cases of major change that will affect the whole. Sometimes, you also have people who are not in leadership officially but still control things behind the scenes. So, it is important to teach people that this is not the right way. Of course, it is obvious that those who are motivated by power and not the Spirit will rebel. At this point, leadership must make a stand.

Be open to change form and position! The premise is, if the form is not from the Bible, then do not be afraid to change it to something more Biblical. If the position is not one that is done out of your giftedness and out of servant-hood, then pray that it might become so, or be willing to change or step down from a present position. With study and humbleness, the transition can be done.

Re-evaluate leadership (Elder/staff) personnel's gift mix! If a person became an Elder under the old nominating and voting system, there is a likely chance that person was chosen and not gifted for the position of elder. There should be no office, but function. If you are not functioning as a shepherd or overseer, you should not be officiating as an elder of the flock. Again, we will look more deeply later in the chapter on Leadership and shepherding.

Streamline by-laws to meet minimum State requirements. In most cases, churches have chosen to use secular means to fulfill State qualifications required of them in their registration as non-profit organizations. In doing this, they looked for a way to meet these requirements and, therefore, looked to commonly practiced norms of the secular world, and used their _Roberts Rules of Order_.

Let us be smart and fulfill state requirements without going against the form and principles of Biblical form. Most states require certain information and procedures to be done, but are not specific in content. In most cases, the State requires the declaration of purpose, leadership, and certain procedures, such as, one meeting. The State does not require a church to vote, or have a Chairman of the Board.

LOOK AT YOUR STATE REQUIREMENTS AND BY-LAWS OF A CHURCH. Only fulfill the minimum amount of information needed. In the appendix you will find an example of bi-laws that goes hand in hand with the ministry team concept.

Conclusion!

It is important that each person in the church "be on the same page." This must first start with the Eldership. If the leaders are not on the same page, then old problems will arise, or new ones will eventually happen.

What does it mean to be on the same page? Does it mean that in everything everyone has to agree on every issue at all times? That would be great, but in a fallen world, and with human choice, that is impossible. But, it does mean that everyone is in agreement with being on the same page for the sake of unity and unhindered forward growth. Being on the same page in regards to purpose and philosophy of ministry.

What does it mean to be on the same page?

1. It means that everyone agrees on the essentials of the faith.

2. It means that everyone agrees on the direction of the philosophy of ministry.

3. It does mean that everyone agrees to not fight over things or matters of opinion or selfish wants and personal agendas.

4. It does mean that everyone will know where their place in the body is and trust others to fulfill rolls.

5. It does mean that, if someone is not in agreement with the overall direction and plan, that they will either find a common ground, or find another fellowship that will meet more of their needs and/or likings.

6. It does not mean that opinions do not count, but that they should not ever go as far as to cause division in the body.

7. It does not mean looking the other way when essential doctrines or matters of faith are challenged or questioned.

8 It does not mean that everyone needs to go through basic foundational doctrines and discipleship. This is important so that everyone's basic needs are being met and that no one will be left behind in the nurturing of the body. This will insure everyone is on the same spiritual page.

9. It does mean If anyone is out of the loop and has not been involved in the church life, then it is dangerous and prohibited for them to show up and have a deciding say in the church or its policy

10. It is also important that transfers likewise go through all the steps that everyone else has been through, and that a transfer not be given any duties or responsibilities in leadership until they have had time to go through the basics and for the leadership to get acquainted with them. Each situation should be taken on an individual basis, but transfers too should be on the same page as everyone else, or problems may occur at a later time.

In an established church, it will take time and effort to try and get everyone on the same page. It will take negotiation, and even disagreement, but if everyone has a heart of love and cooperation, it will happen. The leadership in every step must take the lead in vision, unity, and insight in handling people who may object or refuse to cooperate. If it is a matter of opinion, the leadership must not allow a person or a few to rule or derail the process. But, with the love and guidance of the Holy Spirit, the church can and will go forward to meet the needs of the people now, and in the future.

It is important that communication lines be open, and that agendas and procedures be open and not done behind closed doors. Everyone needs to be informed and given a chance to make their opinion known with love and restraint. The use of tapes and written material should be employed to insure as in 8 above the people are informed about the changes and direction of the church, and that enough time is given to get people on the same page.

The Healthy New Church
Chapter Five

This is not a chapter on every detail of planting a new church, but it is a chapter with information that I think is needed (and hopefully helpful) on some issues that will help build a Biblical and firm foundation when one begins a new church. In my study and seminars with established churches, I have noticed that most of their problems stem from their founding days. They sometimes begin with assumptions and procedures that were common practice, but not necessarily Biblical ones. During my time of assessing each situation for the purpose of suggesting what needs to be changed to help in its growth and retention of members, I found that, in most cases, the whole structure and foundation needed to be changed. Again, the reason these structures needed changing was they were built on faulty, non-Biblical foundations from the beginning.

In many of our churches, a "domino effect" has taken place over the years. The men who began these churches were taught to do things in certain ways, which perpetuated the trend. In other situations, men saw how other churches were founded and followed suit. Sometimes, the problem arose when new churches were started solely by a nucleus of established church members who just duplicated their old church (and often, their problems!) This is not always the case, but more times than not it was; it's a natural phenomenon.

Of course, all this was not a diabolical plan by those who started these practices; however, the substitution of secular forms replaced that of Biblical norms and, therefore, what followed has been less than effective and became a breeding ground for divisive behavior later in the church's life.

So what I want to accomplish in this chapter is to give some ideas and observations that may help new churches begin with the right foundation; a foundation that will close the back door from the beginning, and provide a structure of leadership that will conduct itself on Biblical principles, not lean on post-modern traditional forms.

Benefits of a New Church!

> **A new church is free to try something different from the status quo. It is free to go beyond the traditional forms that may bind us in most of our churches.**

Free to experiment. Usually, the new church is free from some of the trappings of an established church in regard to being able to begin with new ideas and programs. Of course, there is usually openness and freshness in regards to what the church will look like in its approach and makeup. This is not referring to new doctrine, but rather about new methods of "packaging" the gospel. A new church is free to try something different from the status quo. It is free to go beyond the traditional forms that may bind us in most of our churches. I am not talking about relativism, which tampers with the truth and doctrines of the Bible, but forms of operation, which may deter or retard growth in the body. These are forms that do not originate from the Bible or from first-century practices, but from recent modern procedures. We will go into this in more depth later; to some extent, we have already explored this in earlier chapters.

It also gives an opportunity to try new things that may meet needs in a new place, in a new way. The "status quo" will try and protect its way in an established church, while in a new church, there is a chance to break away from these bonds of protectionism.

Chance to establish own identity. What is a *New Testament Church*? Over the past two millennia, leaders of the faith stepped forward to call the existing church to take a look at itself, to try and get back to what it was at first - or as nearly as possible, figure out what the church was supposed to look like in the eyes of Jesus and the Apostles. The church has always had the responsibility, in each generation, to check who they are and if they are in line with God's intentions. In the first three chapters of Revelation, we see that, even at the end of the first century, this was already a problem. We see how important it is to be a church about God's agenda and with God's heart in the fellowship. It is when the church re-invents itself that it is in danger of losing its candlestick, or blessing of the Holy Spirit. It is obvious that God wants a loving and dedicated church that follows and maintains the direction set down for it by Christ and the Apostles.

Today, we again must look at the church to see if it is in line with what Christ intended it to be. As we have already seen, the church is not to be a democracy or organization but a family led by its pastor/elders/shepherds (Ephesians 4:11).

> **To do this, the church must develop a new vision that will allow change to take place. If members are selfish about their local traditions, then they will not be able to part with them for the sake of the new believers.**

It is in the new church that this is most easily done. It is in this arena that establishing a church on the basis of discipleship can be fulfilled. Again, it's possible for the established church to do this, but it will require the whole church getting on the same page at the same time; not impossible, but more difficult. But, it is not guaranteed in the new church either, especially if it leans on the foundations of an established, controlled church as its model, or mother, or is established by those who only know the post-modern way of doing things. When I say post-modern, I am referring to a church that uses 19th century democratic methods to run the church rather than methods set down by the first-century leaders.

A new church usually has the ability to reach different people. In some cases, established churches that have lost their vision for others and have ceased adapting to reach them will usually be stagnated and resist changes that would enhance their chance for bringing in new people. There is hope, however, if that church reevaluates its goals and directions and decides to allow change throughout the congregation. To do this, the church must develop a new vision that will allow change to take place. If members are selfish about their local traditions, then they will not be able to part with them for the sake of the new believers.

A new church that begins without any of these problems frankly does not have to deal with them and, therefore, just begins the process of discipleship as its foundation. The advantage of a new church is that it can target specific groups of people in their city. Now I know the argument about needing to have unity and diversity within the same group. This is ideal, and as the people grow, this may eventually take place if a lot of factors fall into place. However, to reach out there needs to be a more cultural, sensitive approach and even various methods and worship.

Develop a healthier foundation. As has been said, it's far easier to begin new concepts in a new church, than in an established church. If you have new people, you have no traditions or old ways to change; you just establish your own. (That is why, when you begin with people from failing churches or negative situations, all that carries over to the new congregation.) From the start, you disciple people and they think that is the norm. It gives you an opportunity to have new procedures and not be tied to things like *Roberts's Rules of Order.* So it is very important - any attempt to include any of these old ways must be put down at once. <u>Always remember, whatever you do in the beginning, will later become the tradition.</u> So, be sure your foundation is Biblical and healthy.

Because of this freedom, there is a better chance for developing a healthier foundation, assuming the old one, if negative, is not carried over. But in many church plants, the daughter becomes like its parents in all of its success and failures. However, if a new church starts without the trappings, it has a better chance to be healthy. The goal then is to have healthy churches birthing healthy daughters. But, in any new church plant, there should be individual planning and new thinking about what kind of congregation the new church is going to be. If the new church can be born pregnant, or at least have that as a part of their vision, then the kingdom as a whole will grow.

Beware of old leaven when starting a new church.

What is this old leaven? In the New Testament, Jesus referred to the old leaven as people who were destructive forces in the body. It was commanded that the leaven be removed from the assembly or it would destroy the very fabric of the church.

If the new church can be born pregnant, or at least have that as a part of their vision, then the kingdom as a whole will grow.

It is hard to describe exactly what the old leaven was in regards to what they specifically did, but we can be assured it was individuals who held to pharisaical attitudes and doctrine, doctrine and attitudes that were in opposition to the Christian movement. The intent was to force the new faith to act and believe like the old faith. Also, it probably included sinners who refused to refrain from sinning and repentance. Basically, anything that would hinder the growth and progression of the Christian faith is an element of leaven in the body.

What can the old leaven do for (or against) the new church? This leaven can also be applied to present day situations. I have seen where old members of one church would go and be a part of a new work. This is not always a bad idea, if those who go with a new church, go with an attitude of cooperation with the new leadership. Usually, the first people involved in the plant may expect to become part of the leadership rather early. If they don't fit the philosophy of the new plant, then the church is already beginning with the foundation of possible problems that may mature into major ones in the future.

What to do with old leaven? If the transplants do not see eye-to-eye, then they should be asked to *please* not join the new plant! There's no need for problems from other churches to enter into the new church. Difficult people who have problems in other churches will often tend to cause problems in the new church. Why start a new work on the wrong foundation?

It is important that anyone in leadership be aware of those who want to join the new plant. Anyone who begins with the leadership should agree with the philosophy and direction of the new plant from the beginning, and should be chosen as you would any team or staff member. It is far easier to discourage at first, than try to remove later.

So be bold enough to ask the hard questions - and *be willing to say* "You will not fit." The tendency, however, will be to open up to all so you can have large numbers; i.e., "any warm body is helpful." That is nearsighted and dangerous. You must always think of the future, and the implications of those who start with you.

If the church planters are starting on their own, or the church begins with only a team with no outside help, then the new plant will be easier to get established. If the focus is on non-Christians, the new plant will be easier to get up & running. But, if many of your people come in from established churches, or from a church plant, make sure they are "on board." To help this happen, the planter must have a clear view about the direction in which the church will be going and about what methods they will use.

How to prevent old leaven from taking over? First, it's better to never let them in from the start, as we discussed earlier. If this "old guard" does creep in, then it must be dealt with swiftly, and with love, but there is a 'window of opportunity' here. This exclusion is usually done before the church goes public. After that, it will be very hard to exclude. In this case, the members must be clearly taught the direction of the new church. If it comes to the point that a person is not in the right frame of mind, then he/she must be worked with. If it is a new believer, it is usually not a problem; transfers are the main source of potential problems. Do not let them be so, because they can be destructive to the whole.

Who makes these decisions? If the planter is an individual, he must be the one to do it at first. In the case of a team, it would be wise to let the team be part of the procedure. This will develop teamwork and a sense of understanding; this is the right direction. It will also help keep each other in check.

Be patient with evangelism when starting.

Starting too soon - examples of failure. Back in the middle 80s, when I was a student at Fuller, the big buzz was the "phones." This was a way to call a lot of people and get a percentage of them to a church service. Sometimes this was used to get a jump-start, and get a nucleus started upfront. In most cases, there was success in getting a critical mass out for that first Sunday. The success or failure was determined by how much of the nucleus was ready to handle the mass. In many cases, lots of people were curious but at the same time discouraged by what they saw or didn't see that first Sunday.

A new church may have problems with starting big before the foundation is built. I have read and talked with some new church plants that used techniques like massive phone campaigns to bring in a lot of people on the official opening day. This can be a great event but with eventual mediocre results. Time after time I have read that the campaign was successful, with hundreds of people showing up at the opening event, but over the next few weeks, the attendance decreased from maybe 400 to 50.

> **Launch when you're ready to sail, closing the backdoor from the beginning.**

Most of the time, the new plant is not able to handle the first rush of people. The first impression is worth a lot, and when you lose a lot of people like that, it will be hard to get them back later.

Launch when you're ready to sail, closing the backdoor from the beginning. The mistake many churches make is to start mass or heavy evangelistic campaigns too soon. If there is no way to take care of the newcomers, then you do more harm to the future reputation of the church, and may cause some people to feel the church does not really care or is inept about their duties. The result is that they will go somewhere else or nowhere at all. If you have a trained nucleus ready to worship, disciple, and care for the children, among other things, then you may be ready for the outreach. Please be ready, and have all your spiritual and physical ducks in a row before you begin your public launches. The first launch is to be done for the building of the nucleus; the second launch is the big public push that advertises. It is the time you pull out all stops.

Church Planting Team and the new church

Why a team? It seems that when we look into the events of the new church, we see that most missionaries or church planting efforts are sent out as teams. We see Jesus sending out the 70 two by two. We see Paul, as he goes on his missionary journeys, being accompanied by at least another person, and in most cases, a whole team. Years ago, most of the evangelistic associations across America would hire or support a single family or person to start a church. Today that is still done in many cases, but a shift has taken place in that churches are now developing teams to do the work. One of the reasons for the single person was economics. A team would cost a lot more to fund, and usually the whole team needs to be on the field working toward the establishment of the new church. It is obvious though, that more heads are usually better than one.

With a team, you have the support and division of responsibility that makes the effort much easier than being alone. From the beginning, you will have the manpower to meet more needs and get a faster start on the training and leadership. This makes it important that you have the right team members.

> **Choosing the right team members is so important. As we have discussed, it is crucial for the health and success of the church to have a sound beginning,**

Even with a team, there needs to be a main leader or catalyst. Some people may believe they all can work together as one and as equals. In accountability they are working together but practically, there has to be a "Paul" on the team. Usually there is a key person who has the vision and goes out and gathers his team. There never is any question about his leadership, since he handpicked the team and was the impetus for the church plant. If an association or group of churches sponsors the plant, then they usually choose the person and hire him to do the work. In this case, it is important that, if they are going to have a team concept, the first player be of a personality or type that fits that position. It is also important that that person has the say in whom he hires or brings on the team. If he is new at this, the association should help in the mixing and matching by looking at those who will be involved. We will discuss more about how to choose the right team later in this chapter.

Choosing the right team members is so important. As we have discussed, it is crucial for the health and success of the church to have a sound beginning, starting with those who will be involved in the church plant. There should be some obvious considerations made before the team is chosen. Let us look at some key factors that will help the working relationship of the team.

First, being on the same page is as vital as it is in renewing the established church. As the team is chosen, usually the place, and sometimes even the strategy and philosophy, have been determined. If this is the case, the team is off to a good start. What do I mean by "being on the same page" in the new church? Before anyone is involved, there must be an understanding and acceptance of the philosophy, direction, methods, and leadership of the organization or team. If any one person is not in agreement, or is in opposition, then there will be conflict and disorder. This should be agreed upon from the start, and if it cannot be, then any one person should not be considered as a team member.

But, there are some things that need to be taken into consideration when developing the team. This even applies to established churches as they hire ministers or staff for their church. Most times, churches never take into consideration the giftedness or personalities of those they will be hiring or adding to the team. This is why there are so many conflicts within leadership in our churches. If the members of the team are not on the same page, there will be conflict and positioning of power.

Second, knowing the personalities of each person is crucial. In most cases, differences in personalities have not been taken into consideration in the church. Just like people churches have personalities. In the new church you will be establishing that personality by the philosophy of ministry you adopt. Even when a minister is looking for a new church or a church is looking for a new minister, then realize that your personality or goals may not fit, if so, then both need to move on and not feel bad about it. In the world of business, it is now common practice to make personality profiles and instruction a part of the hiring and training of employees. In some cases, these profile studies is a determining factor in the hiring of a person. Is this discrimination or wise decision-making? It is not always wrong to discriminate in certain areas of life. Everyone does it to a point. When I was 16, I wanted to work and make some money to buy a car. The closest opportunity was on my neighbor's, farm. He had a job of loading hay in the fields. The next day I started at 8:00 a.m. They took me out to the field and said, "Let's put these bails on the trailer." After struggling with my first one, they knew I was not bailer material, and there ended my career in farming. At that point, I was not physically able to do the work. Was it discrimination against me? Yes, and rightfully so. I could not do the job, and it would have been wrong to expect them to keep me on.

> **A smart leader will want to have others working with him that will complement or add to the mix.**

Is it right to determine who goes on the team by personality type? If, for instance, you have two "D" personalities in the mix, you have potential for conflict, especially if no one knows about the process. Or, there may be problems if you have an "S" type person in the lead role and a "D" in a subordinate position. (The "D" and "S" refer to the personality DISC model.) This mix can work, but it will take a lot of effort to keep the conflict at bay. This is not to say you cannot have multiple personality types on the team; the fact is, you should. As long as those involved know who the responsible buck stopper is, the team can work well together. It is important to have each person go through these questionnaires before and as the team is being developed.

Third, knowing each team member's giftedness is a must. This is just as important as knowing what personality type each person has. On a team, you do not have all quarterbacks or all centers. The same is true with any ministry team. The only way you would have all members alike is if you are planning on having a church plant. At that point, which will occur much later in your ministry plans, you would add those people to the mix with that as a purpose. Or, as a person rises in the system, you would equip them to go on their own in a new work.

In developing your initial team, you may want all your staff to have the gift of leadership and another gift that will fit their position. Or, let's say the preaching minister will have a gift of leadership/teaching, one associate will be gifted in evangelism, and another shepherding, while all should be able and willing to be disciplers. A smart leader will want to have others working with him that will complement or add to the mix. Early on, someone must decide what each team members gifts and personality are, and what things they will be doing in the church plant. From there, the leader must envision others who might work with him on others that will the team, fill the areas you are weak in, or others you want to delegate. It may be that the leader has a lot of gifts and can, or feels he can do, a lot of things well. This may very well be true, but it will not be efficient to grow a church if he does it all alone. It may be self-satisfying for the leader but it will not be best in the long run for the church and everyone involved. The best scenario is that the leader finds or trains others so he can be the overseer in the beginning. Then, as the team is developed and working, each person can settle into what they feel they're best gifted for.

The whole concept of discipleship is to always be reproducing yourself, for the ministry of the leaders is to help others become and fulfill their God given destiny. Everyone's destiny is to work together in the body, helping others to fulfill their place in ministry, and always working yourself out of a job. Those who choose to be in higher levels of leadership fail when they think they should do it all. It is not the leaders that will be remembered for doing it, but those that have inspired others to do it all and continue on in a much larger way, repeating the whole process again and again.

Also important in the mix is the spouse of each person. It is vital that the couple is a team in their own eyes. Now in some cases, you find that some ministers have the idea that they are the ones being hired, and their spouse is not to do anything. This has evolved out of the misuse by congregations that expect the spouse to work as much as the one being hired. If she or he is doing the work, then they should be paid for it. The spouse is obligated, like any other member, to use her gift in the church. It is wrong and harmful if the spouse stays home or refuses to participate in anything of the church. This is the extreme that should be avoided, but also, if the spouse is expected to do something that you would naturally pay someone to do, then that person should be compensated as well.

> **The ideal is that the husbands and wives see themselves as a team. The church is made up of women and men, and they both have needs for shepherding and discipleship.**

The ideal is that the husbands and wives see themselves as a team. The church is made up of women and men, and they both have needs for shepherding and discipleship. Later in the second section you will see a system of discipleship where men disciple men and women disciple women. In this case, in the beginning the first women should be disciplined by the women in the team. Any church planting team that only includes the men will not be as successful as they could be without the spouses helping in the beginning of the process.

Earlier we mentioned Mels Carbonell's contribution to redefining personality types, but he has made a greater contribution by combining classical personality types with one's giftedness. This is important in that persons with the same gift will use that gift differently than others with the same gift because of the personality they bring to the mix. In a church plant team this is very crucial, as it is in any church staff team or ministry in the church. In the

Walk in Discipleship series, all the people in the church will go through both the personality and giftedness questionnaires. As a church or person goes through this process, they will be able to help each individual know where they fit in the body and how they should learn to react with other people. With this knowledge, there should be less of an opportunity to have conflict, and more of an opportunity to serve each other successfully.

Building the team as you build the church. In some cases, there are not enough funds to provide for the whole team in the beginning. If you start with just one family, then add the others as soon as possible, and definitely before you make a big community push in evangelism. During the developing of the nucleus, one family can handle it, but as you bring people to Christ, start with the idea of teamwork from the beginning. You might be surprised; in some circumstances, leaders will come from those who have been recently converted and not from trained religious professionals. It is important to remember that any team member be committed to discipleship, since this will be the core and foundation of the growth. Yes, great worship, great childcare, and powerful evangelism are a must, but "making disciples" will be the glue that will holds it all together.

Perpetual church planting team! Another option would be to develop a perpetual church planting team that will go from place to place planting new churches. This may work best if part of the team stays with the established church, and the next church will have some of the first team. Those who have the gift of starting, but not of growing the church, will be a part of each plant. When this takes place, it is up to the first or mother church to continue the process. It may be three years after the foundation is established, or even later, as the situation allows. This way the church in theory starts as a pregnant church. (See more about this below in the Mother-Daughter section.)

Individual church planter

Husband-Wife team. Any church planter that goes it alone and does not have a committed spouse to help in the process should look to maybe an established church, where they are hiring him to take over the position that has already been established. There are different jobs and pressures in a church plant than in an established church. As we have seen above, it is important to have this commitment between spouses in the team, as well as in an individual family church plant. If the spouse is not committed, then do not risk it. There are other opportunities to serve the Lord and His kingdom.

> **But, we can say that any spouse, in any situation, be it a job or ministry, will only be successful to the degree the other spouse will support**

You've heard it said that behind every good man is a good woman. That has truth in it, but it is also true that, in some cases, behind every failure of a man there was a failure by the woman. Neither is completely exclusive, and in many cases, the spouse has nothing to do with the success or failure of her husband. But, we can say that any spouse, in any situation, be it a job or ministry, will only be successful to the degree the other spouse will support them. Otherwise, if they are successful, it may be at the expense of the marriage.

It is easy for the husband to hear the call from God and the wife, for some reason, not. In this case, there should be a lot of prayer and honest discussion between the two. I have seen a lot of ministries stopped or never started because the spouse does not have the same commitment toward the calling. If the wife is truly following the Lord in her life, then it may just take time and prayer to have her come to supporting you and the idea. In some cases, she may see something you do not see, and you need to listen to her. Or, there may be some housekeeping that needs to be taken care of in your relationship first before you both begin this adventure. It all starts at home. In some cases, it is a matter of including your spouse in the dream and in the ministry. Leaving her out will tend to move her to resist your participation. In church planting, it is crucial for both to be committed because it is such a different lifestyle and, in many cases, more of a risk and less stable at first. The main thing is to see both of you as a team and keep the communication lines open between you and God.

The wife most times wants to feel secure in her relationship and in basic needs. If she feels that her and her family's needs will be jeopardized by the endeavor, then she will resist the mission you have been called to. If you are engaged and looking to getting married, then be honest up front, and share your calling. It may be that, if what God is calling you to be is completely opposite of what your special friend is interested in; maybe you should evaluate your relationship.

The dangers/pitfalls of single church planter

<u>Loneliness is an obvious result of a couple or individual going it alone</u>. It is not a sin or wrong for a couple to go it alone. One of the most successful husband-wife teams was Carlos and Carol Fields of East Tennessee. They planted at least 10 churches by themselves over the years. Carol worked but also helped in the church with the youth and other things as need be. The biggest thing was her support of Carlos' dream and calling to plant churches. I know at times it was lonely for them to go it alone, but they continued to fulfill their mission.

<u>Lack of gift mix is another potential problem with the single church planter</u>. I was privileged to help Carlos in one such plant, and we had time to talk about things together. It was obvious that Carlos was a catalyst, a self-starter, and enjoyed starting a church from scratch. But, he also realized he was not so gifted or inclined in shepherding and staying for the long haul. I believe he could have done it, but he chose to get things established and then hand the work over to others to continue on. This was okay because Carlos used his gifts to the fullest.

It should be obvious that one person does not have all the gifts and cannot be expected to successfully carry the whole responsibility, but the individual planter must, by the nature of the venture, do a lot, if not all, in the beginning. This is one reason the growth pace of the church usually will be slower. In some cases, the church may never overcome the barriers of a one-man operation. Churches that stay small usually see the minister as the lone workhorse, and expect him to do it all. This may begin a tradition that may not be overcome in future generations. A team effort will usually, by design, prevent this from happening.

<u>Burnout is one of the results of a one-couple or one-person plant</u>. The whole weight is on their shoulders, and the responsibility is great. Much time and effort is required, and if either of the participants are not prepared or committed, it will be hard to carry through until the end of the start-up stage. (The start-up stage is where there is no church leadership in place except for the planter or team before some others join the staff or there is mature men to fill the positions.) In some cases, the wife may burnout because of the strain on the marriage, especially if the wife is not so involved, or if it was not her dream or idea to be a part of this type of ministry. If this is the case burnout will happen, and the whole endeavor will usually crash and burn. If it is a hard field, or slow growing, and the results are not quick, then the

possibility of frustration will set in. Again, if discipleship is started from the beginning, then a person sees results immediately.

Lack of accountability. In an association plant, the individual is usually accountable to the sponsoring association or mother church. Usually this is in terms of finances and of getting the job accomplished in a timely manner. Beyond that, the individual feels they are accountable to God. In some cases, this can cause problems if the person or couple has a hard time or is not willing to be accountable to anyone. In a team, there is built-in accountability. Only time will tell if the couple or person is successful, and has been accountable to God, His word, and His mission. Since we are usually talking about independent works being established, then there is a time when the sponsors, if any, would usually relinquish their accountability. One would hope that, in the big picture, we are all accountable to one another to some point. But in an independent and autonomous system, there is a point where each congregation takes on that responsibility with God and God alone.

The benefits! Some of the benefits are obvious. Financially, it is easier to fund such a project. Secondly, if it is low or slow growth potential, then the manpower in a team may not be warranted at first. If there is a great need for multiple plants in an area, then the more that can be started the better. In some cases, there may be no church anywhere near the proposed site or no funds available unless as mission support, then this may be the best scenario. Any efforts to establish new churches in areas where there are none are a needed task for God's kingdom.

The single church planter! Now by this time, someone has already thought, "What about Paul, he was single." That's an assumption, but let's make that assumption. Even if he was single, he did not do his work alone, as we have already talked about and as you can surely see in his journeys around the world. If you have the calling to go into foreign fields or needed areas to start new works, it is better to find like-minded and called brothers to go with you. Ask God for a team. The work is hard, and the examples in the Bible seem to show two or three are better than one; that is, if they have the same vision.

> **The work is hard, and the examples in the Bible seem to show two or three are better than one; that is, if they have the**

Mother-Daughter Church Plant

The need! One of the most efficient ways to start a church is the mother-daughter birth. Most churches cannot or will not start another church. The small, struggling church cannot start one without destroying the mother church in the process. The chance that the larger church will start a church is slim because they want to become bigger and bigger. Usually a healthy, mid-size church will take that chance and be successful at it. No matter how big or small, if it is not done right, the result could be a disaster for both parties.

The healthiest from the start are those that are planned right and launched right. How do you do this? Let us look further.

The advantage! You have the support financially and logistically, and in most cases, the mass of people, a leadership already developed, and usually the team in place before the plant begins. That is, if the plan is viable. In many cases, people volunteer and just do it. In some cases the birth takes place and the mother gives some assistance, usually financial. But, there must also be the needed accountability and leadership support in the beginning. If it is done correctly, all that will be minimized before there ever is a start.

If the new baby is big enough, then the start will be healthier. If a church sends off 25 people to start a church, they will have a tendency to struggle, and the church will be small for some time. But if the church can send off 75 to 100 or more people trained and ready to function, then the church will be able to grow exponentially. If the church can be started with 150 people, then you will be setting a foundation for a 500-plus church in no time.

Building the foundation before final launch.

The method! Daughter-child plant.

Challenge the people! This is not for every church, and probably not for most churches, but for those who have this vision, God will bless them tremendously. I would not recommend this move for churches fewer than 500 to 600. A church that has 500 members could loose 100 and not be hurt. A church of 600 to 650 and above could easily take 150 and make a start. Some may want to wait until they're much larger to do something like this. The main point is that, when the launch happens, those leaving should be ready.

Before all this, all the people will have to see the new plant as a mission of their church. This will take a lot of challenging and a great commitment from the leadership to see this through. It will especially take a commitment from the senior minister and associates. If he is the type that sees only big numbers, then he may not be motivated or may even feel threatened to do something like this. If this is not a problem, then this challenge may take some time to encourage everyone to get on the same page.

If the church were a new plant itself, then it would be great to have this as a goal in the future. If you are living in a town of a 1000, this may not be a realistic goal, but if you're living in a city of thousands, then it is a worthwhile quest to follow and pursue.

Find the leadership! This should be easy if the church is establishing the *Walk in Discipleship* program that you will look at in depth in section two or have already implemented in your congregation. The leaders will naturally come to the forefront during this two- to- three year ministry of discipleship. This will include those leaders in the shepherding families and in each ministry area of the church.

There may also be a need to find someone to be the minister or staff, and this may have to come from outside. If so, then the mother church should go ahead and hire the ministers for the new church. There may already be someone on staff who will take that challenge, or the next time the mother church hires an associate, it should hire one that has the desire to take over a new church. This should be done two to three years prior to the launch of the new birth so the process and growth will be together.

Train the people! This too should be easy if the church is already discipling and shepherding one another. It will not be a matter of adding, but multiplying. If the church has 600 people and 100 are committed to planting a new church, then you only allow those who have already been trained and gifted to be a part of it. It is also important that this transition does not happen until there are enough workers and ministers ready, so as not to hurt the mother church in her growth or stability.

Find the location! This is a crucial part of the move. This may have been one of the first things done in determining who will comprise the new congregation. If you have shepherding families working, then there may be a sector or family that is in a part of town that could handle another congregation, a place where the mother has reached out and developed a sector but where a new church would better meet the needs of that sector or community.

Distance! You've seen a different church on each corner, much like a Burger King and McDonald's at the same intersection. That is okay for denominations, but not for a mother-daughter. Find a place across town in another community. This is all dependent on the size of the city you're in. The bigger and growing cities will not have any problem finding the right place and distance.

Prime! More crucial is the actual location. In many of the cases, when church plants happen, most have been in a place the mother or the association could afford. That usually would be on a back road, or a location where there was a decline in population- basically cheap, but not advantageous for the work. It's best to rent until the best place can be afforded. If that place opens up, make land purchase the primary goal, then be concerned about what goes on it later when you are ready with a large enough mass. Location is the first important decision in the success of the new church, so do it right the first time. Look for a place where there is visibility and traffic, or where there will be visibility or traffic in the future. Be sure though, if it is a future site, to check with the local planning commission to see what are in the plans for the future. Look for future roads and developments or re-directing of roads. What may be a prime location today may not be in five or ten years. Plan and ask questions because if you don't you will enter in blind and set up the church for failure or mediocrity.

Growth potential! Another important factor is the growth and health of the community you're targeting. Is the area changing? Is the area declining in its growth? Are people moving out and going to other parts of town? Is it a graying community, or are there new developments being planned? Are the schools in decline, or are they growing? All of these are factors that need to be taken into consideration before you buy. The great deal may be a bad deal in disguise.

Separate and name congregations before they go! At least six months to a year before launch date, start having the new church meet at different times. Have them go ahead and develop their identity, their worship, and their staff. At this point the leadership is still shared by both groups, but more and more responsibility and decision making is being separated. One of the first things they can do is to decide what their name is going to be. Let them decide by themselves, without any influence from those who are not going with the plant.

Help them go! There needs to be a sending off and celebration time. So when it is time for the official move, have a celebration, an official sending off, with services either in the new facility, an independent joint facility, or both at the mother church and then the new church. There is no right or wrong way, as long as you have it done. You might have a church shower where people will give a little extra to help in the establishment of the new church.

Let them go! This should be the goal to have an autonomous healthy child. When the children leave the nest, the parents should let them go and stand on their own two feet. If the plant has gone as scheduled, the new child will not go until it is ready. It should have its leadership in place, and be large enough to support itself financially. The mother should not leave it alone financially for a few years, and the building or place they will be worshiping in should be funded in part by the mother and child together, until such time as the new church can go it alone. With 150 or more people, there should be enough to take care of the staff needed.

But remember, the two should keep a warm and supportive fellowship with each other. Maybe have fifth Sunday rallies, or periodical fellowship times, so the church is not a lone congregation. The church is made of all the congregations that exist. We will do better if we realize this and think of ourselves as the body of Christ. Christ wants the church to be one, and that does not mean only one within your four walls but one with all His churches. Let us make the effort to come together and develop that spirit. The mother-daughter relationship will easily provide an opportunity for this to happen.

TEAM PLANT

Another method is the team approach. Again it is wise to prepare the team or planter first. In many cases this is overlooked while the main consideration is the place and funding. Be sure everyone is on the same page. From the beginning, it will be important that everyone sees that making disciples is the prime directive and direction of the discipling church. The mother-daughter concept is corporate discipleship in mass. It is where the mother church is reproducing itself in every way, while at the same time allowing the new church to develop its own personality without giving up the foundation of discipleship and core leadership principles.

The first thing to do is to choose or hire the new team of leaders. If the mother already has the shepherding families set up in sectors, then it is easy to allow one or two sectors to become the basis of the new congregation. If so, then you already have the superstructure developed. The small groups, the shepherds, and system of discipleship are established. All you have to do now is see to it that you have the senior leaders ready to lead. The best way is to hire or appoint an existing staff or leader into the position. This person may work directly under the senior minister of the mother church and with the new plant. From the beginning, the leader is in the mix and will keep it from derailing or from bringing in someone that bucks or does not understand the system. This should take place at least two to three years before the launch date, if possible. He should be a part of its development from the beginning. The idea is that he is beginning the church from the day he becomes involved. The benefit is that he has the structure, support, and even a majority of the people already in-house to start. Bugs and procedures are worked out in these developmental years before they go public or launch from the mother church. It is a true gestation and birth process.

Another option is that the existing minister or pastor will go with the new church and find someone to come in and take his place in the mother church. This again is all according to the personality and goal of the senior minister or pastor.

If it is a church start where there is no mother mass then the first thing after the team is established and trained is to get an initial nucleus to start with. This is the 12 or 70 or even the 120 factor. If 120 to 150 could be trained and separated into the new plant, then you will have a healthy, growing congregation from the start. As was noted above, this can be from sectors or families that have been growing and mature enough to commit to this concept. Or, it may be opened up to the church at large, or a combination of both.

Build the nucleus first

1. *Be patient.* Ideas come and go, but if your church has this dream of being a mother in a church plant, then their needs to be wisdom on when and how it is to be done. Wait patiently for people to catch the dream it is usually a new concept to most people. To some leaders, it is hard losing people, especially if they are concerned about their growth and

numbers. The vision has to be shared and caught by all. If you are a church plant and young in your development, then even from the start, make it a part of your long-range goals to be involved in mothering. In some cases, this may be premature, but if a mother church started a new church, then it would be natural to also make this part of your philosophy. In anything that is done, whether it is implementing the *Walk in Discipleship*, planting a new church, or building a new building, try as hard as possible to have everyone on the same page.

If there are individuals that are negative or destructive in everything that is positive, then there must be steps taken to deal with those people. The goal is to serve and fulfill God's command to make disciples, and if an individual is a consistent thorn, then the problem is with that person, and he must not be allowed to control the death of the church or allowed to go with the new church plant. But in some cases, if there are some that do have concern and caution, then it is always important to listen and try to be on the same page. The goal of a mother church plant is not to get rid of all the dead weight by suggesting they go with the new plant, but rather deal with them as we have said above.

2. *Take the time.* It may take years to get to the point of producing an offspring. The church has to be healthy and full of trained leaders so the event will not harm the mother. That is why the program of *Walk in Discipleship* will be so helpful in preparing for this endeavor.

3. *Equip them well!* Be sure that those in leadership and at every level of giftedness are ready and trained before they are allowed in the church plant. Encourage each person that becomes involved to be involved in using his or her gifts and talents. This is why it is important to have the mother church healthy and those who stay behind to also be diligent about their service and gifts as well. A church that operates on the traditional percentage of 80% watch and tell the 20% who do all the work what they should and shouldn't be doing will fail to fulfill this dream. If your church is a typical church like this, then you will have a long time to be patient. You have to get at least 80% mobilized, or any endeavor like this will fail.

4. *Develop the framework of the church.* If the mother church is structured like is suggested in the "Walk in Discipleship," then there will be a framework to transfer. Now there may be different types of worship, and there may be new ministries developed based upon their location and community, but the basic framework of discipleship, shepherding, and training leadership will all be basic to both.

Second launch. This is where the new body goes public and on their own. By this time, a place has been purchased, or a place like a school or theater has been rented, like a school or theater to begin meeting. I would suggest that there be no launch until at least a property has been bought. It might be premature to build. The new church needs to grow and get a public momentum and then build after this is established. I suggest the land being purchased, for this will make a statement to both the new church and the community, but having the building built may be too much of a burden. It also is good to allow the new church to have this goal to work towards. This will give the church time to grow on its own, and to grow a stronger identity going into the building program.

If a church starts at 150 members and is discipling and evangelizing, then it won't take long for it to double or triple if it is in a growing community. At that point, it will have a vision of how big a building it will need to build. Buildings can be a great help, but at the same time can be a deterrent to growth if built too fast, too small, or in the wrong place. The building is not the cure to growth problems, or the panacea that will keep it going. The church already has to have in place the people and discipleship that will continue the growth. If that structure is not in place, then the building will be the focus, and when it is done, then the momentum is lost and the people settle into a rut. This has happened time after time.

The example! I read once about a church in Florida that had a vision to plant churches in her city. The church determined to grow no more than 650 people, but at the same time plant new churches. Their plan was that every time they reached 650, they would take 150 people and start a new church. This then would bring them down to 400, and then the growth would start again. Then at 650, they would start another church. At the time I read about them, they had started nine congregations, and attendance at the churches ranged from 400 to 1500. Overall, these church plants yielded about 5000+ members among all the churches. What a testimony to church growth they became.

Dream your dream, visualize your vision, build your team, and go with the direction and power of the Lord.

Church Splits and the new church!

As we have seen some churches have Planned Parenthood, and some just have illegitimate births, that is, splits. In both cases, new bodies are formed, and God will bless both if they both will yield to His will and guidance. Sadly splits do happen and in some cases the results are minimal, or at times disastrous, to each church and the name of Christ. The thing to remember is that it will happen, there will be division and splits in this world we have now. The hope is that whatever the reason for the split, the new churches can become a glory to God. How do the two churches recover after the split? This is a book in and of itself, but I do want to suggest a few points that may help those who have, are, and may be going through a split.

For whatever reason the split takes place, you have for the most part two different churches. There are usually those who stay and those who leave. Those who stay usually continue their same old ways, whether good or bad. Hopefully they will take a look at themselves self as a congregation to see what went wrong and how they can fix the problem or become a better bride for Christ in the end. If they point their finger only outward, then they may miss an opportunity to see things that may need changing in their congregation. In most cases both sides can only see the other's fault in the matter, and this is unfortunate and sad. In any case both have the opportunity to become what God has intended for both to be. Let us look at some things that may help either body go forward and become the church they were intended to be.

First, determine to forgive. Just like with individuals, God will not bless us with forgiveness if we fail to forgive others. This is the same for both sides in the church split. Any given congregation is made up of individuals that make good or bad decisions. It is obvious that the health of any church is based upon the sum of its members. If you have selfish, divisive individuals, then you will also have a selfish divisive congregation. To heal this, there must be admittance of fault and repentance and forgiveness. Even if one is in the right they must in the end let the bitterness go. Usually the split is not over doctrine, but over personal conflict and personality or personal agendas. In this case there, needs to be healing before either body will be able to go forward and serve God in a healthy growing situation.

Second, determine to look inside yourself. Each church as a whole, and each individual, member must look inside themselves own self to see attitudes that may need to be changed. You also might look inside and see that maybe the other side did have a point or an issue. In some cases, there may be healing and reunion, and in others acceptance of each other as brothers and sisters in Christ.

Third, look inside the Bible for direction. If the split was over doctrine issues, then be sure your part of the body is based upon the biblical foundation. If you find that it was not over doctrine or personalities but rather over differing philosophies of ministry, then accept that there can be differences in style, but not in allegiance to Jesus as Lord. For instance, let us say that half of the congregation wants to worship by using southern gospel music and the other wants to have worship around contemporary songs and choruses; then both need to celebrate the differences. Now I use this as an example, but in no way condone a split of churches over music style. The better way is having two different services, but if a split does happen, then realize that neither style is right or wrong. We will discuss this more in depth later in our chapter on Worship.

Let us not forget Jesus' prayer for love and unity in all that we say and do, and that includes the church; at all times.

Planting Churches on the foreign field

The biggest mistake I have witnessed in my years in foreign mission work is the transference of our methods or democratic forms to the churches planted around the world. We have already issued the fallacy of the democratic church in its form and structure. Why do other countries hold us in distain at times? It is because we have tended to force our ways on their culture. We have taken our flawed model of the church and expected them to accept it. I propose that the model the first church developed was and is transcendent of culture. I still think it is the same today. The first church was not based upon American, or even democratic Greek forms of the day.

I believe the missionaries of the recent past saw that part of their mission was bringing democracy along with the planting of churches. This was a mistake and still is a mistake today.

I remember the first time I visited Poland back in 1975. When you were introduced to a brother in or out of the church service he greeted you with a holy kiss on each side of your cheek. I also noticed other differences between their church and the American church in terms of warmth, worship and dedication. I returned in the years of 1979, 83,85,89,92, and then full time missionary from 1995-2000. During those years Poland and the rest of the former Soviet Union eastern countries went through tremendous political and cultural changes, and still are. What I observed is an example in many areas. As these countries opened up to the west, their money, and influence things began to change. Now when you go into most of these churches you will find it hard to be greeted with the holy Kiss. You will see churches that look more like US churches than Polish. Another thing that has changed is the excitement to hear the word of God no matter how many preached. I was in services where you had as many sermons as you had preachers, and there was no concern about time; they were there to hear God's Word and worship. Today you see more of 30-minute sermons as the norm and only who is scheduled will be able to preach. Are they better off? I some cases yes, but in many cases think not.

What I am saying is be careful when you plant or help churches world wide not to try to Americanize them at the expense of helping them become Biblical New Testament churches. It might be that as we go around the world we might learn something from our brothers and sisters that will help us grow. I know in my mission endeavor that has been the case. We do not have all the answers. When we come across that way we then will lose our audience and ability to help.

As you go through the rest of this book you will see how the discipleship model I am suggesting is more New Testament than the model we have propagated. I think it will be accepted better than the democratic model of the past.

A healthy growing church will grow to the level of their dysfunction. Churches that do not grow are usually dysfunctional in some way. Now most churches have some dysfunction, but those that do not grow have more dysfunctional tendencies than those who are growing. How can a church become healthy in their dysfunction? That is the question to answer for the next part of Church Growth Pie.

PART TWO

Church Growth System
The Pieces of the Pie to help the church Grow!

THE
CHURCH GROWTH System (Pie)

Introduction to Part Two

The right ingredients are imperative to a successful pie; the same is true for church growth. Of course, there are basic things like flour and heat, but amounts may vary, as much as the stars. But, some ingredients just won't work. I found that out when I made my first mud pie with my next-door neighbors. What I have tried to share so far, and what is to come, will result in growth - if followed. Of course, you must have the basics, and equally important is "the filling" (what goes into the pie.) You may have the right crust, but if the insides are spoiled or tasteless, then the basics won't matter. The church may have the basic "crust", but if it does not have the right "fillings" (ministries), then no one will remember the golden brown, flaky crust.

In this section, each piece is important, and if anyone is missing, the church will then be deficient by that amount. As mentioned above, if the piece has the wrong ingredients or is improperly blended, then the result will also be wrong and, in many cases, useless! As you take each piece, I hope you are able to apply it to your church.

What we are talking about is developing a system, not a bunch of programs. Most churches have programs that work independently from each other with ineffective results. But I propose a system where all parts are coordinated and working together, for the same purpose and goal, and that is making disciples.

The Nature of Leadership
Chapter Six

Li Hung Chang (one time leader in China) said, "There are only three types of leaders: those who are immovable, those who are movable, and those who move them!"

Harry S. Truman, U.S. President, once said: "A leader is a person who has the ability to get others to do what they don't want to do, and like it."

The litmus test of a leader is simply whether or not anyone is following his teachings and directions.

It is easy to look throughout history and find examples of great leaders - great men and women who have stepped out and gone above others to lead them to higher levels. We can see great charismatic leaders who have moved people and nations, whether to the right or to the left. Is there a difference between charismatic natural leaders, and spiritually-gifted leaders? Even in the religious world, one does not have to look far to find great charismatic leaders who lead from their own charismatic personalities and who bubble over with spiritual fervor and wisdom. Both seem to gather a following of people, but what makes one leadership type valid (in terms of Biblical standards) and the other questionable?

The leader must be gifted in: (Ephesians 4:11-13)

Spiritual leadership! Oswald Sanders said, "There is no such thing as a self-made spiritual leader. A true leader influences others spiritually only because the Spirit works in and through the leader to a greater degree than in those he leads." Personality without the person of the Spirit will lead to personal agendas, and to misled people. Many problems arise in the church when talented leaders are placed in leadership and given authority without the power and anointing of the Spirit. God would rather have a person with fewer abilities, under the guidance and power of the Spirit, than the most "qualified" spiritless leader. If this were not the case, then why would we need the Spirit? In the secular arena, you merely need to find the best-qualified and talented leader.

For example, look at Moses and his inadequacies. In his humbleness God could use him, maybe even more than someone who was full of himself. To God, a person open to His leading is more apt to be more useful than a person with talent - who is "full of himself". A leadable servant can be used because he is teachable.

Spiritual teaching! What is the main task of a leader? Quite simply, the leader is to show and teach others where they should be and how to get there. To do that, the person must know how to teach. Does that mean enthralling people via a powerful lecture? Maybe, but spiritual teaching is more than that. It is teaching people with spiritual power and direction. Again, let us not confuse a talent with a gift. A person may have all the skills to effectively deliver and teach people to the point they will learn, but is the method of teaching as important as the gift? The apostle Paul himself admitted he was a lousy speaker or lecturer, but what he taught was powerful and life changing. Paul was consumed with spiritual fervor and power to teach through the Holy Spirit, and his willingness to yield to God made him one of the most powerful and effective leaders of all time.

Spiritual insight! Knowing leadership principles and procedures will only feed your ego, if you lack the spiritual insight to make them effective. This is why it's dangerous to merely put "talented people" in positions of leadership. If they do not have the spiritual insight, then they will not be equipped to truly guide in times of debate of the truth and trials in leadership. This is also the reason you don't put a novice in the faith, in certain leadership positions too soon. It takes time for a person to develop insight in the Spirit. It takes time to get to know what the Spirit wants and needs to teach a person. A novice or recent convert has not had the time to be taught these insights by the Spirit through the study of the Word and Christian experience.

Many churches make the mistake of putting people in positions of leadership in order to get them involved and keep them coming back. This is the biggest mistake a church could make. It is here that churches set themselves up to fail and have problems later, because you can put a person who is operating from the flesh and not the Spirit into a leadership role, and the decisions he/she makes will be detrimental to the church and the individual.

Knowledge is important and comes through our study, but wisdom is what we do with that knowledge. That wisdom comes from having and yielding to the Holy Spirit within us. Paul's prayer for the church in Colossae, and for each person, especially each leader, was for God to "fill you with the knowledge of his will through all spiritual wisdom and understanding" (Colossians 1:9). This takes time and humility, so don't rush it.

Life Application: How can we know if the potential leaders have these qualities? Having them go through a year of apprenticeship will help you see their gifts of leadership in practice. For those who are already in leadership, you must evaluate yourself in the areas above and as well as in those that follow. Be honest about yourself. If you do not fit these criteria, then be willing to reconsider where God wants you to serve in the body.

The leader must be a Servant-Ruler.

Attitude of servant! We do not read "Moses my leader", but "Moses my Servant"! I would add, you are not becoming an officer or joining an office; you are becoming a servant, or performing a service. So it is not participating in the office of the elder, but in the service of an elder.

In Romans 8:12, the leader or manager is to serve with earnestness, diligence, zeal, and eager effort. The English fails to give all these meanings, but in the Greek, one can see the kaleidoscopic facets of the word. This service should not be a drudgery or task to put up with, but should be looked at with eagerness and excitement. If you have no eagerness or zeal in your service, then you need to check your motivation or gifts. You may have all the qualities and just need to be encouraged and to realize what great opportunity you have to serve the living God and His people.

What if a person has all the gifts, but does not want to serve? He may have been in leadership before but has no desire to do so now. It may be that, sometime in the past, he was hurt or disillusioned while serving. Or, maybe he was placed where he was not gifted and it didn't work out. This person needs encouragement and counseling to see what the problem was so he might be restored to service.

Not lording, but guiding! The word that is used for the term *leader* also has deeper meanings in the Greek. A leader is a person who is a manager; one who cares for and gives help. The concept even has the idea of engaging with the one being taught. You not only lead from the front, but you take people by the hand, like a friend, and *guide* them to where they need to be. Although the word does indicate that a leader is a person with authority, he is more like a father rather than a boss or ruler.

Sacrificial! What does it take to be a leader? It takes sacrifice. If you feel put out that you have to listen to another bleeding heart or spend all this time in study or with people, then it is important that you evaluate your service and commitment. It is not a sin to decide not to be a leader, but it is wrong to *say* you are, yet *fail to be committed to the task* and those you lead. Jesus said it well: "Whoever wants to be great among you must be your servant, and whoever wants to be first, must be slave of all" (Mark 10:42-44). To be a slave means to sacrifice. A servant leader is a slave to those he serves.

> Life Application: 1. Pray for God to give you these qualities. The leadership should take the time to pray for each other and for future leaders. 2. It is important to realize that only Jesus was the perfect leader. Not one individual will be perfect in leadership 100% of the time, but the Bible has given us some guidelines on how to be the best we can. Therefore, pray and seek His way in your leadership.

The leader must be an Example in: 1 (Thessalonians 1:3-7). "Just as you learned it from Epaphras, our beloved fellow bond-servant, who is a faithful servant of Christ on our behalf."

Character! Paul was Timothy's mentor, his example in so many things, one of which was his character. In 1 Timothy 3:2, we see a leader that must be above reproach. Now, what is the practical meaning, to "be above reproach" today? It means that a leader must do nothing shameful or disgraceful. There must be nothing sinful in his Christian life, especially at the present, which is known to the public. Now this, of course, does not apply to the time before he was a Christian. It is important that the elder or leader have a character that will help the new and struggling Christian find strength as an example of what a Christian life should be like. If a leader's word cannot be trusted when he says he will do something, then how can this be a good example for those he is trying to lead?

Action/Using Gifts! Can the people whom you shepherd <u>see</u> your dedication, as you participate in the life of the fellowship? Are you faithful at meetings and during church services? Do your actions demonstrate that you are serious about your faith? Can you be relied upon to be there when you're needed, when you say you'll be there? Are your gifts evident, and are you willing to use them to glorify Christ and help the body grow?

Life Application: 1. First, think about your reputation and your current actions in the life of the body. 2. If any changes are required, then ask God to give you the power to repent and to change, both as individuals, and as a leadership team. 3. Are you willing to use your gifts and your time? If not, then check your commitment. The church needs your participation, not your title.

The leader must be an enabler by:

Helping others to discover their gifts! The saddest thing in any church is for its members to find out, too late, that they have a gift that was never discovered, developed, or used. In most churches a majority of people don't know what gifts they have, or what the Spirit wants them do. The task of the leader is to help each person bring his or her gifts into service. Power without tools and talents will also lead to discouraged disciples. The Spirit is smart in what he gives. He knows the talents and interests of each person because those qualities also came from the Creator. It is also true that, in some cases, the Spirit gives us gifts in spite of our shortcomings and lack of talent. So, it is the responsibility of the leader to help each one in his/her discovery and implementation of that gift in the body.

Life Application: 1. Is there a system to help people discover their gifts? Is it proving effective for every believer? 2. If not, what must you do to get it started? Teaching on the kinds of gifts, workshops on how to discover your gifts, and apprenticeship in areas of service, are places to start. Explore more ways to get the job started during your leaders' meeting.

Encouraging them to use their gift! Encouragement is the biggest human factor that will spur someone on to fulfillment of his or her gifts. Discouragement, or even a lack of encouragement, will quench the Spirit of involvement. It surprises me how negative people can become in the church. The negative person can derail or destroy any progress in an individual's life or in the life of the whole church. To some people, discouragement is not a derailment but a challenge. Although this is the exception, some people bear down the hardest, but will give up if continually discouraged. My 7th and 8th grade teacher told me that I was stupid and would never make it through college. Many students would have given up (and some did) because of his ignorance. I have always wanted to show him my college diploma and my three graduate degrees, but I just prayed for him and all the students he discouraged. Paul tells us to encourage one another, for the days are short.

Life Application: 1. Each shepherd should be responsible for taking the time to encourage each member of his shepherding group to use his/her gifts.
2. Acknowledge in public how well people are doing in service of their gift.
3. Don't underestimate what a person and God can do together.

Giving them opportunity to use their gift! Does your fellowship make it easy for people to serve in the ministries of the church? Some church leaders will discourage the use of gifts, because it will require more time to create and watch over certain ministries. Churches that have the vision to grow will make every effort to see that people can serve in their areas of giftedness. If the Spirit gives certain gifts, then the leadership has the responsibility to see that there is opportunity in the life of the church to fulfill these gifts. It is important that discovery of giftedness precede service, or even the implementation of certain ministries. If there are no gifted persons, then no ministry should be started.

Life Application: 1. List all the different ministries available for people to use their gifts. 2. In this list, do you see where the option can be expanded to allow for more opportunity? 3. The best way is to gather each person based upon his or her gift and let each to explore how to use these gifts in the ministry of the church and the community. It's better to find the gift and then serve, than to create a place of service, and try to find a gifted person to fill it afterward (See appendix for membership involvement forms).

A leader must be a visionary that has:

Foresight. Most people are not visionaries. This is why most people are not leaders in their time. The leaders of a local fellowship must have the foresight to lead their group to where they need to be. You are not responsible for the world, but you are responsible for the flock God has given you in your part of the world. Some people may have bigger visions and God will direct them. Most people in leadership lack the foresight or direction for their people. They just go on as usual, never knowing that God has more in store for each of us. It is the leader's job to see that and to help each person find his or her place. The leader with foresight will be able to see the result of what he's teaching, and know how to lead his people there. The individual and the group may see and capture the vision, but it takes visionaries to see it first, and share it. In many cases, the senior minister or pastor comes to the table with a vision. If this is the case, it is extremely important that he take the time to work with the leadership to help them see this vision. In some cases, the senior minister has no specific vision, or has had one but was discouraged by some non-qualified leaders who would not listen to any new ideas. This is where he needs to spend time talking with God and his fellow leaders.

Insight! What vision do you have for the people God has given you? What are they capable of in the Lord? They have the insight about what are right and wrong directions. It is also important that unity be maintained. God will not give leaders conflicting visions. The people on the day of Pentecost saw a group of uneducated Galileans, but Jesus long before saw their potential. We must see that potential in ourselves and in others. It is important to always ask, "Whose vision?" Of course, there never should be any conflict with the spirit of the Bible and the vision God has for His church.

Courage and fortitude! A visionary leader must be willing to step out in faith when others are, at first, afraid to try. A visionary can see the first, next, and last step, and is willing to take that first step and sacrifice to see it to the end. He is also able to know when to quit and/or when to redirect, if needed. It is important that, no matter the opposition, he must be faithful to God and rely on Him to confirm and carry out the vision. Some will try to attack any vision or progress because that is their carnal spirit and choice, but it is always important that the pastor/leader be open to others and their opinions. They may have insight that may help in the vision.

Life Application: Does your church have a vision of God's plan in your part of the world? 1. Take the time in prayer and in discussion to explore God's vision for your fellowship. 2. If the senior minister/pastor has a vision, pray about it and work together to see how it can work in your fellowship.

A leader must be a Lover of:

God and His Word! Do you love to read the Word of God? The elder or leader must be a man of the Word. How can you teach and guide the fellowship in the right direction and protect them from heresy if you are not in the Word yourself? Loving and knowing God is the only way we will be able to know and love the Lord better.

People! Even though an individual or a group may oppose the leader's vision in the church, and may even despise you at times, the leader must still speak the truth in love. A leader can have all the words and knowledge of the Bible, and know all the right leadership techniques, but if he does not lead with love, then Godly results will not be forthcoming. A loveless leader becomes a controlling dictator, selfishly taking people where he wants.

The work! Do you find yourself complaining about the people, the time you spend, and the effort you have to make to be a leader? Do you loathe going to meeting after meeting? Then maybe you do not love your work or ministry. If you do not, then you will not be fit or joyful in doing your service for God. God wants someone who loves his work. I'm not saying you have to love everything or every situation, or that you may not be sad or tired at times, when serving. If your general outlook is one of dread, then it is likely you are not where you should be in your work for the Lord. God wants us to rejoice in what we do. He wants us to have a desire to be in this position to help others grow to their potential.

Life Application: 1. Pray that God will give you compassion for others and a deeper love for His Word. Spend time with His Word and with His people. 2. If you have a hard time being with people, then evaluate your place in this ministry.

The leader must be a Disciple that:

Continues as one. Always remember that we are all disciples and that we all need to continue to learn from someone who is more knowledgeable than we are. It is always important to ever learn and grow. You should seek out a person that can be a mentor to you. You should never have the attitude that you don't need someone to learn from.

Reproducing yourself and discipling others. "Go make disciples of all nations." This is our task until the whole world knows. In every area, and in every field, disciples must be made. This should be the goal of each leader- to reproduce him/herself. This provides more leaders for growth. If you want to control how much the church grows, then don't reproduce. But, the church that grows will always have an apprentice at every group in the church. Every class, every cell, every Sunday school should have someone in training. Some are afraid that if they train someone else, he may be better and take over the job. That's quite right, and that's the goal! What you leave behind may be more important than doing everything yourself. Jesus could have done every-thing perfectly, but he pulled back and let His disciples or trainees do it. In the church, we should not be concerned about competition, but multiplication. I win when we all win. The church wins when we all win.

> Life Application: 1. In whatever role you find yourself, try to encourage someone to come alongside and learn how to do what you're doing. 2. Then, deploy and set apart this person into his own role. This is not only in official leadership positions but also in every fabric of the life of the church.

The Purpose of Leadership! Ephesians 4:12-15

Feed and care for the sheep. The people with whom Christ was most angry were those who were in leadership positions but failed to lead, those who were "hirelings". Leaders who fail to take care of God's sheep will be held accountable very highly in the judgment. Paul warns leaders not to take this duty lightly, and especially for the wrong reasons. Some people take upon themselves these responsibilities without really knowing or understanding the importance of this position in the Church.

What is at stake? The first thing at stake is the committed souls of those who depend on you to lead them to maturity. Most people in the church are not leaders and will never be, but they need good leaders to lead them. Second, you as a leader will be accountable for what you do (or don't do) with your flock. If you are a self-centered leader, and fail to take care of the people, then God will judge you harder than the non-Elder/leader.

Why? Most people want to trust and believe in their leaders. Most people will believe and listen to them, often without any resistance or question. This is why it is important for the leader to know the difference between right and wrong and where to lead the sheep. Therefore, if they are led astray, their blood will be on the hands of the leadership. This may sound harsh, but we are talking about eternal life and death. I have seen people who were once active members, but who are now bitter and will not darken the door of any church because some leader (or leadership) failed to fulfill their duties as leaders and shepherds. Now, of course, there are those who refuse to be led. Even if this is true, this does not negate the responsibility of the leadership to lead. One of the successes of leaders is to realize those who want be led and deal with them.

> Life Application: 1. Pray for your leadership and those who are in leadership. 2. Evaluate your current shepherding activities. Some churches do not have any way of looking after or shepherding their people. If this is the case in your church, start praying for that vision and commitment to begin this ministry. 3. If you are being responsible, then evaluate your effectiveness. (More of this will be discussed in depth in Chapter eight.)

Equipping the Saints for the work of service! (v. 12a). In many of our churches today, the work and service in the church is delegated to those who are hired staff or ministers. The idea that "we pay them to work" has hindered most believers from fulfilling their God-given duties in the church. It is true that those who are being paid should spend their time in full-time service. The question is - *what kind* of service? The church that depends on its leaders to do it all will not be the kind that will grow to its God-intended level or potential. It will also produce a spectator church, without every member participating. As we plainly see in this text, the goal of the leadership is to equip or train every "saint" member in the body to participate by using their gifts and talents. This equipping is realized in at least two ways.

Have some level of understanding of the basic tenets of the faith. Christians must be equipped with the Sword of Truth. They must know what it means to live a Christian life, as well as how to live it in daily circumstances. They must be able to spiritually survive in a world that is hostile by hiding the Word in their hearts.

Every member should be equipped in using his or her gifts and talents. Everyone's needs are met when everyone is equipped to serve one another. Learning that the mature attitude is service, not only receiving, will help the body grow more into maturity and unity, as well as in numbers.

> Life Application: 1. There must be a planned course of basic studies and materials to train and equip each person in the knowledge and application of Biblical truths and practices. This is, of course, solely based upon Bible truths and methods. "No direction" will lead you "no where". 2. Every member should have someone guiding him/her in the development of his/her gifts and talents, and equipping him/her for service. An apprenticeship program is the best way to train and deploy servants.

Build up the body! (v.12b). What does it mean to build up the body? It is a sad state when many churches are seen as a place of fighting and division, not love and harmony. The body of Christ must be concerned about "building up one another". This is to start with the leadership. If the leadership is in disarray, then what will the church become? The leadership must first build up each other, then provide the atmosphere and opportunity for the rest of the body to be there, to minister to one another.

> Life Application: Gene Getz's book, *Building Up One Another,* is a good place to start in studying and applying some of these principles. Use the topics as sermon themes and then apply them in the home Bible studies during the week.

Promote and create unity! (v.13a). Once the church is taught how to build up one another and how to live as servants, then the body will grow into unity. What kinds of unity should the leadership be concerned about? It is important that, in each of the areas below, unity exist. If any one of the two has disunity, then problems, fighting, and division will occur.

In the truth, doctrinal purity! One can look back over history and see disunity among believers concerning doctrine and what is truth. The important thing for the leadership is that they know the difference between what is essential and what is not. Many have lived by the idea that, "In matters of faith or essentials unity, in the matters of opinion or non-essentials liberty, and in all things love." The problem is deciding the essentials of the Christian faith and the non-essentials or opinions. In most churches, for example, the essentials include the deity and resurrection of Christ. To have unity, you must agree that Jesus is God and that he rose from the dead for our sins. Non-essentials include such things as the kind of music, worship style, or the decor of one's meeting place. The leadership should bring the body to an understanding of the essentials and not allow matters of opinion or non-essentials to cause division.

In relational unity, one with another! How do we promote unity within the body? Lives must be transformed from the old way of thinking and living into a new way. The leadership is responsible when there are problems between believers. It is the duty of the leadership to be peacemakers and to see that certain relationships do not grow into divisive problems. The reason Paul commanded the Corinthian church to expel the brother was to protect the body. The leadership is to see to it that the people are accountable to each other and treat each other in a Christian way. Ephesians 6:25-32 gives a good example of how people should relate to one another in the body. If the believers are failing in these areas, it is up to the leadership to step in and help them treat each person correctly. Personality conflicts in the church usually cause more problems than doctrinal issues or matters of the faith.

If a family has an older teenager and younger siblings, and the older teenager insists on engaging in destructive behaviors that will harm the younger ones, it is time for tough love, which may mean the removal of that older teenager. This also applies to the church family as well. A disruptive, non-repentant person should also be given spiritual tough love and be asked to leave. If and when there is repentance and change, then he/she may return.

> Life Application: 1. Always pray before a decision, and don't argue over non-essentials. 2. You may want to evaluate the way you make decisions in the leadership and church. If it is by democratic vote, then some type of division is usually the result, unless all agree. It is rare that 100% agree, therefore, conflict usually arises. Think about making decisions based upon consensus.

Help believers become mature! (v.13b). For the people to become mature, they must have leaders who have already attained some sense of maturity. This is why a new Christian should not be an elder. The position requires maturity in both life and the faith; therefore, a leader must be mature in these two areas. This is important because these two areas are where the people in the church need to be maturing.

In their knowledge of the Word and faith! A man may be mature in daily living but not in the areas of the faith. A babe in Christ is a babe, no matter what age physically. The leader must always ask, "How can I help the people of my flock grow in the knowledge of the Word and faith?" A leader in the church is not there to fulfill his agenda, but God's. He is not there to lift himself up, but to help others be lifted up and become mature. To do this, the leader must be a person of the Word and faith.

In their daily lives! He also must know his people; where they are in their walk and their struggles in life. The leader must spend time in the lives of the people. He must be able to relate to their hurts and struggles. To do this, he must get to know those for whom he is responsible, within his flock or area of leadership. The goal of bringing a person to maturity is not how much knowledge he has, but how he puts that knowledge into practice in his day-to-day life.

Life Application: 1. The leaders should be continually growing. Seminars, good books, and tapes will help. The senior minister, pastor, or seasoned elders should take the time to keep the leadership in a position of learning and increasing in their maturity. 2. Each leader should commit some time each month to getting to know their people and their needs. (More practical suggestions will be covered in the Chapter on shepherding.)

Help protect the sheep! (v. 14; Acts 20:28-31). God was very angry with shepherds who did not protect His flock. If you choose this position, then you choose the responsibility to protect those whom God has given you to care for, and lead. In verse 14, we see what the sheep need protection from. This then is the responsibility of the Elder\leader - to help protect the sheep from:

False doctrine! Seasoned saints should have a firm foundation in the Word. If they have had years of good teaching, then it will be so. In your fellowship, the leaders should know the history of those in the church and what they need. It is very important for those who are new Christians and transfers to know the difference between truth and false doctrine. First, do not assume that people who transfer in or move from another church have had the background needed to know the difference between false and true doctrine. It is important that the leadership find out what the new person knows and believes. Secondly, it should be obvious that new believers have no basis or tools to know the difference between the two. It is the responsibility of the leadership to see that both groups are taught and guided. This can be done best through discipleship and shepherding family groups, which we will look at more closely in a later chapter.

Deceitful schemes and men! Just 20 to 40 years after the church began, we see Paul striving with false teachers in the church. The problem, many times, arises when unqualified persons are placed in positions of leadership. If people are not qualified, then they will most likely make decisions based upon the flesh, not on the Spirit and Word. If the leadership and the people know the difference between true and false doctrine, then they will be able to recognize the false teacher. A fellowship that is trained to search the Scriptures and check whether everything the leaders teach is true will be a fellowship that will not be led astray. Again, the biggest warning concerns those who come from the outside. Transfers, visiting preachers, tapes, and books should all be examined with a firm footing in the truth.

> Life Application: 1. Leaders, do you know what your church bookstore sells or what tapes your people are listening to? If you offer a tape or book to your people, then you are saying we believe this to be truth. 2. Treat a transfer just like a new believer, no matter where he comes from. Get to know him and what he believes. Be sure he knows what your church philosophy is before you allow him to be a part of leadership.

Create an atmosphere of love and work (v. 15a). In some cases, local leadership creates the opposite of love. If there are disagreements, divisions, and fighting among the leadership, how can it lead the church into loving relationships? How the leadership works and lives with each other will determine how the rest of the church will function in their daily lives with each other. If the local leadership truly loves Christ's sheep, then they will be cared for and looked after spiritually.

> Life Application: 1. If there is any bitterness or division among any leaders, then there must be healing, forgiveness, and a willingness to come to consensus. 2. If there are any problems in the church, the leadership must be out front trying to be peacemakers.

To help the whole body to grow! (v. 15b,16). The leader must be concerned about the growth of each individual and the body as a whole. If this is not your aim as leader, then should you be a leader? Biblical leaders are there to help others fulfill their part in the body.

Body Life is realized when each individual part is doing his or her part. Every member doing at least one thing based upon his/her gift will produce a body that is healthy and growing. People will be excited about their part and where it fits. (More on this subject will be covered in Chapter 4, Section Two.)

Building up the body. Each person should be concerned about building each other up, as we have noted earlier. Of course, there are those who seem to only tear down. Usually, this is because they are not converted, have some deficiency in their spiritual life, or have not found their place. When each person is doing something in the body, according to his/her giftedness, the body will be built up.

Love life. Again, all that we say and do should be from a foundation of love for Christ, His sheep, and His church. Genuine Christian love will motivate the true leader to show that love for the flock he's been given. Does the leader love life, does he love his work, and does he love those with whom he is working or serving? If he does, then he will do whatever it takes, and those he serves will see the love of Christ in all he does.

Choosing and Grooming Leadership

Chapter Seven

> "Spiritual leaders are not elected, appointed, or created by synods or churchly assemblies. God alone makes them. One does not become a spiritual leader by merely filling an office, taking course work in the subject, or resolving in one's own will to do this task. A person must qualify to be a spiritual leader." (Oswald Chambers)

Procedures of choosing leaders!

There should be no set quota, either upper or lower limits. Those who are qualified should be the leaders, whether it may be two or more. When I first arrived at my first pastorate, I read the by-laws of the church. In the by-laws there was the clause: There will be a minimum of six elders and eight deacons. This was absurd. If there were only four qualified men, then there would have to be two put into service, who were not qualified. What do you think this would do later, when spiritual decisions had to be made? This is man controlling, not God. The potential in a situation like this is that the deacons could out-vote the elders and make an incorrect decision.

Recommendations should only be for the purpose of consideration by existing leadership, not for final decision. No one should be nominated or voted on for the eldership. I have seen this method produce popularity votes. A person may unduly be forced to become a leader because a nomination (or the good will of the people) pressures him. Church leadership should not be decided by the majority of the people based upon personality and longevity but upon the filling, giftedness, and direction of the Holy Spirit.

How can this be done?

From giftedness! Leaders should be confirmed due to their giftedness, not personality, tenure, or popularity, but by having gifts that meet the criteria of their ministry. For an elder, the main gifts should be leadership and teaching. It should be obvious that if a man does not want to teach then he should not be an elder.

Volunteer/desire. Leadership roles should also be open for people who want to personally make their desire known. Leaders will rise to the top if the church has a mentoring and discipling mentality. Make it easy for people to volunteer for different positions.

Evaluation Pool. The elders should always have their eyes open for those who may be material for eldership/leadership positions. The best way is for the existing eldership to be observant of those in the church that are growing towards this type of service and approach them. This is best done from within the family systems suggested later in this book.

From prior functioning or past performance in ministering. Why should a church place the highest responsibility in the hands of an unproven person? This is why a leadership candidate should not be a novice, either as a Christian or as a member, before he is given the responsibility. No one should be an elder until he has been in the body at least three years.

This gives everyone time to see the candidate function and know his gifts, as well as to get to know him as a potential leader.

Candidates should go through at least a year of apprenticeship before being ordained as an elder. The apostles spent three years in apprenticeship before Christ let them be leaders. The person being considered for this role should have experience and confirmation from his service that he is qualified. If either he, or the existing leadership, sees that he is not a leader\ shepherd, it is much better to learn that fact at this point, in this trial period. The only exception to this is if they had been an elder previously and has proven himself. When I say previously, I do not mean in another church. If they are transfers it is important that they go through the apprenticeship year just like everyone else.

Elders should qualify and screen candidates before they enter into apprenticeship. All recommendations or requests should be prayed over before they are accepted into apprenticeship. If the whole church is involved in discipleship procedures, then the persons considered should have already shown an aptitude and gifts for this service. It is important that, in every area of the church, there should always be individuals who are disciples in training or involved in apprenticeship relationships. This can best be utilized within the family systems. You will learn more about this in the next chapter on shepherding.

Candidates must desire the position and accept the year's apprenticeship. This is the first of the qualifications. If the person is forced to be in this position, or feels hesitant after being approached, then he is not ready for this work. There is nothing wrong in encouraging people to be leaders, but they should not be unduly forced to take any position or function in the fellow-ship. If they have any doubts or hesitation, perhaps the Holy Spirit is not leading them in that direction at this time.

The apprenticeship will include both study and active participation in the duties of an elder or leader. The apprentice will go through this course of material or other like material for leadership training. The apprentice will also attend and observe elders' meetings and procedures. He will also be actively involved in teaching and shepherding activities.

After the term of apprenticeship is finished, and if both parties agree, then the candidate is brought before the congregation so they can affirm this person as their leader. The church has a voice, so it can object if anyone knows of any reason why this person should not be an elder\leader. In certain cases, some people not in leadership may have some information that will disqualify this person at this time. The leadership should also be wise in hearing any complaints against anyone. There should be more than one witness, as well as evidence. The leadership should try to ascertain if there are any ill intentions from the accuser. If so, the leadership should wisely consider all things. Also, none of this is to be done in a public meeting. Those who have reasons for this person not being ordained should privately submit, in writing or personally, their reasons to the elders. Also, the one in question has the right to be given a fair chance to defend himself against these objections.

Time limits; is it Biblical or just another result of American democracy? Should there be any time limits set for those in the ministry of eldership? Why do churches set time limits on their elders? Historically, I think there are two main reasons churches have placed time limits on their eldership. First, the custom was adopted from operating systems like *Robert's Rules of Order* - or from examples from our government. Secondly, the practice also became a practical way of getting rid of bad or unwanted leaders.

If the leaders are chosen, groomed, and taught correctly, then it is more likely the leadership will not need this aid to get rid of them. Yes, there are always exceptions, and a mature leadership should be able to deal with these as they arise. If, at any point, a person knowingly falls or disqualifies himself, then he should step down or be asked to do so for the sake of the congregation. If elders are chosen by qualifications, they should only be dismissed by a lack of those qualifications.

There is also the consideration of the sabbatical. In Jewish/OT tradition, there was to be a break every seven years. This has been applied to certain professions. This concept might also be adapted into the eldership of a local congregation. Whether it is three or seven years (each congregation may decide), the idea of taking some time off for spiritual renewal is valid. The person should be encouraged to take this time and renew his walk, take some courses of study to grow in certain areas, or just rest from the responsibilities. Following this time of rest, he would then be expected to resume his duties as leader. Once qualified, and if not disqualified, a person may be an elder for life if he desires.

REMINDER NOTE: If you are an existing elder, but realize that you no longer desire to be or qualify as an elder, be mature enough to step down.

Elder Qualifications
I Timothy 3:1-7

1. Desire - "Sets heart on being" Why?
2. Above reproach! Why?
3. Husband of one wife. Why? Does this mean one only, or merely one at a time?
4. Temperate\Self-controlled. Why?
5. Sensible and a wise thinker. Why?
6. Respectable, and well behaved. Why?
7. Hospitable, kind, and open. Why?
8. Able to teach. Why?
9. Not a drunkard. Why?
10. Not a violent man or quick tempered. Why?
11. Gentle or considerate. Why?
12. At peace with self and others. Why?
13. Not greedy or preoccupied with money. Why?
14. Manages his own household well. Why?
15. Not a new convert or neophyte. Why?
16. Good reputation with unbelievers. Why?

Desire - "Sets heart on being." If a person has all the other qualifications and does not have this one, he and the rest of the leadership should take notice. Desire is _number one_ on the list, because it is at the center of the person's heart and drive. The desire is the result of the Spirit's influence in the person's heart. No desire, no Spirit leading. Or there may have been some leading or desire in the past, and the Spirit has been quenched for some reason, whether by a bad experience, or by an individual's preference. If this is the case, the person may need some counseling for healing or debriefing to help him overcome his problem. He may also need time to heal. At any rate, it would not be wrong to encourage him.

Why is this important? If the person does not have the desire, he will not put his whole heart into the ministry. Also, he will usually burn out and/or develop bitterness if forced to take the ministry.

> LIFE APPLICATION: If a person seems to have all the other qualifications, he should be encouraged to explore the idea of considering this ministry. He should be encouraged to pray and seek the Lord to see why he does not have the desire at this time. If after all this, there is still no desire, by all means do not coerce or push him into this decision or ministry.

Above reproach! Impossible to be criticized! In what are we to be above reproach? I think practically, in those qualifications that follow in this same list. This of course, is where everyone would say, "Everyone can be criticized for or about something." Yes, but is it something petty or a personal grievance from someone with an "ax to grind?" If it is any of these things, then it may either be ignored, or prayerfully considered. Yes, we all have skeletons in the closet, but are they such that they will destroy the witness and ministry of the eldership? By all means, if the criticism concerned something which occurred before the person was a Christian, that should not even be considered, if the person has changed and rectified the problem. Even if it happened when he was a young believer. If it has been dealt with and a part of the past then consider their walk now.

Why is this important? If there is genuine criticism, and if the people who will be following do not have respect, then they will not follow this individual, perhaps eventually, the entire leadership. The situation might also bring dissent and division, as well as foster the possibility of poor decisions within the leadership.

> LIFE APPLICATION: If there are any questions about any of the areas below, and the candidate or the eldership have any reservations, then it is advised that the person be guided and discipled in these areas so as to help
> him meet the qualifications. It is also advisable to start teaching young boys these attributes and qualifications and how to develop them in their lives.

Husband of one wife. Does this mean one only, or one at a time? Does this preclude a single person from being an elder? This is possibly one of the most controversial, difficult, and misunderstood qualifications in the list. Given our divorce rate, up to 50% of the men may not be eligible because of this one qualification. So do we ignore the question - or rationalize it? Some believe the scripture means to have had only one wife "ever"; i.e., no polygamy and no divorce. Furthermore, under this idea this would disqualify a widower that remarries! The text cannot support, nor does it say "ever;" therefore, there may be some exceptions, or at least a better understanding to the term "one wife." Some theologians believe that, during the time of this writing, polygamy was rampant in the society and that this situation would promote a natural requirement for having only one wife. The text does not negate this position. There were, of course, exceptions to having more than one wife in your lifetime. Death holds no bonds to the believer concerning re-marriage, for the person is free in this case. Secondly, the Bible seems <u>not</u> to bind a person from service, (though many theologians & preachers disagree) if the unbeliever decides to leave the believer, and if the other person (in this case the woman) has committed adultery (*1 Corinthians 7:1-18 and Matthew 5:31,32 ; 19:1-9*). There are two other considerations. If the person is divorced and has tried to reconcile but is not re-married and does not desire re-marriage, then he may be qualified, since the passage did not mention divorce, but one wife. Secondly, I believe that in principle, this should preclude any divorce that happened before the person became a Christian.

Why is this important? It is important because a person in this position must be an example to the rest of the body if he is going to be effective leader. If the divorce was especially the fault of the candidate and it was due to his immaturity and lack of commitment, then this man would not be fit for leading the church family.

> LIFE APPLICATION: Although this is a sensitive area, the hard questions must be asked concerning the past of the person. Be sensitive, compassionate, and non-condemning. This is not the unpardonable sin and should not be used as a weapon against the person. This is a time of ministering and teaching. This is an obvious place of disqualification while in the eldership. If he is going through a divorce, on un- Biblical grounds, then for the best of all concerned, the person should be counseled to step down from this position, (but not from Christianity!) "In all things love."

Temperate\Self-controlled! Meteorologically, "temperate" is weather that is neither hot nor cold. A self-controlled person is neither hot nor cold in their relations with others. Have you been in a meeting where a person either won't participate, or loses his/her temper and destroys the whole spirit of the meeting? The self-controlled man is a Spirit-filled man. You cannot be ill-tempered and spirit-filled at the same time. God wants Spirit-filled men leading His flock; if they are not spirit-filled, and they cannot control their temper then they should not be considered for this ministry until they are led by the Spirit. When they are led by the Spirit, then they will be able to control their temper

Why is this important? An uncontrolled man usually destroys the unity and spirit of the meeting. If a person is not self-controlled in his personal life, he will find it difficult to control himself within church leadership. Again, we come to the point of example. An uncontrolled tongue or lifestyle is very obvious to the flock, the unbeliever, and very harmful to the leadership.

> LIFE APPLICATION: If a person has a known temper, this person should be counseled on how to control it and let the Spirit take control. This is why a year's apprenticeship will be of help, especially when you have not seen a person in certain situations. Having the candidate as an apprentice in your meetings and in certain given tasks will help the existing leadership evaluate if the person has more work to do in this area. If the person is already in this eldership ministry, it is up to the others to remind and admonish him to be filled, or step down for the good of the leadership, until he can control his temper. A one-time outburst is not what we are talking about; it is a consistently uncontrolled temper that is the problem.

Be a sensible and wise thinker! A sage, a wise man! This should be an assumed part of being an elder. Being the spiritual leader and overseer is an important task and responsibility that requires one to make decisions and judgments in the life of the church. Not only should they be wise in the truth, but in practical matters as well. Christianity is for us to practice in our everyday life. A person without the ability to think wisely will make decisions based upon the flesh and immaturity. This naturally will lead to problems in the church. This is a good reason why a novice should not be considered. (Remember, however, age alone does not make a person wise.)

Why is this important? It is obvious that immature counsel and decisions will hinder the growth of the church and each person in the flock. They will also hinder the work of the Spirit. Growing people will find it difficult to follow a foolish leader; unfortunately, young and immature ones won't!

LIFE APPLICATION: Again, a person should prove himself in situations where he is to make decisions. He must take responsibility for decisions he makes. Sometimes leaders are afraid of giving duties and responsibilities over to others for fear of failure, but delegating responsibilities is a part of discipling and of good training. Failing is much less a problem than not being allowed to learn from our mistakes! . Also, you must remember that it is not man's wisdom, but Spirit-filled wisdom that is needed.

Respectable, and well-behaved! How does this person act and react in public? Is he rude, or a coarse joker? Does he have any social problems or idiosyncrasies that may hinder his witness? What does he do when he goes to his son's or grandson's baseball game, or when he himself plays on the church team? I have seen some of the worst sports in Christian ball leagues.

Why is this important? It is not a very good example as a leader and not a very good example for the non-Christian in their midst. This is where the world has a right to talk about hypocrites in the church.

LIFE APPLICATION: 1. If a person has these problems, or any problem like this, the first thing to do is to remove himself from these activities. 2. Pray for control and wisdom on how to act. 3. Have someone else remind you when this is taking place.

Hospitable, kind, and open! The elder or leader is to have the ability to be hospitable and kind to others. He should not be a stingy person, but a giving person. This is not to say you are not to protect your privacy and family life, but you should be able to open your heart, home, and time to those you serve. A man who is ruff and gruff is not mature enough to be in this position.

Why is this important? The leader needs to be a person who can socially open their heart and life to others. If you look at the time of Jesus, people were expected to be open to others, even strangers, if there was a need. The leader in the church who does not want to be open and friendly should not be a leader and should find some other ministry in the church. This may sound harsh, but you have people's feelings and emotions involved. You have impressions, and this is what most people see or make decisions on first. If a leader is not hospitable and friendly, this will more likely offend and push away new seekers or prospects. So do not suggest they be greeters either.

> LIFE APPLICATION: 1. This does not mean you have to have the gift of hospitality, but an openness to be friendly and hospitable. 2. If you find it hard to do this, then pray for the compassion and willingness to open up on occasion. 3. Team up with another person or family that does have this gift and work together to minister to those you lead and shepherd.

Able to teach! Along with desire, this is probably the most overlooked quality. Sometimes churches will overlook this aspect because of a person's age or tenure. If the person is not able, or is unwilling to teach, then he should not take on this ministry. There is no shame in not being a teacher, but there should be if you are an elder. Some have the ability, but for some reason refuse to teach. Until they are willing to participate in this ministry, they should not be a part of this ministry. But, it is also important that being able to teach does not automatically qualify a person. If the other qualifications are lacking, then have them teach but not be a part of this overseer/eldership ministry. Remember, one is not a failure if he is not a teacher or elder, he just has not been given that gift. God is concerned about us using the gifts we're given and not feeling like a failure in the gifts you don't have.

Why is this important? The main duty of the elder is to be a teacher of the Word. To be sure the flock is guided and protected, he must be able to rightly divide the Word and teach it to others. Unless the elder can teach the flock and guide them in the Word, he is not doing the work of the elder, and therefore disqualifies himself from this ministry.

LIFE APPLICATION: Sometimes a person has not had the experience of teaching and, therefore, does not know if he can. This again is where a year apprenticeship for the elder\leader is important. In this time a candidate can participate in various teaching opportunities. If the person can, but refuses to or has no desire to, maybe he needs to be encouraged or reassured that he can, but until he is ready, he should not be an elder.

Not a drunkard! This is obvious and should be easily understood. The debate comes between abstinence and non-abstinence. It is true that, if you never drink, you will be assured of never getting drunk. There is, however, no prohibition in the Bible against drinking, only the warning against drunkenness. The principle can be applied to anything in life. If there is a substance that controls you, it is a sin at that point. A person, who becomes controlled by any substance, including recreational drugs, should also be disqualified at this point. Now this stand may seem strong, but what about any substance that controls you, like cigarettes? Now, course, it will not cause a debilitating response; like alcohol, it may though be a bad example a leader does not need to deal with. You be the judge.

Why is this important? Again, the elder should be the highest level of example to the flock. If alcohol or drugs control you, it is impossible to be controlled by the Spirit at the same time. The leader is to lead the flock down the same path Jesus did, and you are going in the opposite path when these substances control you.

LIFE APPLICATION: A person who has such substance abuse is usually dealing with other underlying problems that need to be dealt with. This too would underline the notion that this person is not qualified for this ministry at this time. A <u>recovered</u> alcoholic or drug addict should be considered based upon his progress. Even though drinking is not prohibited, it may be wise to abstain so as not to put oneself in danger, and also possibly keep someone else from stumbling. Of course, smoking cigarettes does not hinder your thinking, but it does show that you are under the control of that substance, and that is not a good example to others.

Not a violent man or quick tempered. This should be obvious. Jesus was the example of peace and patience. Likewise, His shepherds should be also. This is a person that has a problem in controlling himself in times of conflict or personal disagreements. This is usually a person who is out to have control and will fight when he does not get control. This person is usually immature, both spiritually and emotionally.

Why is this important? Have you ever seen a person who in public, away from the church, loses his temper or becomes violent? When you do, you lose respect and trust for that person because when he deals with you, it may be in an unpleasant manner. These people are those that others try to stay clear of and avoid. This creates a big problem if this type of person is in the eldership. He is to be the prime example for the rest of the people, especially the youth. Also, the elder is to be an example to other potential leaders. If they see this person lose his temper and become violent in church meetings, then it will turn sour the stomachs of those that see the temper tantrum. No person that cannot contain his temper or violence should be allowed to become or continue as a leader. There is too much at stake if this is overlooked and pushed under the table.

LIFE APPLICATION: 1. This is an observable trait that must be looked at, both in the life of the church and out of the church. 2. If a candidate or an existing elder has this problem, then he should be counseled, and if it continues, he should not be allowed to be an elder. If already an elder, he should be dismissed until he can prove himself able. 3. The person may put up a fight or hold a lot of power, and it might be hard, but with prayer and openness to the qualifications, he should step down or seek the help he needs. 4. If you are a person with this problem, be open, honest, and willing to do what it takes to be a truly qualified servant.

Gentle or considerate. The elder must not be a harsh or rude person. This is especially important when it comes to teaching or mentoring. I have seen teachers who are belligerent and inconsiderate with some people they are teaching or mentoring. Even in times of disagreement, gentleness and consideration are invaluable. A soft answer turns away wrath and keeps communication and teaching opportunities open.

Why is this important? A harsh teacher helps learners to turn off and tune out what the elders are trying to teach. When people are in search of a church home, they are very sensitive to how they are treated, so it is important that those in leadership be considerate to people's needs and life situation. Even those who have been in the church for a while will choose to leave if they are treated badly. This is especially increased when the leadership seems insensitive.

LIFE APPLICATION: 1. Remember, as an elder/leader you are a servant first. 2. Remember, if you offend any one of these, God will hold you responsible. 3. Don't become paranoid; there are those who will be offended about anything and everything, so take each person individually. If you are honest, you will know if the fault lies with you. If it does, make amends and beware of your approach. 4. If inconsideration is a chronic problem, you might remove yourself from leadership until you have changed.

At peace with self and others. Many people do not have peace within; they have unresolved conflict. They may not have peace with their Lord due to lack of repentance or self-absorption, and they may not be a peace with others because they have not resolved a conflict between someone in the church or community.

Why is this important? A person that is not at peace with self and God will not be free to lead and make quality leadership decisions. They will unconsciously be focused on their own self-interests. If there is conflict, there will be disharmony and division. If there is lack of peace with a fellow leader, there will usually be conflict and disagreement on issues in the decisions that are made. They will be looking out for their own good, or protecting their own interests, because of the lack of peace between them.

LIFE APPLICATION: 1. Find out what is hindering your peace with self, God, and others. 2. Make every effort to reconcile the problem through counseling, repentance, and change of ways. 3. Approach those with whom you are not at peace and try to mend the relationships.

Not greedy or preoccupied with money. Where is your heart? Wherever your pocket book is? Money is not evil, but the love of it is. The person who is in leadership should be able to set a good example of giving and charity. A greedy person is often selfish and, at times, a ruthless person in his dealings, preoccupied, or controlled by the money. Needing money to survive is a given, but greediness is a sin and an attitude that money is the priority. This greed leads person to making decisions that do not reflect a good example. The money is in control not the Spirit.

Why is this important? First, it may cause a problem in a person's allegiance and priorities. Secondly, it can be a bad example when people see you, during the week, make decisions based upon greed. It is also a problem when making money is your number one priority, to the point that concern with finances is excessive and compulsive. This may lead to behavior that may hurt the person in being able to have the time to serve and also hinder his example to those that he leads.

> LIFE APPLICATION: This is a problem that may require a lot of counseling and help for the person. It may even be a problem that needs repentance and total commitment to God rather than money.

Manage his own household well. The church is a family, from the church as a whole to even the smaller units of the whole. The elder/leader is a manager of God's flock. He is to shepherd and take care of those under his care. The basic unit of the church is made up of each family in it. This is why it is important that the elder is successful in the basic unit of his family. If he can't be a leader there, how can he be a leader in God's family, the church?

Why is this important? If there is conflict in the elder's family, not only will it be a bad example, it will also prove to be a distraction. When you have problems at home, it will affect every other area of life, even if it is secret to those on the outside.

> LIFE APPLICATION: 1. If this is a problem, the candidate should not accept the position. If an existing elder, and it is to much of a distraction or problem, then you should take a break until it is under control. 2. Maybe marriage counseling will be the best thing. It is suggested you find someone outside of your staff to do it. 3. When children leave the home, or are late in teenage years, they begin to make their own choices, and sometimes they are against all that you taught them. Should this be the case, it should not be held against the elder candidate, assuming you know they have trained them right, and all else is in order.

Not a new convert or neophyte. What constitutes a new convert? How long and how much should a person know? How much should you take into consideration the age of the person in both physical and spiritual realms? A person who is less than three years in the faith is definitely a new convert, but time is not always relevant in some circumstances. The person may have been a Christian for a number of years and is still feeding on milk. It is how much they know and what they have done with it that counts. Some may be fast in their learning and in their yielding to the Spirit in their development. It may be advisable to follow the 30-year-old rule in making a person an elder, but I hasten to not make this a hard and fast rule. Each person is different, and one 30-year-old may not be as ready as one 25-year-old. Do not make 30 a magical age; if people are not ready, they are not ready. Sometimes they are not ready at any age, so it is also important that physical age be relevant and be combined with spiritual age. A 50-year-old new convert is not as qualified as a 30-year-old who has been a growing Christian for 10 years.

Why is this important? It is obvious that this person will not and cannot make the right spiritual decisions; even if they are wise in age, they may not be wise in spiritual matters. Spiritual growth and regular maturity should be combined in the person of the ministry of elder. I do find that most people kind of laugh when they hear of a Mormon 20-year-old elder. People just realize that you usually can't make those wise decisions at such a young age.

> LIFE APPLICATION: Time, education, and maturation are the answers. The existing leadership should hold off such a person, while encouraging and giving him tasks and training that will help him grow into this ministry that he desires. A major problem comes with new churches. Many churches are pressured to rush and choose elder/leaders. A minimum of three to five years is advisable, and generally no less than 30 years of age. There needs to be time for the people to trust in those who will lead.

Good reputation with unbelievers. How does the community regard your leadership, both corporately, and individually? Is there a leader or apprentice with a bad business or personal reputation?

Why is this important? If the leadership is corrupt, then the whole body is corrupt. The world is very aware of this in today's political atmosphere. They also look very closely a (the experiences in the recent past of preachers being brought down by their actions. You can do all the evangelism you want, but if the leadership is known for their hypocritical leadership and lifestyle, the unbeliever will not choose to be a part of the church, or even Christ. The people of the community are watching.

> LIFE APPLICATION: 1. It is hard to put things back together once things are broken. It will take time and sometimes restitution to begin the healing. 2. Each case must be looked at individually because there may be circumstances and history that were not accurate. 3. Also, how long ago was the offense or the making of the tainted reputation? If there was and is an effort to take care of the situation, then consideration must be made individually.

Ministry of Deacons
I Timothy 3:8-13; Acts 6:3,5

Full of the Spirit. Here again, the main qualification is to have the presence and power of the Spirit. This passage in Acts does not specifically refer to the function of deacons in 1 Timothy 3, but does not limit the scope of 1 Timothy. *Diakonous* Servants likewise should be serious, honorable, and worthy of respect.

Dilogos - two-tongued or two-faced, not honest or dependable! This is one of the most important qualities you want in any leader. If you cannot trust them, it is dangerous to the health and stability of not only the leadership team but also the whole church in general. Do not make the mistake of saying or believing if we give him the responsibility, maybe he will change. Expecting them to change will only happen if they have a conversion and let the Holy Spirit control them and their attitude.

Not be addicted to wine. Not a prohibition to drinking, but an admonition to discipline and control oneself. This is not the place to debate the potential evils of drinking. It is obvious that if you never drink you will never get addicted, and you will never make a person stumble if you're a servant and drink, as was mentioned in the elder's comments above.

Not be greedy for gaining money. Not be your number one priority. All of us require our needs to be taken care of, and everyone probably knows of people that are only concerned about money and riches. Jesus did say that where your riches are, there would be your heart. In His leaders, Jesus does not want someone that is controlled by or dedicated to money and riches. Again, I am not saying that having money is wrong, or being wise in your gathering of money is incorrect. But, if you're controlled and possessed by it, then you can be more occupied in that pursuit and not the pursuit of the ministry you're in. It all comes down to who is in control, and that could include drugs, tobacco, or anything that may lead you astray from being committed to God.

Husbands of one wife, and good managers of their own household! Please look to the answer for the elder above.

Women/Deaconess

Should there be a problem in calling or putting women into service as deacons? Does this passage give us a hint about women deacons' qualifications? The Greek word _diakinos_ means male and female servants. There is no word _man_ mentioned in verse 8. The sex is assumed, and could be general for both sexes. Verses 11 and 12 are specific in application. So in context, it seems that we're talking about men and women deacons. Some congregations that place the deacon on equal grounds with the elders in decision-making and polity may debate this. Since this is a non-Biblical practice, it should be a non-issue, but more will be discussed on this issue later. This verse, in the midst of these qualifications, seems to show that this is a special warning for the women deacons, or some may interpret wives of the deacons or elders. Some scholars, though, have interpreted verse 11 to be wives of the deacons. The bottom line is that both should be examples.

I believe there were women deaconess in the New Testament, take Phoebe as an example. If they are removed from making decisions that the elders should make, and they use their gifts in service areas of the church then they should be recognized for their work and service. So what are some more considerations that women can be deaconess in certain areas?

1. _Deacon_ is a Greek neuter word; that is, it is sexless, and simply means servant. It becomes tied to a certain sex when it is mentioned with that sex within its context. We see this example in verse 12.

2. Deacons were not to make the decisions that the elders were in matters of spirituality, and are not in the position of being overseers of the congregation, but are over special and specific areas of ministry. If those ministries were fulfilled, then so would be the work of that deacon in that area.

3. Being mainly a service, task-oriented position, not an overseer, there should be no conflict for women being involved in ministry teams and, in some cases, in leadership where it involves ministries to women and children. Except for the position of elder, the women can and should be considered leaders in their gifted areas of ministry. If the women are under the authority of the elders, and all deacons should be, then there should be no problem in women serving with a title.

Women as Shepherdess! In the family system that I suggest in Chapter 8 of this section, qualified men are to be shepherd servant leaders over a family group. In that group there are both men and women. Both men and women must be shepherded by someone. In this passage in First Timothy the women are told to lead and teach other women. They are being their shepherds. No authority is being usurped over man, but the work is being done none the less with the women, by the women, under the supervision of the elder/shepherd. It should be no problem to recognize the women for what they are doing as co-shepherds when all this is taken into consideration. Don't worry; they are *not* to sit on any official team or board as decision makers, rather they are recognized for the work and dedication they're involved with. It is recognizing their function. It in no way gets out of hand as long as the leadership identifies their limitations. Again I think a woman's only limitation is in the eldership/overseer ministry.

> Life Application: 1.There are many ministries in the church that are and can be lead by women. If they are being led by women then they are doing the work of a deaconess. If so then recognize them as such. 2. If there are places of service the leadership thinks should be led by men only then let it be so. One such place is the eldership. Women make up more than half of any churches workforce. Honor them and recognize them.

Leadership principles that enhance growth

Improve your leadership and each member by recognizing your weaknesses, correcting your mistakes, and improving your strengths. This should be a theme for every area of church life. What is the leadership's weakness? What areas need correcting in your overall program? How can you make those things you do well even better? This begins by recognizing one's personalities and gifts. Knowing both will help you know how to deal with people.

Commitment of time! You cannot be an absent elder or leader. In one northern church I served in, there were five elders. From October 15 until April 1 every year, three of them went south to Florida. After almost a six-month absence, they came back complaining that they did not like it when there were so many new people they did not know. If you do not have time, that does not make you a bad person, but it should preclude you from accepting the position. You can be qualified but never be available. What good does that bring to the leadership or the health of the church?

Know where people need to be spiritually, how long it may take, and how to get them there. Make long-range plans for the growth of each individual and the church. What should they know in a year, or in three years? Plan out your sermons and teaching materials to meet these goals. Have some way of evaluation to see if people reach their intended growth level. This, of course, is just a tool, but many churches do not think about their growth.

Be observant of those who are in trouble or latent in faith. The leader that fails to be observant and keep their ear open for possible problems will, in the end, have bigger problems they may not be able to handle.

Be sensitive to needs. Meeting and being aware of both spiritual and physical needs are important in the growth of any congregation.

Always ask, is what we are doing working and producing growth? Have a means of evaluation so that you can know if things are working well. Ask people who lead and who participate how they feel it is going. Are they learning, and do they see better ways of doing the task? If it is not working or fulfilling its purpose, then change it, or quit doing it altogether. (See appendix for evaluation form.)

What are we not doing that hinders growth? Sometimes it is not what we are doing or doing wrong, but what we are not doing at all. Look for needs not being met, and through the gifted people, find a way to meet the need. The best way is to find what gifts people have, then find a need to be fulfilled. Usually we do it the opposite way, and force people to fulfill task without having the gift to successfully accomplish the task. The Spirit gives the gifts based upon what he sees, so let us look to His guidance.

Know what the surrounding community thinks about you. Take two probing surveys in your community. (Both will be found in the Appendix.) The best source are those who have come and gone from your fellowship. They will be able to give you an insight into what others are thinking. Sometimes people just are not happy anywhere and are constant complainers. In most cases, people do see things that are missing in your fellowship; things that need added or changed to better attract and keep the sheep in the fold. A church that has become very inward and cliquish usually cannot see this like those who visit, so be aware and open.

The next best indicator is how the non-church person views you. These are those whom you want to target for the gospel. How do they view your individual church, and how do they view the church at large? Knowing this will give you information that will help you plan outreach to meet their needs.

What creates leadership crises and problems?

Church splits are happening at an alarming rate across America. Many, people have said if you find a Baptist, you'll find a split in the making, or at least in their past. Of course, this is not always the case, but there is a truth to it in almost every denomination. Being an independent missionary force me to travel and be on the lookout for new possible sources for support. At the end of our second tour to Eastern Europe, we had 10 churches supporting us. When we returned, we learned that two of them had split, two lost their ministers, and two more that we were cultivating for new support had split. Upon our return for our third tour, we found that the new church we were to work with had, just two months before, had problems, and a new church was the result.

Why? Many churches give their reason for the split. In one it is music style, in another it is personality styles, and in yet another there are too many new people who upset the traditions. But are these the real reasons?

Very seldom is the problem over basic doctrine. In almost every case, the root problem is twofold. First, and basic, is that mankind has the tendency to divide and fight instead of compromise and unify. We are selfish beings, and that tends to come to the top in our relationships and dealings with others. The second root problem in the church is that there is usually a lack of maturity and stability of those in leadership. Whether it is a recently developed leadership, or one that has long standing leaders, the problems usually arise because of the following factors in the selecting and ordaining of these leaders. These may not be all the problems or solutions, but if a church would follow these, they would be on their way to a healthy foundation and church.

Let us list those problem areas:

The person <u>did not desire</u> the position. Remember how your church has chosen its elders in the past. Usually these men were compelled by the need or by a very strong nomination process, usually very difficult to resist. In many cases, if there is no desire, there will be no passion. No desire, no leading of the Spirit. Therefore, this lack of desire will produce frustration, and usually in a short time, burn out or callousness.

> Solutions: 1. Change your method of choosing from nominating to mentorship. 2. Stress and encourage from the pulpit the need for a desire in the work of elder. 3. Provide an opportunity for men to come forward. 4. Existing elders can approach men who demonstrate the qualities and gifts to consider this ministry and who have proven themselves as family shepherd apprentices.

The person <u>was not spiritually gifted</u> for this type of leadership. No spiritual gifts, then no spiritual skills to do the job as God directed. The Holy Spirit gives the desire, the gift, and then the success. No desire, no gift. If no gift, then it is not God directing but man. If a person is placed in leadership without consideration of their giftedness and desire, you are open for failure and division, or at least mediocrity.

> Solutions: 1. Have each member complete his or her personality and gifts survey. 2. Select and ordain leaders based upon their gifts and success in that field. 3. Have them be apprentices before they are officially become or are recognized as a leader. 4. Be willing to say no, this is not for you right now, and redirect them to another ministry or task.

<u>Was not qualified.</u> A man may have the desire, even the gift, but still not have the qualifications to make it valid. If the person is not above reproach, or has a problem with controlling his temper, his leadership will be undermined and impotent. But not being qualified for one ministry does not mean the person cannot serve in some capacity. We're talking about leadership at this point, and it is important not to put immature people into positions where they may be a hindrance to others and themselves.

> Solutions: 1. Have someone continue to mentor or disciple them in their areas of weakness. 2. Encourage participation, but also responsibility, in their personal lives. 3. Remember, in all things love.

Thinking there is an automatic rite of Passage! There may be a mistaken view that being old enough and being a deacon for a period of time qualifies you for the position of overseer. If the ministry and activities in the church are based upon one's gifts, then one will not expect a man who has the deacon type of gifts to ever become an elder. It is not a shame to be a servant deacon all your life. The position of a deacon is not an automatic stepping stone or proof that you have the gifts for overseer. Now sometimes God can and does give new gifts. As we all mature and show responsibility, God can, and does, give other gifts to meet needs at any given moment in the life of the church. Again, the major difference between the leadership of an elder and the service of the deacon is threefold. The person should desire the position, be able and willing to teach, and show the maturity to handle the ministry of elder. If they cannot and will not teach, then they never qualify for the leadership of elder. You do not experiment with being an elder; you do that in the apprenticeship stage.

> Solutions: 1. Never teach or imply this idea to younger men. 2. Encourage one another to find and use their gifts. 3. Encourage one another to aspire for the character of the eldership's qualifications in everyday life.

People wanting the position for the wrong reasons! Some people want the position for power or recognition. Others feel they are due the right to be in the position because of family pedigree or what they have given. There may even be more wrong reasons not listed here, but these are enough to bring a congregation down to ruin. These people do not have the congregation and Christ in their best interests. They usually are prideful and selfish, and this is a recipe for disaster.

> Solutions: 1. If you are one of these people, repent, re-evaluate, and maybe step aside. 2. Reorganize, and put men in this position that are qualified. (See # 6 below for how to do this.) 3. Realize control is to be in the hands of the Spirit and in guidance of the Scripture, not in any one man.

The leadership is operating on an inadequate operating system, e.g., *Robert's Rules of Order* or democratic procedures. Many of the problems in the church today stem back to how we are set up. Usually, it is an organization developed around democratic procedures as we have mentioned earlier. Once upon a time, and even still today, the government asks churches to provide by-laws, especially if they are to be incorporated. Since this request was based upon secular government, the church went to secular sources, like the one mentioned in the opening sentence, to find out how to meet the request. This seemed to be a logical way, but in fact, was unnecessary. What it did do was open up a box that has plagued the church ever since. Voting has a 100% chance of division. Anything we can do not to have division is important. Except for politics and many churches today, leaders in other areas of life are not voted on. You don't vote on a doctor or a plumber. You equip them, qualify them, mentor them, and test them before they become whatever they desire to be. The same is for the church and its leadership. You must not nominate and vote on men, but rather grow them and confirm them. The democratic way circumvents this process, and you have a100% chance of getting the wrong man in the position.

Solutions: 1. Throw out and stop using *Robert's Rules of Order* as a basis of your structure and meeting. 2. Cease voting, and adopt consensus as a main means of coming to decisions, with the Bible as the guide. 3. Streamline your by-laws to the minimum. 4. Don't use terms like *board* and *chairman*. 5. Use Bible names and procedures to conduct meetings and order.

There is just general neglect and laziness for the duties of the leadership. This is a grave sin. Luke warmness is one of Jesus' biggest points of anger. An elder or leader who is neglecting their flock, or not providing food and protection for the people, is in danger of being derelict in their duty. The work of an elder/shepherd is grave and should not be entered into lightly. When a group of elders doesn't even know what they should be doing, it is either out of ignorance or they just don't care. I hope that most congregations are just ignorant about what they are to do, not lazy and comfortable. Any problem that arises should be taken care of by the leadership, especially before it develops into a crisis. People management is always the responsibility of the leadership. The wise and qualified leader will have a better chance of handling the problem with spiritual means and wisdom. A lazy leader will just push it aside with some excuse, or even worse, not think about or deal with it. It will become more of a problem, and come back to destroy or deaden the congregation.

Solutions: 1. Leaders that go through discipleship, mentorship, and leader apprenticeship will already have proven their willingness and effectiveness to serve. 2. You will observe neglect and laziness in other areas of their lives 3. The process of encouragement, discipleship, accountability, and mentorship will help a person develop out of these tendencies. 4. What you expect from people you will get.

Again, I propose that 90% of the problems in the church today are based in our leadership. I also propose that of the healthy churches, 90% of the time they have identified healthy leaders and placed them in every area of ministry, or they are working on that goal with a leadership that is in charge and leading.

Each existing leader, and every future leader, needs to be willing to make the tough decisions! What are the tough decisions?

About your place in the church! If after this study you find yourself saying, "I was put in a position that is not suited to my gifts and desires," then be strong enough to step down and find what you are gifted for. There is no shame in admitting you are in the wrong place. It is a sin and a mistake to know it and refuse to change, especially if it is due to selfish or prideful reasons. If you do not have the time to teach and shepherd then find the time. We all do what we think is important. If you refuse to teach or cannot teach, then be willing to make the hard decision, step down or refuse altogether.

About the direction of the church and its leadership. Most churches exist in neutral; that is, they are not moving forward in their growth and outreach. They're not meeting the needs of their church and the lost community around them; they just operate church business as usual. Be willing to say this may not be the direction God has intended for us. I am willing to go back to the Bible and see what pattern God has for the church. This takes honesty, fortitude, and a willingness to lay everything on the line.

About mistakes of the past. God is only concerned with the future. If you can deal with the past, repent and change if needed, then God will be there to take you and your leadership to the highest level. God wants a church and leadership that walks in His will, so be sure that it is God's direction, and not yours, in everything you do.

I am excited about what has happened in the church throughout the centuries. I am excited about what can happen in the church today. Throughout the centuries there have been breakdowns and successes. There has been drifting from the Bible's plan, and times of renewal orchestrated by the Spirit, and men faithful to God's Word and methods. Time after time, God has moved men to go back to the truth and His way. Like Martin Luther, Menno Simmons, and Alexander Campbell, those who are reading and following the principles of this book will have a chance for renewal. I am not saying this is the only way, but I do believe these methods are Biblical and, if followed, will produce success for God. I have been observing all over the world, in different denominations, men and women moving back to the Bible. While working as a missionary in Poland, I met a brother in Christ from England, Paul Paulson. Paul grew up in the Anglican Church, and is presently a part of the Methodist Church of England. Paul wrote *Normal Christian Birth*, which in my opinion is so close to my tradition, and I believe in the truth of the Bible, that I could have written it with a good conscience. I thought at first he should join us in the Restoration Movement, but no, he is where he is supposed to be; he is helping restore the church where he is.

Each leader and congregation has the obligation to see to it that they are in the stream of the New Testament. It is when man's ideas and methods become the standard that God's church becomes less than it should be. With dedication to God's ways and methods, we can see in our generation the return of the church to its intended form and vitality. When the leadership is about doing and being in God's will, it will grow and be blessed.

I have found that the growth of the church will depend upon the growth and maturity of it's leadership. This is why it is important the leadership understand their crucial place under Jesus' leadership. It is His people/sheep you are taking care of if you're a leader in His church. When the leadership forgets this and destroys the flock or stands in the way of it's growth in anyway then let him be accursed. For there is trust from God to you as leaders, and if you break that trust He will hold you responsible eternally. So it is best to take your pride, crucify it and follow the Bible and it's ways. Now I am not talking about men who do not know everything, but wills it God's way. I am talking about men who think they know it all and want control without being a servant. You're not Lord. Let His people go, and you be honest and go your own way. This may offend you and make you mad. If it does, then repent and step down until your wiling to be a servant first.

Discipleship Principles

Chapter Eight

The Height of Evangelism

Most evangelicals stress and ask, "Have you been born again?" They make this the most important and, in some cases, the height of our experience. It is true that this is the beginning and is, most times, the single high point in a person's walk with Christ. But nonetheless, it is not the last question you should ask and be satisfied with. The problem with

> If you look at Jesus and Paul's teachings, it is not only the beginning that is all-important, but also the finish.

this as the only test of a person's relationship is that it, many times, circumvents the importance of making them disciples and the commitment they should have to being disciples. If you look at Jesus and Paul's teachings, it is not only the beginning that is all-important, but also the finish. Many evangelicals see a person's commitment at conversion as the event that ends all events. But it seems that, in the New Testament, salvation is a process that begins with conversion but is sustained through discipleship. It is not those who say Lord, Lord, but those who do the will of the Father. Saying Lord, Lord can be evident in many modern day conversion events, but doing what He says is proven and cultivated in lifelong discipleship. Paul writes in Romans 11 about the importance of the believer continuing in the grace and kindness of God. "Behold then the kindness and severity of God; to those who fell, severity, but to you, God's kindness, if you continue in His kindness; otherwise you also will be cut off." The best ways to continue in His kindness are to disciple His people, and teach them to observe God's ways and wishes.

The Crises Revealed! Turn on your TV nightly news and all you will hear is crisis here, and crises there. When churches are in crisis, it is even bigger news. All through church history one can see crisis after crisis, but what do you expect when man is involved? You say, "It shouldn't be so," and you are right. The major crises in many of our churches today are not individual indiscretions but wholesale neglect of the command to "Make Disciples." I have been involved and in contact with a lot of churches and, in most cases, they are carrying on Church business and functions while clueless about the primary reasons and results for existence. The only reason to build buildings is to aid in making disciples. The only reason to have ministries is to make disciples. The only reason to have services and classes is to make disciples. Everything we do in the church should point to making new disciples through evangelism and growing disciples through ongoing discipleship (Matthew 28:19,20). Again, everything we do in the church should fulfill these two verses. Ask yourself every time you want to do something in the church, "How will it help make a new disciple or continue to help develop the disciples?"

The Crises Relieved! Only when a church realizes their need and duty to make disciples will it ever have a chance. In some cases some realize it, but others either do not want to take the time, or do not make the effort, to see to it that this task is primary and the center of their existence. The remainder of this chapter will help illustrate and encourage you to make disciples. I suggest that you also acquire two other books to help you and your church get excited about discipleship; Juan Ortiz's book, *Disciple,* and **Dietrich Bonheoffer's book,**

The Cost of Discipleship. **They will change your lives, or make you feel guilty if you don't change.**

Small groups and discipleship!

Is it enough to have small groups and cell groups in the church? A church can have small groups and a cell ministry but at the same time be very lacking in genuine discipleship. If there are no specific goals for discipling, or if the format is just providing another time and venue for a Bible study, then discipleship may be lacking.

In most churches, a person is taught if they attend, listen, and participate in the discussion. This is not the New Testament view on being taught. In the Great Commission, it is obvious that Christ was not concerned about delivering information only but about changing behavior. "Teach them to observe everything that I have taught you." Matthew 28:20 Small groups that just provide another opportunity for study or in some cases just fun will end up short on the command to disciple. These

> **In the Great Commission, it is obvious that Christ was not concerned about delivering information only, but about changing behavior.**

types of groups does meet needs, but does not provide a person the opportunity to achieve a higher level of commitment like discipleship. A Bible study usually ends in a completion of the text and the gathering of knowledge, but if the goal is to disciple, the result and goal is changed behavior. It must be intentional and expected that a person is to change their life when they follow Christ throughout their Christian walk. Jesus expects it; why does the church not expect it?

Usually the church is afraid that people will turn away and not participate. The New Testament church today is afraid to hold people accountable. Mormonism is the fastest growing religion as of this writing, and they have very high expectations of their people. So, I think the mainline churches can expect more of a commitment from their followers and not lose them because of a higher level of commitment. They may lose those who were chaff, but not those who are truly serious about their faith and commitment to Christ.

This is not heading towards cultic control of the people, but rather an expectation from the body that people will be encouraged to live a life of obedience to the Lord. It means that each church should have in place a means and a heart to disciple, with the expectation that everyone involved will work and walk as an obedient follower of Christ. Paul's writings are full of expectations for his disciples. Are these expectations not also for us today? "I urge you therefore brethren by the mercies of God to present your bodies a living and holy sacrifice... And do not be conformed to this world, but be transformed by the renewing of your mind..." (Romans 12:1,2)

This renewal of a new mind is done best when the church expects this type of commitment from the beginning of a person's conversion, and when it is modeled in its leadership. My booklet, *The Most Precious Thing in the World*, will aid any church in helping a person understand that becoming a Christian is to become a responsible disciple. The transition from the initial conversion to committed discipleship will be accomplished if the ideas are presented in the beginning. In this way, the new convert will just accept it, and it will become a part of their walk. Let us not be afraid to call people to commitment. Jesus did, and so should we. The problem is that many in leadership and the church do not have this commitment and, therefore, do not want to commit others to it. If they did, they would have to be committed as well. It is so much easier to be laissez faire and find an excuse for the lack of commitment.

What is the purpose of the Church? Most would say, "Saving the lost," as we saw in our first chapter of Part One. That would not be wrong, but is that the whole of it? No, I think it is only half of the mission, or even a part of the overall mission, but by far not all.

When I have asked where the purpose of the church is found in Scripture, I would usually get the answer, "In Matthew 28:19,20," and in my opinion, that is correct. I think everything the church should be about is found in these two verses. I will explain more on this point later as we take a closer exegetical look.

> **In our world of churches today, the mistake is making evangelism the high point of our concern. This I have seen has caused the church to be nearsighted in their focus and approach to continued disciple making.**

In our world of churches today, the mistake is making evangelism the high point of our concern. This I have seen has caused the church to be nearsighted in their focus and approach to continued disciple making.

The problem started, in my humble estimation, with the misinterpretation of the Great Commission in the King James Version. The King James did a disservice by translating the verse, "Go teach all nations," when in fact it said, "Go make disciples of all nations."

When I ask a person what they think of when I say teach, I usually get the answer of classroom lecturing or the dispersing of information from a teacher to a student. That is the western view of teaching. As long as information is shared, and hopefully understood, teaching has been accomplished. The hope of most teachers is that those listening will take to heart the information or message and do something with it, but this outcome is unexpected in most cases. So when the King James four centuries ago said, "Go teach all nations," most people had the understanding that when someone went and taught about Jesus, the work was done. If people responded to this message or teaching they were baptized, and their task was basically finished. Even if there were no response from the hearers they would, in a sense, have still fulfilled the task by preaching to them.

This has caused a lot of false assumptions in the church since then. If we teach and even if we baptize, we have really had success, but the task is still not done. This is why we have a lot of people in the churches today that have made a decision but are truly no different than they were. They may even have a lot of knowledge but in essence, are no different than when they first began. If the benchmark of growth is the knowledge one has, then we may have been successful because the teaching has been done. But, if it is more than that, then maybe we have fallen short of the mark.

Over the past few hundred years, churches, and even missionaries, have gone into a majority of the world and have operated under the assumption that if they teach people about Jesus, then they have fulfilled the Great Commission. If some people accept and receive Jesus that is a bonus. That is not enough; it is not what is truly said and meant by Jesus. Therefore, the Old King James has done more of a disservice in this passage than any other aspect, except maybe not translating baptize as immersion, because it has given workers the false assumption that they fulfilled their work when they preached the gospel and maybe got some converts.

As was said, the result is that many have "received" Jesus, but most have not become His true disciples. The command in the Greek, and in most recent translations today, is worded "Go make disciples," not "Go teach." Again, this action is totally different in its meaning and results than just "teaching." To make something means there is raw material and

> **If a person understands *all* he has to do is believe (note the Bible never uses these words, and so we shouldn't either), then any future behavior or action is logically irrelevant.**

there is an end result from that material. When you make a disciple you have raw material, a new believer or non-believer. Your result is to take that new person and help them become a mature and founded disciple or follower of Christ. This takes more effort and time of the church but, in the long run, will produce a more committed person and will set the groundwork for future healthy disciples and their churches. If a person understands *all* he has to do is believe (note the Bible never uses these words, and so we shouldn't either), then any future behavior or action is logically irrelevant. On the other hand, if the person is taught that they are to be a follower or disciple who obeys, then the chance of that person becoming a new person willing to obey God and live a Christian life is much more likely.

But the making of disciples is the correct translation. "Go make disciples of all nations." What kind of results or change of approach could you see from this translation? The results would be phenomenal. First, there would be no confusion about the goal; second, no confusion about the strategy; and third, no confusion about the outcome.

Why are we to make disciples?

First, it's a command, not an option (Matt. 28:18-20). This should all be a "no brainer," as some would say. It is so obvious that this is what we are to do and be as God's people. Let's look a little closer into why we should be making disciples. The Great Commission- God commanded it, and that settles it. Ah, another cliché that has a bite and truth, regardless of the fact that these are Christ's last and foremost words on the subject. This alone should be enough. If we do not respect the orders of the Commander-in-Chief, then who will we respect and follow?

Leaders, and especially most people, would say, "Yes, we know it is a command," but there is no evidence they truly believe it by their actions. One of the churches I have been associated with over the years has proven the point. In a five-year period, 95% of those coming into the church have been by transfer. Now there have been some baptisms, but these have either been children of current members, who count in the Lamb's book but do not reflect on the fulfillment of the Great Commission, or a few Orientals who have come to Christ at the effort of a mission group within the church. It is more like a great omission rather than commission.

This church, like many churches, is stuck in their world. They worship, they preach, they teach, and they are even encouraged to invite people to their cell groups or worship service each week, but they are not equipped or led to "GO." In actuality, the Great Commission is an option in this church. It is not their main focus to make disciples but to have church as usual. If the person is comfortable coming to an existing group, there will be success. The problem is, the only ones to come are those who already had contact with the church or people just looking to find a church. A total non-believer will not come to Christ this way 99% of the time. This is not the way to make disciples but rather just shifts disciples from church to church. This is not what God intends for the mission of the church.

All this can change, though, when the leadership has the vision to equip and deploy others in the church. We will be exploring how to do this in the chapter on evangelism.

Second, Jesus' example shows us another reason why it is important to disciple. Jesus either wasted His time and gave us an example we could not follow, or He in fact showed us the method He wanted His church to follow; not for a decade or century, but until He comes back. Are we His disciples? Most would say, "Of course, we are Christians." If we can say we are His disciples, then we are foolish if we do not follow his methods, as well as His other commands. When we try to improve on the Master's method, we begin to step on a slippery slope.

Third, we see Paul's example in discipling. Paul's whole ministry was one of discipleship. Were it not for his work and relationships with others, we would have a bleak picture of how to apply what Jesus had done earlier with the other disciples, and later in the wilderness with him. Jesus gave us a glimpse of the divine method and Paul gave us an example of its possibilities with all people everywhere. Jesus was the architect and blueprint, and Paul was His foreman or crew chief. Jesus built the foundation and Paul took the materials and methods and put them into action. We are no less responsible to carry out Christ's mission than was Paul. We are not to be irresponsible and try to build on any other foundations and methods than those laid down in the New Testament.

> **If the church is not discipling, and if it is not mentoring its leaders, then it is being built with little or no foundation. Being politically correct may be Biblically damning tomorrow.**

But someone might say, "Oh we're in the 21st century and the church needs to do things differently." I would say, "They still build houses today with foundations, walls, and roofs don't they?" Now you may have different décor or material, but the basic foundation and ideas are the same. So it is with the church. If the church is not discipling, and if it is not mentoring its leaders, then it is being built with little or no foundation. Being politically correct may be Biblically damning tomorrow.

Fourth, the process of making disciples God's method for world evangelism. What was the Lord's mission? What was His reason for coming? To seek and save the lost, was it not? Making disciples is the best and most productive way of accomplishing this through the church today. Don't forget that, in the command of the Great Commission, the first thing is evangelism. The second thing is that it is to be done everywhere, giving everyone an opportunity to follow Jesus as His disciple. If it is done right, discipleship comes full circle when those who are made into disciples make other disciples, as we will see later in this chapter.

What does it mean to be a disciple or Christian? At first, it may seem obvious that both are the same. In the Bible, those who were disciples were Christians, and vice versa. To be a Christian is to be Christ-like. If that was actually the case and the result, I could stop here, but, sadly, in the real world today, everything is blurred. _Christian_ is a term that has been twisted and misused. To be a Christian is to be an American, or not a Muslim or Buddhist. There is no real line drawn on what it truly means to be a Christian. This being so, we see that to call yourself a Christian is to say very little to the world.

But when you call someone a disciple, you know what it means. Well, most know this; "I am sure even the truck drivers on route 10 know this as my professor, Dr. James Strauss, used to say. So what is a disciple of Christ? I am not referring to the denomination, but to an individual.

A Disciple is:

•A Follower! Red is red, and a disciple is a follower. Not just hearing, but actually doing. To follow is to become or to do. You cannot be a follower and not follow. Oh, how simple all this is, but yet we make it a non-issue again because we do not want to offend anyone, but in fact, most people want a cause, or deep down are willing to follow something or someone if they truly believe in their worth. In many churches the concepts of being accountable, to become, or to follow our teachers need to be reinforced and expected. If the church members are followers of Christ, then it will be easy for others to follow also.

In Mark 2:14, we see Jesus' calling of Matthew. Much like he did with His other disciples, Jesus asked Matthew to follow him, and immediately he did. I believe Matthew knew something of Jesus before this call. This was not the first time Levi met Jesus, nor did that Jesus place a power over Him he could not refuse. To become a follower today, each person must see Jesus and believe He is someone worthy of them following and committing to. Matthew saw Jesus, and only through seeing our following, will others want to follow.

> We have very few true learners in the church today. The reason is they are not expected to learn, they are not trained to learn, and they are not given opportunity or experience to learn.

Learner! A true learner is one who actually does something with what he hears. No teacher will consider his student successful if the student does not acquire the pertinent knowledge *and apply it*. You do not learn a lesson until it makes a difference, makes a change in attitude, or reforms a habit. The person that stands in the street and gets hit does not learn their lesson if they go right back into the street and get hit again. We have very few true learners in the church today. The reason is they are not expected to learn, they are not trained to learn, and they are not given opportunity or experience to learn. It is important to remember that, "just learning information is not what is meant by being a learning disciple". Peter learned from Paul that it was not acceptable for him to be prejudiced against the Gentiles. Now, if he would have heard and then continued being prejudiced, he would not have been a learning disciple. This is the same today as we read the Word of God and hear a Biblically challenging sermon. The problem is that, in many churches and with many people, they are not reading and hearing challenging sermons.

In my nine years of football, I learned that if you did not learn and execute the play, you did not play. It did not take me nine years to learn this; it would have been miserable sitting on the bench all those years. How many people spend nine years or more and never learn or execute anything in the church? I am afraid sitting on the bench may put them off the team forever.

In Matthew 11:28-30, Jesus is saying it is beneficial to learn from Him, and that if we take His yoke, we will be wiser than to keep our own yoke. We all find it hard to admit when we are wrong. We become stubborn and think we must do it our way. This pride or stupidity brings about more hardship in our lives and keeps us from truly learning. Nothing wrong in failing, but it is wrong to continue to fail by refusing to learn from your mistakes or sins. Jesus gives us the invitation to come to Him and learn, but why do most people refuse this offer? Anyone that has a chance to learn from a master would jump at the opportunity. I have dabbled in painted landscapes for 26 years, but I have never learned under the guidance of a master. The old classic masters are all dead, but there are those who have learned their techniques and can teach them today. If I had the money, time, and chance to sit underneath their teaching, I would. We have that opportunity with the Bible. The Bible is our textbook, and living, following disciplers today can help us learn. People learn from Jesus in two ways today; through His Spirit's divine Word, and through those who commit their lives to following it. Find an elder, a righteous man or woman, and sit at his or her feet, as he or she sits under Christ. Or, be someone's Discipler and help that person learn to learn from the Master.

•**Obedient!** It is obvious that to be followers and learners, you have to be obedient. In this politically correct world, being obedient is relative and mostly passé in this post-modern era. To obey or not to obey, that is the question. "Be ye perfect as I am perfect." Most Christians have dismissed any chance to fulfill this command. Therefore, whether one obeys or not, it is not that crucial with this type of mindset. In the Great Commission, when you teach a person to observe, you must teach them to obey. So a true committed disciple will learn to obey everything He taught us. It may be improbable, but if we do not try, we will never know.

> The same is the case with the Heavenly Father. If we, His children, refuse to obey Him, can we say we truly love Him?

In John 14:23-24, we see what Jesus and His Father think about obedience. Children don't be fooled; if you do not try to obey your parents, you truly do not love them. You may say you do but your continual rebellion says differently. The same is the case with the Heavenly Father. If we, His children, refuse to obey Him, can we say we truly love Him? And we know that if children are not taught and given examples of obedience, chances are they will not learn to obey. Obedience, even in the Christian realm, does not come naturally because we are not by nature holy. There are two ways we can be obedient. One is by discipline, and the other is by the power of God's Spirit working within us. Jesus gives us this hint in John 14:25 when He promises a helper, the Holy Spirit. This is still the same today. We need to learn and be disciplined, and as we do this, we need to yield to and depend on the power of the Holy Spirit to help us. In almost every case, new Christians will need two helpers, the Spirit, and the Discipler.

A Becomer/Imitator! The biggest complement is that someone imitates another. Paul says to be imitators of him as he is an imitator of Jesus. In my tract, _The Making of a Disciple_, I write, "You can obey without becoming like the person. Becoming is the same as transformation into a new person, but a person can do things outwardly without truly being changed on the inside. You can do an act of love without truly loving. Many, people act for their own benefit, not from a sincere heart. A true disciple becomes like the Master, both inwardly and outwardly. A metamorphosis and new creature is what God wants and intends from His church and each individual believer. It is important to realize that the process of discipleship is a partnership between the Holy Spirit, Discipler, and Disciple. Without the trifold partnership, the Church cannot truly become like the Master.

When you look at Ephesians chapter three you can see the closeness each of us should have with the Godhead. The text is clear that we now have access to all three in the Godhead. A disciple must realize that we can now go before the Father, and each disciple/Christian should daily be on their knees. When we realize that all three come to be in us then we can see what awesome privilege we do have. Knowing that we are in God's presence should motivate us to be the Disciples God wants and we need. When all this happens, we will in fact become more like Christ.

A Reproducer! To leave the task finished at developing a Christian's life or helping a person come to maturity is only half the battle. To stop with one person or a few only makes the person rare and on his way to extinction. The reason making disciples became a low priority is that, somewhere back in the past, Christians changed from making disciples to care taking church members. A true disciple will see that his task is not over at his assent to maturity, but at his making others into disciples. This is not to say a person has to reach the highest pinnacle of maturity before he makes a disciple. If so, then we would have found another excuse not to evangelize or disciple. In everyone's walk, there is someone who is younger and less mature in the faith and in need of his or her help or encouragement. Paul told Timothy in 1 Timothy 2:3 to go find others who you can disciple and who will also in turn disciple. The circle will be complete when you see ones you have helped help others help others become obedient disciples. When one sees the grandchildren in the faith produced, one sees the process a success. I see this happening in our ministry in Cuba. Our team there have caught the vision to make disciples. Those that they bring to Christ through our material and of course the Holy Spirit are our grandchildren in the work. What a blessing to see this happen

How do we make disciples?

Bring people to a saving knowledge and commitment to follow Christ! (Colossians 1:28). What you win them with will generally determine who and what they will become in the future. If you convince a person that all they have to do is say a little prayer and receive Jesus into their heart, in their mind they have done all they are required to do. I know this is a popular theology, but it is very shortsighted and dangerous to the new believer or convert if they think this is it, they have arrived. Jesus, nor His Apostles, used this method. They always asked for commitment to follow and obey, and we should do no less. If a person understands they are to be a disciple, a follower, then they will be willing to follow because that is what they committed to when they came on board. If a convert came into the church understanding all they have to do is receive a person or idea, then they have accomplished this important event, but it does not often translate into a person that is committed to follow as a disciple. The only way it can is if that teaching is given right after the conversion, but it is still hard to say, "Oh by the way, you also have to do this." Put it up front; Jesus does not want merely receivers, but followers. Tell them and be honest with them. You will not lose them, but if you do, Christ never had them.

> If a convert came into the church understanding all they have to do is receive a person or idea, then they have accomplished this important event, but it does not often translate into a person that is committed to follow as a disciple.

Bring converts to a point where they are mature or adults in their faith (Ephesians 4:11) This is the next step in the process, and is not an overnight deal, nor a six-week class. It is a lifelong adventure that starts immediately upon conversion. This is qualitative growth. Maturity is the goal and outcome. But if this is the only goal, and the next goal is pushed to the side, the church will become worthless to the rest of the unsaved in the world.

Make disciples of your church. If you are in an established church then the goal is to get everyone involved in being discipled. This, of course, will take a lot of time and teaching. Some people will refuse and not want to participate. If this happens, then make it known that they will not be able to be in leadership or have any grave responsibility in the church .if they don't. You shouldn't bar them from coming, but you can make their wiliness to participate a litmus test for being in any type of leadership. If it is in a new church then all you do is make this a norm from the beginning; this is who we are and it is just what we do. And if it is not what you want in a church, then you may be happy some place else, as we alluded to in section one.

> **Just making a few converts is not enough. You must make those converts into self-propagating disciples. To only win one generation and not help them win the next is shortsighted and ultimately self-defeating.**

Make disciples of all nations. The Church also accomplishes Christ command to make disciples when others are trained and deployed in all nations and to every people group. There are to be no off -limits or untouchables in this world. All people are precious in His sight. The goal of the Church and missions is to see that every nation is evangelized and equipped to evangelize their own people. Just making a few converts is not enough. You must make those converts into self-propagating disciples. To only win one generation and not help them win the next is shortsighted and ultimately self-defeating. At this point of writing I have 15 different languages in process. Spanish is complete, excluding this book, and the others again are in process. Please contact Fishnet Publishers for what books and languages are ready. I tell you this, to tell you that I am looking for those natives in these language groups to step up and help me train and deploy disciple-makers in their countries. It will only be successful when indigenous natives steps up and take on the task of making disciples. Our mission is not about the business of training and keeping control, but rather, training and releasing. Foreigners will never be able to do as good a job as the native in reaching their people group. Now there are exceptions to the rule. In some countries the time is limited for those of foreign decent, therefore the missionary needs to prepare the natives to take on leadership and to be equipped to carry on the mission to make disciples in their country of influence.

How to have a successful journey?

People oriented, not program oriented Discipleship is not another program or study to go through. Rather, it is intended to be the fabric and foundation of all we do in the church. It is about helping and loving others. It is about helping them grow and looking out for their best interest in the Kingdom. A parent who neglects their children is looked down upon in any society. Unfortunately, we have a lot of children in the church that are being neglected. Don't be one of those neglectful parents or church families.

Spirit led, not man led! It is so important that those who lead and work for the Kingdom be led by God's Spirit, not man's, and that includes each of us. If we believe that God is God, and that we truly are men and women of faith, then we will be successful in

God's eyes if we let Him lead us through His Spirit. It is when man steps outside of God's direction that we make mistakes.

Mentoring more than lecturing! It is easy to lecture or just share ideas with each other, but true discipleship is intentional and repeatable. It is intentional in that you intend for there to be change and action taken as a result of your time together. That includes those who are mentors as well. But it is important that the disciple sees examples of the Christian life and walk by being mentored and guided in Christian disciplines. It is repeatable in that what they see you do and teach, they can teach others. If this discipleship ends with one generation, then it was ultimately a waste of time in the long run. If it is not repeatable, then again, what lasting good is accomplished for the Kingdom?

Making disciples is not a program, it's a ministry! In most of our churches, discipleship is gated off as just another program to be added instead of being the fabric of what the church is all about. If it is just another program or set of material to go through, when you go through a course, you're done. What I have written and you are studying is only a means or beginning. Making disciples is what the church should be about. It is a lifelong process.

Be committed to see it through! As you have waded through this book and process, it is not hard to see this is work, but anything that is worthwhile is worth the work. The important thing is to see the plan through to the end. We can jump from program to program year after year and still, at the end, be no more mature or larger than when we began. Usually this happens when churches change ministers every two years, or never quite finish what they start. Some people have said, "Let's start a shepherding program," but a year later, nothing has been done. They found it took too much time and commitment to truly do the work. Is not the church deserving of our time? Yes, so let us rise to the challenge, see the course, and make disciples of all nations.

"Discipleship: Friend or Foe?"

In some churches, the thought of discipleship brings fear and trembling, or at least contempt for something that is foreign or threatening to their situation. Some churches have tried this or that cell or small group and, for some reason, had a bad experience in the process. After that, they decided no more, too risky. What are some of the reasons people have for staying clear from discipleship as the central ministry and not just a program?

So what are the fears and misconceptions about discipleship?

Takes too much time to implement. Yes it takes time, but I propose not too much time. What you treasure will be where you spend your time. Everyone needs to do a time budget. When we want to know where our money goes, we list all of our expenditures. Where has all the time gone? Make a list of your day and where it is spent. How many hours are wasted on insignificant things, events, and hobbies that, when they are all done, produce nothing lasting? Now I have hobbies, and I would like to spend more time doing them, but I set my priorities concerning them. And let me say, hobbies are not evil, but when they consume all your time they can become your lord, and this is when they become wrong.

> If God has equipped each of us to do ministry, then is it not right that we take the time to allow Him to use us?

Everyone has the same amount of time; no one has a market on it. But some have a better use of time that leads to productivity. Time is a gift from God that we need not waste. But I am afraid that when He returns part of his judgment on the Christian will be wasted time that could have been spent on Kingdom things. I am not just talking about activities, and being involved in things every time the door is open. I am talking about being responsible with the time and gifts He as bestowed upon us. If God has equipped each of us to do ministry, then is it not right that we take the time to allow Him to use us?

Discipleship can be done in eight weeks. This is a result of our day, fast and shallow. The quick fix soothes our conscience, and now we can go on to something else. It is easy, but it is superficial. Again, making disciples must be seen as the foundation of the church's purpose, not just a fixture, and not just another program to be discarded. You cannot bring people through a study alone and think they have been made into disciples

Not everyone needs it, especially older Christians. This is another copout for mediocrity. Just because people have been involved in going to church all their lives does not mean they have ever been committed disciples. Some would be considered to be pillars in a church but have never changed from day one. I have found that it is not age that is the factor, but an open heart. I have seen a 71-year -old elder in central Mexico cry and say, "I have finally found what it means to be a Christian by learning what it means to be a disciple," and I have heard a 30-year old say, "I don't need any more, I've done enough." Discipleship is understanding what God wants of His people and helping others, as well as self, fulfill His will and follow his commands. That expectation is for everyone that claims to be a Christian.

Takes too much effort and manpower. Yes and no! Yes, it takes much effort and much manpower to see that everyone is discipled, but it is worth it. The problem is that in our conventional churches only 20% usually do all the work. So it is feared that, "Oh no, here we go again, more things for us to do." But if done right, in the long run it will be less for the few, and a little more for the many. If everyone does one thing based in their giftedness, then no one will likely burn out or get overworked. This is how God intended the church to work.

It can create cliques and division. Yes, it potentially may, but so does any other group that meets together. You do not do something because a human may make a mistake. You do something because it is right in and of itself. You don't refuse to feed someone in hunger because someone might abuse the act of kindness and become a glutton.

> **But true discipleship is here to stay if God's leaders and disciples are committed to Him. It is when the church or individuals get sidetracked that they jump from fad to fad.**

It's just another fad. As you know, fads come and go, and if discipleship is just another program added to the other programs, it too will be another fad that will fade away. But true discipleship is here to stay if God's leaders and disciples are committed to Him. It is when the church or individuals get sidetracked that they jump from fad to fad.

Although it was Jesus' method, some people have thought, "We cannot do it His way because we are not Jesus. Then Jesus came and wasted His time showing 120 people how to make disciples. Jesus said we would do greater things. Now, I do not quite understand all of what He meant, but what He did was natural for Himself, and what we can do through His Spirit is supernatural. If we are in Christ, and following His will, we can and will do great things. We can do things the way Jesus did if He is truly motivating us and we have the faith and power within us to follow.

It may run people off. Well yes, this may be true, but who does it run off? When commitment is required, some people will not want to commit and therefore leave; that is okay. Jesus did not run after the rich young ruler. He did not say, "Well, okay, you can follow me anyway, just don't go away." No, He let him go. This is the problem today we are afraid to offend anyone. Now we should feel this way if the persons leaving is over our way or selfishness, but if it is over asking for commitment and being strong in following God's work, then we must stand, even if others do not want to stand with us. But what you will have is a truer, more dedicated, and more committed church, and that is what God wants for and from His church.

What are some reasons bad experiences happen?

There was not enough training. In the area of who becomes a leader, the church has of late had a bad track record in training and equipping leaders for service. It is much easier to assume and hope those who are nominated or chosen will be qualified for the position. Being in church or Sunday school does not automatically equip a person to be a leader. Usually when something new is introduced, there is very little training going on before or during the process. People will rise to the level of their training and expertise. To be successful, there must be training and mentoring taking place.

> For whatever reason, failure precedes success. It is in failure or lack of experience that you are taught. If you learn from your mistake, or better yet others' mistakes, then next time you will be able to see the finish line.

Not enough committed or mature leadership. This again is a result of lack of prior mentoring or discipleship. Very few men are really ready and able to do the work because they have never been challenged or mentored towards maturity. We do not ask for commitment and, therefore, do not get it. Most people will go with the flow towards the least resistance. That does not mean they will not go in another direction if challenged and equipped to do so.

Gave up too soon before results were evident. A major tendency is to give up too soon. There are numerous stories out there about people who gave up too soon. A little more effort, skill, or encouragement, and they would have made it to the finish line or completion of their goal. I know I have done it, and when you find out it could have been done with a little more effort and time, it disappoints you. For whatever reason, failure precedes success. It is in failure or lack of experience that you are taught. If you learn from your mistake, or better yet others' mistakes, then next time you will be able to see the finish line. You will be able to say, "Let's try it again, but do it right." In mentoring and discipleship you can minimize failure by saying, "Let's try it again." Don't give up too soon; God sees the big picture, so trust Him.

Some person or circumstance derailed the process. Not everyone was on the same page. Rogue people who do not want to get involved usually are the ones who causes a division. The most frustrating thing in my ministry has been when shortsighted, faithless people get in the way of God's work. I had a case where the church went through my training with great success. Almost 100% of those who were in attendance committed to being involved in family and discipleship groups. Even all the elders were willing to participate. But one day, one of the elders decided he had had enough and became a source of division. It only takes one person with negative or selfish attitudes to destroy what a whole group is enjoying.

Usually, it is those who have not surrendered their leadership to God and want control. This is a sin, and a shame, but they need to be challenged for the good of the Kingdom. They may get mad, but the Kingdom and others are worth it.

When is disciple making finished?

When there is maturity! When will that be, and at what age can we say a person is mature? In this sense, it is relative in comparison in that each person is growing at their own pace and commitment level. For the most part, we will always need to be involved in discipleship. We can say we are done when we can say we have learned and observed all that Jesus and the Spirit have to teach us. So, even mature Christians have a need to continue to be discipled.

> When individuals, and even the church as a whole, are reproducing themselves in a responsible manner, then discipleship has come full circle. It is important that it becomes a never-ending circle.

But there are benchmarks that show a person is on his way to maturity, or has developed a mature mindset. First, the mature person is open to change. Second, he does not get defensive when challenged. This does not mean, however, that he does not defend himself if he is right. Third, he treats others, as he would like to be treated. Fourth, he is fair and non-judgmental. Fifth, he is able to control his tongue and temper. There may be other elements of maturity not mentioned, but these are a good place to start.

We can see God's idea of maturity in some passages. Please look up and list standards of maturity. (Titus 2:1-8; Galatians 5:13-26)

When there is reproduction. Any organism is usually mature when it can reproduce. Now you might say that a girl of 12 is physically able to reproduce, but she is not mature in other ways, and you would be right. The important point here is that responsible reproduction is a sign of maturity. When individuals, and even the church as a whole, are reproducing themselves in a responsible manner, then discipleship has come full circle. It is important that it becomes a never-ending circle.

When we're in glory! Of course, it may go without saying that when we enter into glory, discipleship will be finished. But, as I write this, it comes to me that it will only just begin. Just think of being able to finally sit at Jesus feet, walk with the Apostles, and be able to ask them questions. What a time it will be! Everything will be revealed and evident.

The Nuts and Bolts of the Discipleship System
Chapter Nine

Discipleship seems like a large task. In some ways it is. When you have to go back and start over, it does take time to change structures (and minds!) This *has to* happen when you introduce this program to an existing church. When you are working with a new church, or a church that has yet to establish a leadership, then it is much easier because there are no stringent forms that may need to be changed or altered.

Attitudes and procedures needed to help the program succeed.

First is <u>time</u>! In the beginning, someone will have to spend time developing the infrastructure, but once it is set in order, it will continue to work.

<u>Some will have to do more tasks in the beginning</u> to get the new structure in place. This is where I have seen churches and individuals give up and the system fails. It is new and it will take time to get it going. Just think of all the programs and things your church has started and finished over the years. This is different because it is a ongoing process and not just a onetime study. It will take some of the leaders or teachers a little double time to get it going. To make it easy I suggest you might have to merge some existing Bible studies with this material, you will keep people from time overload.

<u>The longer you take to get things started, the harder it will be</u>; keep the fire burning. Time in delay will be one of your worst enemies.

> **Just like communion, preaching, and baptism, discipling must be at the center of the church's existence and everyday life.**

Second, is that everyone understands the vision and the command to make disciples. To be successful here, the vision must be stated again and again - in different situations. As we have already noted, people need to see that this is not just another program, but the very fabric of the church, and that this ministry of discipleship will be a continual process that will be established to <u>shepherd</u>, and keep the church growing. Just like communion, preaching, and baptism, discipling must be at the center of the church's existence and everyday life.

<u>**Reminders must be made from the pulpit**</u>**. Keep the vision before the congregation through sermons and other events.**

<u>**Elders and leaders involved must keep sharing their enthusiasm about the new ministry system.**</u> In most cases what comes from the elders and rest of the leaders may be as, or more influential than the lead pastor. People expect him to champion the cause, but when the grass root leaders step up then the people will more likely follow. When you begin the ministry system you might have all the leaders stand up in front of the congregation and vow to make this happen in the church. This will implant in the rest of the congregation the importance of the new system.

Have times of sharing in church about those who are going through the discipling process. Nothing is more endearing and exciting than success stories about what God is doing through the small groups in discipleship. Have times of testimonies of what is happening in some of the groups.

Third, is that everyone is willing to eventually get involved. Everyone has to be discipled. New people, both converts and transfers, are started immediately into the program. Any existing member should go through the discipleship training as soon as possible. In a new church, this should be the assumed "track" for everyone.

Unity and shared vision are the responsibility of the leadership. The biggest problem in the church today is not false doctrine, but disunity. If every leader is not on board then also a segment of the congregation will not either. To be successful there must be a solid front of unity from the leaders.

Anyone in any ministry (elder, deacon, etc.) should be involved in the process. What we are talking about here is being an example. Who do leaders lead in the church? Sheep, that's who. That being the case, then whatever the leaders do, or not do, will affect what their sheep do. Even one leader who goes his own way can cause major damage to the process. Most would be surprised how people follow different leaders and not others.

> **Who do leaders lead in the church? Sheep, that's who. That being the case, then whatever the leaders do, or not do, will affect what their sheep do.**

Not all will be teachers, but all need to be discipled. "No discipleship? No leadership responsibilities." When the ministry system is in full implementation I suggest that you limit eldership to those who have been in the discipling ministry system. In an established church, if all are not totally committed, then this will take effort and time to get everyone on board. If they refuse to see the need then maybe it is time for them to be asked to step down. You cannot afford to allow one person destroy the whole process.

Everyone, no matter how old, should be encouraged to look forward to finding and using his or her gifts in ministry. The ultimate sign of involvement is that each person in the church identifies and uses their gifts in the service of the congregation and the world.

Don't force, but continually encourage and provide opportunity. As I said, you can require the leaders, and anyone who wants to be one to be involved in the discipling ministry system, but a regular person in the pew you can only encourage. In the new church you just let people know this is what you do and if they do not want to participate then try to show them the importance. You will not get any problems from new believers if they are taken through the "Most Precious", but transfers are a different breed than new believers. You may have one that thinks he knows all and does not need to be involved in the discipleship. Again if it is a new church then you may ask him to find somewhere else where he will be happier. Better to deal with it now than have division later. Another option is to tell the transfer that he can come but will not be able to get involved it they do not start at this basic level.

Fourth, NEVER do any part of this discipleship ministry on Sunday morning. The ministry will self-destruct and dwindle away. You can have the home small group meetings on Sunday evening if need be, but have it in homes, for this proves to be the most successful. The only exception is the study of church doctrine. This can be done during Sunday school if you follow the rule of finishing it when you finish it. That is, if you do not finish the study on God, then you go into the next week. Therefore, plan on two weeks per lesson. But I stress - it is still better to have discipleship groups during the week where you can have an hour and a half to two hours to give to the study, or Sunday night might be another option if done in the homes. You may say, "Why not at the church building?" For some reason, it's easier to commit to coming to a home during the week than on Sunday night. Furthermore, there seems to be some psychological barrier that people have about staying two hours in a church setting, but in the home it seems to never be an issue. Sunday morning is a free day from family groups. This is a time for corporate study and fellowship. Have electives or other studies that complement the sermon or the general needs of the church. Time constraints are destructive to the methods employed in the discipling ministry.

Fifth, if you decide to use ministries like Global Church Growth ministries to help you in setting up your discipleship ministry, write down any questions or negative responses, and ask your project advisor. It is better to get the advice and direction than to make mistakes. Not all questions will be answered in the four-day training session, so do not be ashamed to ask for help; that is what the project advisor is for. Two heads are better than one, and others have gone through the same process, so wisdom comes from counsel.

Problem Areas

Some objections will come up. Most often it's because there isn't enough information, or there was a misunderstanding about something said in the seminar. Please call and talk this through, because one phone call or e-mail can clear up the problem or misunderstanding and can, as well, save the program.

Don't let negative people control the situation, especially those who were not in the seminar. Tell them before they complain to sit down and watch the videos of the seminar first. Videos of the seminar will be available from Global Church Growth.

Encourage the people to be a part of the solution and fulfillment of God's will, not a hindrance. Those who complain or try to impede the process of implementation of the ministry in any of it's parts, is suspect of a number of things. First, they may just be ill informed, or do not understand enough to get on board, and just giving them enough information will solve the problem. Second, They may have a selfish motive to stop it, or get in the way. These selfish motives may include they do not want to spend the time, they may not want to lose control of some aspect that may be changed in the new system. Third, they are spiritually immature and need to be taught that it is the right thing to do for the church and their self. If they are willing to be taught then you have won your brother, if not, then you will have to evaluate them further. Fourth, they are just carnal, and are not being led by the Spirit. Or lastly an unbeliever in sheep's clothing. If it is anything but the first, then the leadership should not let this person destroy this system of ministry. If they continue to refuse to belong or cooperate then they may need to be ask to not be vocal or complaining or at last resort to go some other place to worship. You may lose the one, but that is better than the many

"How to Start a Discipleship Program in the Local Church"

Step by Step

1. <u>Keep the fire burning from the pulpit. Have some of the people who were in the seminar share (the first Sunday after the seminar) about what it meant for them</u>. Use at least two, maybe three, including male and female - not an elder or preacher, but someone who the congregation wouldn't expect; someone who is excited about what he/she has learned. Be wise about your choice; don't get someone who is *overly* excited.

2.   <u>Meet with shepherds, and divide up the people into families</u>. Also, include in this list people who have left the church in the last year. This will be an attempt to "go" and gather back in, those who have gone astray. But be ready to hear things that may be unpleasant - things the church may need to rectify. This will give the family leader an opportunity to do some healing and share the vision. Share that we are going ahead and making the changes that need to be made to meet peoples' needs. This one visit may do more to bring people back who have gone astray. Do this even if they are going somewhere else at this time.

3.   <u>Have a time where those who missed the training can sit down and go through the material</u>. Do this after the testimonies, but not too far into the future; keep the fire burning. Those who missed it will probably never capture the enthusiasm like those who did attend the seminar. You might go through the recordings with your family as a family meeting.

4.   <u>Challenge gifted teachers and mentors</u>! To succeed, the church must have those who can and will commit to the ministry of discipleship. All need to be discipled, but not all will be Disciplers. In beginning this process, challenge those who are gifted to step out and be Disciplers or mentors to someone. It's suggested that all those willing to be disciplers, be taken through the *Walk in Discipleship*. People do not have to go through the entire book before they are ready. We are talking here about people who are mature in their faith and have a firm doctrinal foundation. The main thing is to go through each stage and set of materials with those who will be leading before they take someone through it. This is ideal, but not always expedient. The best way is to have a time with the leaders before their lesson so they can see how it's done.

5.   <u>Start the initial discipling groups</u>. This group will prepare the leaders, or disciplers, for the rest of the congregation. Those who are already involved in teaching might be candidates for the "first-level" disciplers. Those who are leading existing weekly groups could be trained. Each family leader should look into his family and ensure that both a women's group and a men's group start in the *Walk in Discipleship book*. These first people will be the core teachers and disciplers of the discipleship ministry in the beginning. Each person should buy his or her own book, because this provides ownership for the participant. This first group is not necessarily comprised of those who are, or will become, elders or leaders, but it does mean they should be teachers, both by gift and desire.

6.   <u>Every person in each family needs to be evaluated to see if they are indeed in a saving relationship with God</u>. At this point, everyone who's been determined to be unsaved should be taken through the book, *The Most Precious Thing*. To alleviate any doubts, especially lead each transfer through this book, so you're sure of their stance and understanding with God. In a new church plant, it is advised that everyone, from the very beginning, go through this book.

7.   Have each shepherd visit everyone in his family and give them the "Steps to Spiritual Growth" booklet. After a person transfers or yields to baptism the family leader will visit with each person in his family. This visitation needs to start as soon as possible because it will take some time to see everyone in his group. It's advised that they go in teams to each family's home; maybe the preacher and shepherd, then the shepherd and wife, or the shepherd and a person whom the shepherd might possibly recruit as an apprentice. The church is to provide the "Steps" booklet as a gift. Each new person who is saved or transfers in, is also visited within two weeks, given the booklet, and introduced to his/her family and family leaders.

8.   Have each family leader/shepherd pick out and approach someone to be his apprentice. It is important to remember that all elders are to be shepherds, but not all shepherds have to be elders. If you have people in the function of the apprentice/shepherd, most likely they will become the candidates for the ministry of eldership in the future.

9.   Once each person is visited and given the booklet, then they are organized into a small home group to go over the "Steps" booklet. This is the first stage to the process, unless they started with the "Most Precious" booklet. This will last about four weeks. This will be done in mixed groups, ideally in groups of four couples of eight. Why is eight the best number? When you have four couples you will have a natural division of four men and women who will be separated into their groups of four for the study of The Walk in Discipleship. Each church is different, and the plan may need to be tweaked for your situation. This is where you would bounce off any strategy problems or questions with your Global Church Growth advisor. A person might in fact do "double duty" at first. A leader may have to both be a "Steps" leader and a discipler of the first level of disciples, but as you begin these steps, a teacher and an apprentice of this stage should be in place as well. This may or may not be the family apprentice, but another person that will just be a teacher in this area. This study will take about four weeks for the "Steps" booklet. It is suggested here to also have each new person take the personality test that is available from Global Church Growth; this should take at least two more weeks. Some churches may wish to add another session on where the local congregation is and its goals of ministry and involvement, so it could take a total of seven weeks to go through the training!

10.   Once the groups go through the "Most Precious" and "Steps" booklet, then they are to continue studying the lessons in Christian doctrine in their weekly meetings. Some churches may tend to want to do this on Sunday morning; resist this if you can, because it's been proven that interest and attendance will wane in that setting. In the small group time, you have more time to devote to, and develop, the small group habit. Try to make this more of a discussion time rather than a lecture. You might have different people who are capable of leading different subjects. Ideally, each family should have more than one group at a time. Once the church is brought through these lessons, repeat this process a couple of times each year (spring and fall), as people are added to the church. When people finish the "Steps," they can then enter into the doctrinal study, wherever it is in progress, and finish the next time material is offered. Again, try to avoid doing this course on Sunday morning - with one possible exception. When beginning the program in an established church, it may be advantageous to have existing church members go through the study of doctrine while they are beginning the phase in _Walk in Discipleship._

11.   Once the "Doctrine" and "Walk in Discipleship" phases are completed, give certificates to the people in recognition of their completion. You might also give a little gift at each of these points. This is good for the whole congregation when done during Sunday

morning services. Giving this recognition in front of everyone shows how important all this is to the person, and to others who haven't yet finished, or maybe hesitating to get started.

12.   Have each family meet as a group to develop _family identity_. This should be done in the beginning of the process. Have this as a fun time of fellowship and envisioning. Family meetings may take place every three months. Every six months, you might have a gathering of all the families. At this time, you could offer Bible games between families and fun icebreakers that mix the families up. Again, this strengthens community, fellowship, and solidifies the family units.

13.   As people join, assign them into families and get them started on this journey in Discipleship. Remember to start them in the "Most Precious" Book if they join as transfers. Again, if you are an established church, don't organize any massive evangelistic outreach campaigns in the first year of implementing this program; instead, spend your time developing your base of disciplers. Do encourage people to talk with their friends, as God leads. Don't miss any opportunities that present themselves, but don't make a big push until the church is ready to take care of the added number of people that may come.

14.   After the "core" discipling is done, move to the next phase; study the gifts and revisit the personality questionnaire. The next set of studies involves the gifts and taking the "gift and personality" questionnaire. This will follow the _Walk in Discipleship_ material. This should actually be the _second time_ each person has taken the personality questionnaire. Now have them compare their first and second questionnaires, so that each disciple can see his/her growth and changes over the past two years.

For those who were new believers when they started the discipling process, this will be their first time to take their gift questionnaire. Those who took it at the very beginning may also want to revisit it, to see how they have changed, as well as to see if the first questionnaire proves to be accurate.

15.   People should be encouraged to participate in doing things on Sunday morning, but not to be official leaders until they go through the discipleship. You may get impatient at times, but remember that, especially with new converts, Jesus took three years before releasing them to lead or minister. In an established church, there are some people able to step up and begin leading immediately. Those are the people who've already proven themselves over the years to be capable of some type of leadership.

Things to agree upon!

Everyone must see making disciples as the "prime directive". Making disciples in every area and fabric of the church is important. As we have seen in the first chapter, the purpose of the church is to make disciples, but do most churches understand this, and see it as their prime directive? If not, then what kind of church will you have? If any of the leaders fails to see the need to make disciples, a congregation will have problems in implementing this type of ministry.

Evangelism is not an end, but a part of a whole. It is of the utmost importance that "everyone" sees that evangelism is not the end of the process, but the beginning. (See the Thermometer of Faith illustration found in the appendix of _A Walk in Discipleship_) I'm afraid, unfortunately, once a congregation gets settled into its routines of church life, evangelism becomes a side issue, and "caretaking" becomes the main focus. _It is not to be "either/or"._

Evangelism is the <u>first phase</u> of making disciples. See the chapter on Evangelism for more information and insight.

Everyone must be on the same page! Unity was an important issue with Jesus, and later with Paul. Jesus prayed that His disciples would be one. This was usually the case between the Apostles. Even when Paul approached and admonished Peter, the encounter ended in unity. If everyone is not willing to go in the same direction under one purpose, then conflict can and usually does raise its ugly head. Nothing that is done in the church will be a success unless everyone is on the same page, or wavelength. This is important in the vision and direction of the church. I have seen great movements in a church thwarted by the negativity and power of _just one person_. If what is happening, or should happen is of God, true leadership will not allow a few to rule against it.

<u>Old ways may need to be changed or modified</u>. The biggest obstacle to growth and establishing new ministries or programs is resistance to changing the old forms and ways, and many are unwilling to do what it takes. As long as the old ways are not foundational truths, then we have to be open to the Spirit's leading in each area.

Principles for teachers to lead by!

<u>Study the material yourself</u>. Disciplers must study and deal with the material and grow from it. If that doesn't happen, the discipling will be unauthentic or ineffective.

<u>Disciplers must commit to following the material</u>. This is an automatic result of studying the material, or at least it should be. If you, as a Discipler, commit to go through the material for the purpose of your own spiritual growth and maturity, then the journey will be authentic and valuable for your disciples.

<u>Be an example</u>. Again, this follows; if you cannot be an example, then you will have a hard time being a fruitful mentor and Discipler for the Kingdom.

<u>Stay on track</u>. Be faithful and committed to follow through. _Stay the course_. It is easy to get distracted and give up, or look in other directions. When people find it hard to commit to the process (or to show up on time, or consistently) it will hinder the whole group from being consistent and faithful. Staying on track has to be an <u>expectation</u> in successful discipleship; it is holding others in the group accountable. One of the main tools to discipleship is accountability. Holding one another accountable is important in any phase of discipleship!

<u>Listen carefully to those being discipled</u>. Remember, as a Discipler you are "One beggar showing another beggar where the bread is." No one is better than another. When a person lifts himself or herself up above another person, they lower the process, and the power of God is cheapened. Every person, no matter where he may be on the journey, has something to contribute. Why? None of us are omnipresent, omniscient, or gifted at every level. We all can learn from each other. When we forget this, we are at the place where we ourselves cannot be taught.

<u>Listen to the Holy Spirit's guidance</u>. True Biblical discipleship is not a program, because it should be _fluid_ through the guidance of the Spirit. It is a relationship building block, not just a

program. A program is material-driven, while discipleship is relationship-driven. This makes it different, and potentially more effective. The process becomes derailed when you make it into a program and do not allow, or plan for, relational discipleship. Discipleship is the sharing of lives, a caring touch of another human being, and sharing the truth that binds and nurtures. Without the Holy Spirit's presence, the process will be diminished. Now, of course, you may say the development of the material was Spirit-led, and that's true, but it's _miraculous_ when the Spirit is allowed to lead in its application.

SPIRITUAL GROWTH PLAN
THE MAKING OF DISCIPLES

LEVEL ONE: CONTACT/OUTREACH

The goal is to make the initial contact with the prospect. This may or may not result in conversion, so _do not_ make the mistake of rushing a person into a decision that may be more harmful than constructive. This stage is as varied as there are people and places. In one situation, you may find some things that work well; while in other places, the same event or strategy may not be as effective. This is a great phase to let the Spirit lead and guide. There are, however, some general proven methods (and also some relative methods) that we can suggest.

- **Mailings! One of the methods used today is that of _target mailings_ into the community. This is a good way to obtain some names in the beginning, but too much of a good thing could become counter-productive. If you send out too many invitations then of course, too many people might come. What's the problem with** this? Quite simply if you have more contacts than you can handle, _it's better not to have them_ than to lose them! Be sure you're ready before you use this method.

- Block parties! This is a wonderful way of getting to know the people in your community. It is also not as pervasive as the mailings, but is very effective in making the first contact. Many churches make the mistake of rushing things before they're ready to go to the next stage of evangelism (or confrontation). This is a great way to begin developing relationships and meeting new people. Now a person may be ready the first time you get together. Usually you can tell if he/she is responsive. If so, make the transition from contact to sharing at this point. If this is a group gathering, however, it's probably not the place to start evangelizing. (Approach the person at a later date.)

- Surveys! This method may be used for first contact (or traditionally, information gathering). It's a method to contact the people in a target community. Now the Jehovah's Witnesses and Mormons may have made it difficult for you to open doors, but only if you make a presentation, or try to urge people to make a commitment. But if you're truthful and use the right survey, you may open up some doors to people who are in need, or who may be open to visiting or talking with you at another time. (See the appendix for suggestions.)

- New home visits! This is a proven method that works in new Church starts, in addition to contacts on an ongoing basis for outreach from new or established congregations. You need to contact your local Chamber of Commerce, Welcome Wagon, or City Hall for a listing of those moving into town. In the appendix and in your "Church in a Box" kit[1] you'll find a "Bread of Hope" outreach program to be used with new homeowners in your community.

- <u>Etc</u>. Use whatever approaches you may find to contact and start developing new relationships.

LEVEL TWO: EVANGELISM

- The goal is commitment to follow as disciple!
- Develop as many methods to reach as many people as possible.
- Relationship building is the norm; use other approaches as needed.

(Suggested Material: *The Most Precious Thing in the World* by Dr. Householder. This book is intended to bring a person to the point of salvation by convincing him to be a disciple, not just to receive salvation. More about this level can be found in the chapter on Evangelism, and in the *"Leader's guide* to The Most Precious Thing in the World" by Dr. Householder.)

LEVEL THREE: FIRST STEPS

The text used here is *10 The Steps to Spiritual Growth* by Dr. Householder and the DISC behavioral questionnaire by Mels Carbonel.

- Goal: to get the new convert or transfer started on his/her way to discipleship and to incorporate him/her into the body.

- Presented by a family leader and introduced into their family. Each family leader should receive a name(s) of new converts or transfers who will be going into their family. (See chapter on shepherding for more details) The shepherd leader and/or apprentice should set up a time to visit with the new member to give him the gift of the booklet, *Steps to Spiritual Growth* and welcome him into their family. This is only a chance for the family leader and his wife and/or apprentice to meet with their new family member. This is not a teaching time, only a time for contact.

- Set up at time and day with others to begin going through the steps; it should take about 6 weeks to go through this stage. A small group leader who will continue to lead the person through the discipleship course should teach the *Steps* booklet. Now there can be a person(s) in each family who just takes people through the *Steps* phase if you so choose, but to keep the continuity of the small group, it is good to continue on with the next book within the home small group setting.

- Used as a shepherding tool, and for all to use to help get everyone growing and going in same direction.

> **Suggestions for implementation: 1. Before you introduce this stage, or any stage, develop a team of teachers in each phase before you take the whole congregation through the different levels. 2. Each person needs his own book so that he can make notes and keep reminded of the things that he needs to learn and apply in his life.**

---

[1] The "Church in a Box" is comprehensive program developed by Dr. Householder and Global Church Growth. For more information contact Global Church Growth.

LEVEL FOUR: CHRISTIAN DOCTRINE

- <u>Everyone participates</u>. Those who don't take part will usually cause problems. This is the case in every area of this ministry of Discipleship.

- <u>New believers need the foundation</u>. This is an understatement. Please give them this foundation before asking them to teach or lead significantly in the body.

- <u>Transfers need to be tested</u>. You don't know what baggage they bring. You don't know the background or level of transfers' maturity and knowledge. Having every person go through each book and phase is a safety net for the congregation, and it's the responsibility of the elders to be sure everyone is growing, and that they don't believe differently from what you know to be true doctrine.

- <u>Seasoned Saints need to be on the same page</u>. They may think they know it all, and they may. If they do, encourage them to go through the study so they'll be able to help others go through it in the future.

- <u>This is only an introduction to the basics</u>. It is not intended to be a college-level course, but rather an introduction. As the church grows and people mature, their study grows. It is to be an ongoing process to teach everyone the doctrines of the faith. Don't get hung up on the word *doctrine*; it is another word for truth, or it should be. True Biblical doctrine is what we are to strive for, not denominational or personal doctrines. When beliefs are based on your opinions, they can't be assumed to be truth. It is *only* true Biblical doctrine that we are concerned about and should be following.

- <u>Suggested text</u>. Denver Sizemore's *13 Lessons in Christian Doctrine* is a basic beginning series, but you can use anything you want at this stage. I use it because it is in most of the languages into which my books are being translated. For example, if you're trying to reach out to Spanish-speaking people in your community, you can have everything in English and Spanish to evangelize, teach doctrine, and disciple in one package when you use Denver Sizemore's and Dr. Householder's materials.

LEVEL FIVE: DISCIPLING

Walk In Discipleship Series. This is the basic thrust of this whole chapter. Remember that discipling is not just this set of materials or ideas, but it is the *fabric* of what each leader and ministry must be established upon. Over the years, discipling must be seen as an ongoing process. These first three years are only the beginning. Build and continue to build in each other's lives.

LEVEL SIX: MINISTRY
Discovering Gifts for Service!

- Study and implementation of gifts is the focus. Use the material provided in this program or at your bookstore.
- Take questionnaire for gifts and personality together. During level three you should have taken the personality questionnaire; now take it with the questionnaire.
- Confer with others to see if they see each other's gifts. During (and after) the questionnaire, ask others if this is how they see you, and ask them to give examples. If so, then venture out and use your gift with the direction of the leaders and the Holy Spirit.
- Meet with your gift advisor to see where you might use or pursue your gifts.
- Experiment with other gifts.
- The leadership must organize and provide a place and an atmosphere in which everyone can use his/her gifts.

LEVEL SEVEN: GROWTH GROUPS!

- Growth groups are the same as what are commonly called Cell Groups, with some added emphasis on continued growth of each person and group. What should happen within these groups? What is their purpose and reason for existence? The leaders must continually ask these questions, in order to have continued health and growth in the congregation.
- Discipleship continues.
- Growth continues.
- Both individuals and community are strengthened.
- Family develops and multiplies. The biggest problem every cell or growth ministry faces is that people become comfortable and want to stay in their initial groups. This will kill the ministry at the very start. Be sure to keep reminding the people in the first few years that multiplying is a major part of the goal. This will prevent cliques from forming and inertia from setting in; give people the vision, and keep it out front.
- You notice that this is *level seven,* and not what you start with. The growth group or cell is an ongoing group, but so much will be missed if the discipleship grou**ps do not precede it. The previous levels are specific, and continually utilize the same material, but the growth group will change and move as is needed.**

LEVEL EIGHT: MINISTRY INVOLVEMENT!

–Based on giftedness One of the biggest problems in congregations doing ministry is that the work is not based on giftedness, but on volunteers (or begging!) Except for things like taking up offerings, ministry should be done from one's giftedness. Leaders should not be appointed except through their giftedness. If there is a ministry from giftedness, the leaders should come from that pool of people. Ministries should be started because there are enough gifted people desiring to carry them on.

Group involvement! If the ministry needs a team to function, that team must be made up of gifted people. If you've identified and trained people in their area of giftedness, the natural outpouring is ministry. If it is an existing team, feed it with gifted people. If it is a needed ministry, which should be developed, launch it when there are enough qualified people to carry it on.

Individual involvement Desire! If there is no desire to do anything, there are three reasons that might give us an idea why there's no desire use one's gifts. First, the gift may not be present. When the Spirit gives a gift, He gives a desire to use it. Second, the desire may have been there at some point, but someone quenched it – or else there was no training, encouragement, or place to use the gift, and so the desire waned. Thirdly, the people might never have been shown that they have a gift.

Success! If there is never success in this area of perceived giftedness, it's most likely because the people are not gifted in that area. It also may be that they are not leaning on the Power of God through submission and prayer. Even if we have a gift but do not call on the power of God to use it, we will fail, because God deserves the Glory.

First Steps
(First shepherding visit after conversion or transfer)

After a person has been baptized, or after his transfer, discipleship should begin immediately so as to help his/her new journey as a disciple. Within two weeks at the most, depending on scheduling, the person's shepherd should visit the person and go through the booklet on *10 Steps to Spiritual Growth.*

The shepherd should take no more than one person with him to this first meeting. The person should be either an elder going through mentorship, or a person on his shepherding team, like a deacon or future Discipler.

There are three reasons for this visit.

The first thing to do is to begin the discipleship and give the new member material to start him on his spiritual journey. This will relay to the person that the church family is serious about him, and is there for him.

The second factor or step is for the new Christian or transfer to get introduced to the shepherd and his team. He will know he is not alone and is a part of a body or community that cares.

Third, introduce the person to the opportunities in the church, and to the discipleship tract he'll be following over the next year. The new idea here is simply this: you *do not* want to keep a person busy doing something, just to keep him. Many churches have made this mistake. Every church will be healthier if each person feels and is shown that he is cared for and guided in the faith. What he will do - and become - will be seen in time. To force participation will be dangerous to both the individual and the church.

It is important to make an appointment. You'll need at least an hour, more if possible. This meeting can be done in an hour, depending upon the time and your estimation of the need. Be flexible, be considerate of their time, and do not overstay your welcome.

Spend a little time getting to know his family. Maybe look at the pictures on display, but don't take too much time, (maybe five or ten minutes at first). If, after you fulfill your mission, there is still time, then spend more time getting to know the person.

Find out information about him. Make mental notes of needs or problems you might need to help with, either now or in the future.

Check with anyone who knows the person or has been involved in evangelism with the person to gather whatever information might be helpful before going on the visit.

Transfers also need to be visited in the exact same way. If it's a husband and wife, and even believing children, take each person a *Steps* booklet. Make an appointment when everyone can be at home.

Guide to Sharing the *10 Steps to Spiritual Growth*

Suggested Week-by-Week *Steps* Lesson Plan. There is also a power point presentation, and a leaders guide that can be used in the training. Contact Fishnet Publishers for more detail. The main thing again is to finish when you finish, these suggestions below are just a guide, please do study and use the leaders guide, which is sold separately. You should take 11 weeks, give or take a week to go through this phase of the ministry system.

First Week, Introduction: (Pages 4-9) Read and discuss first few pages of Steps booklet. Share who and what the local church is all about. This is where you can share the philosophy of ministry, the direction in which the church is going, and what it means to be a part of the congregation. The main direction or goal for each person should be stressed on climbing the steps on page 9.

Second Week, Step One: (Pages 10-11) This is foundational for each believer, and if you wish to add more information to each of these categories feel free to do so. But remember this is just an introduction to each of these disciplines. You might take time during Sunday school and preaching to go more in depth. Also remember it is in the small groups that you will be able to go deeper.

Third Week, Step Two: (Pages 12-13) If you talk with most church members about small groups you will have many different responses. First, you may hear "I don't have time". Second, "I hear they form clicks and I don't want to be a part of that". Third, you may have resistance from the leadership because they may loose control over the people.

In my 30 years of ministry I have seen and experienced how small groups helps people and churches grow. Churches can grow by numbers without any small groups and I would propose that the church is just as shallow as it is wide. It is in small groups that people get real, open, honest, and able to get face to face, and not look at the back of a sea of heads. Each member of a small group has the opportunity to open up and share their deepest thoughts and needs. Only in small groups can one be ministered to, as well minister to one another. The more people the church has involved in small groups will determine how deep that church will grow. Now of course you can say what about small groups that only have fun and games? First, they will grow in fellowship and have some needs met that would not be met in a larger setting, but that is as far as it will go. Let me say that a small group that has meaningful material and discussions will both grow spiritually and socially. In this system of discipleship small groups is the barometer of its success. It is in small groups that discipleship takes place. No small groups, no genuine discipleship. It only takes looking at Jesus' methods to see how small groups is His method of choice. Therefore, to put this ministry system in place, as it is meant to be, then make your goal to get everyone in the church involved in small groups. If you take every new believer through the *Most Precious* first, then it will be natural to get him or her involved in the *10 Steps* in a small group setting. Of course you can work with a person one on one in the *10 Steps* if you are in non-church situation.

Fourth and Fifth Weeks, Step Three: (Pages 14-17) This step is very crucial to the development of each believer. I have asked probably a thousand people over the past 5 years the question, "When you became a Christian did you have anyone come to you and offer to help you develop you in your spiritual growth, and learn the spiritual disciplines that will help you grow through discipleship"? Out of that thousand, all over the world, I have only had two people raise their hands. Take your time as you go through this section. The goal is not to go over the material but to encourage each person to put the exercises into practice. To do this I suggest two basic things. First, is that the discipler/teacher does the exercises so they see your serious about it. Second, give the assignments and ask for them the next session. You will want to help them by doing the exercises in the small group time. Especially have the whole group go through the PACT using the James passage.

Sixth and Seventh Weeks, Step Four: (Pages 18-23) First, go over the procedures on "Daily Devotions" on page 19. You might find a passage that allows them to answer the first four "W" questions. Then explain the procedures on page 20 and have the group look for each part of the PACT in the James passage on page 21. It's best to have each one look at his/her own Bible in lieu of using page 21. You might end the session with page 14. Actually take them through this by asking for sharing in these areas, then end in praying in these categories. If there isn't enough time, begin the next session with page 22. Encourage each person to acquire a notebook and to record his/her devotions and PACT discoveries. Have the students to bring examples of each of these exercises the second week. I would suggest at this time that the teacher/discipler share their praise times and journals.

Eighth Week, Step Five: (Pages 24-28) Begin the Eighth week by looking over "Developing the Word in your life" Have them look over the themes in the Scripture to live by, especially note the titles on pages 26 and 27th. Spend the second half of your time by doing a study in Philippians on "12 Promises You Can Trust." Be sure to stress that when God's word gives a promise, then we are to trust and believe it, as was discussed in the PACT study earlier.

Ninth Week Step Six: (Pages 29-33) Read and go over the pages on the different types of testimonies, and ask them to give examples of each. Have them take the time to fill out page 33. If there's enough time, have each person share one of his/her testimonies, either for the believers or unbeliever. If each person needs time to think, then have him or her go home and come back next week and share at the beginning of the session. There are two testimonies to prepare, one to believers and one to unbelievers. It's good to have them share both at some point.

Tenth Week Steps Seven and Eight: (Pages 34-37) You will already have been through the booklet *The Most Precious Thing,* so encourage them to write down some people's names in the spaces, and to begin praying for an opportunity to reach them for Christ. Be sure to go over the ideas for witnessing, and ask them if this seems hard, or easy for them to do. Ask them if they have ever shared their faith in any way since they became a Christian. This is also applicable to seasoned saints. There may be a person in the church that never has shared any aspect of his or her faith with anyone. Challenge everyone to begin thinking and praying about some one who they can begin a relationship, or cultivate one that may lead to a decision to follow.

Eleventh Week Steps Nine and Ten: (Pages 38-39) Read and discuss the "Truths to Stand On." This is an important lesson so that the teacher gets a glimpse of what the person believes. This is a brief statement of core beliefs, and if a person has problems, or other views, then this will let you know where they stand, and what you, or other teachers have to work with. This is more important for transfers than new disciples. Generally the new believer does not know this information, and you should tell them, "Don't worry, as you grow you will learn more about these truths". For the transfer, or even long time member, you must ascertain where they stand. The important thing is not to argue with anyone at this point. Just note it, and issue it if you can, but say we will get back to that at a later date, especially if it will take more than five minutes or more to deal with.

Again, remember that you have a guide that will go step by step with the booklet. It will be your friend if you let it. But also remember to let the Holy Spirit guide you also as you go through the book.

> **Notes to Remember: 1. Do not be overly concerned that some weeks you may take longer to finish the material. The important thing is to get the material into the minds and hearts, rather than just get it done. Each group leader will have to see how his group proceeds. But it is also wise not to linger longer than you should. 2. Have fun, and continue to get to know each other. 3. After you finish the _Ten Steps_ booklet, at the next meeting have a meal, fellowship, and fun time, but no study, please.**

Personality and Giftedness Questionnaire

After your last lesson in the _Ten Steps_, remember to have some fun and games or outing together. Then have them take the appropriate questionnaires. You will have to have some time of training or teaching of the principles of the DISC. You might have to have a specialist to train the church, or have some of the leaders trained. See www.globalchurchgrowth.blogspot.com for more information on training for your church.

Behavioral Questionnaire Have each person take the personality test and discuss the implications. When a person sees and understands their personality mix they should realize that who they are now is made up of their whole life up to this point. But they are not stuck to who they are. Generally a person who is a DIC will be that all their life. But remember there are two aspects of each personality, the good and the bad qualities. The goal is to increase the good part of your personality and decrease the bad part. A D person may be harsh and over demanding on people as he heads to finish his goal. The growth comes when he still keeps his passion about the goal, but he does not step on people to get there. This is where he must grow. Assure them that in the power of the Spirit, and over time, God and His word can mold their personalities as they spiritually grow in Christ.

Giftedness Questionnaire Unlike the Personality questionnaire that is to be given to everyone, regardless of new birth age, the giftedness questionnaire, in my opinion, should not be given to new believers. The only persons that I advise not to take the giftedness part are those who just decided to follow Jesus as their disciple. A few months old Christian/disciple has not had enough time to allow the Spirit to work through them and show them what their gift is. If they take it a few months after their new birth they will most likely get a false positive. I am not saying the Spirit can, and does not give his gifts when people first become a believer, but the questionnaire is best when a person has a history to look back on and see what has been given. If it is taken to soon it may give the person an idea that they have a certain tendency or gift, but really they do not. People forget that our spiritual gifts are not a result of our personality, but an actual supernatural gift from God. When I shared this with Mels in his beautiful Georgia home he concurred it was a good idea.

In this system I suggest you give everyone in the church the personality part, but not give the new believer the gifts part until after a year or two. Now I am not saying that you do not involve the new believer. NO you do encourage them to get involved and pray to God to give and reveal His gifts. By getting involved you will see and know what is, and is not your niche. The new believer is to be encouraged to spend most of their time in developing the spiritual disciplines, and not to be so involved they fail to develop their disciplines that will help them grow. It is easy to get people busy, but many times at the expense of true growth. What habits are begun in the first year will set the foundation for their years to come.

What Mels has brought to the mix is how your personality affects how you use your gifts. This is so valuable to the growth of the church and the individual. You may have a great gift, but if your personality gets in the way it will make it useless for you and the Lord. You may have a gift of administration, but your C personality may be so critical that no one would want to follow your guidance.

Guidelines for Implementing Christian Doctrine Phase

Decide what is to be taught! It is naïve to think that this one course in
doctrine can suffice. This study is only a beginning to the disciples' knowledge of Biblical doctrine. A full-blown Christian education program should always be sure it is continually helping the members grow in knowledge and maturity.

Decide who is to teach! I suggest that, if you have a number of qualified men to teach at this stage, this will minimize boredom (that is, assuming not all of the teachers are boring!) This is a great opportunity for elders in apprenticeship to take some turns teaching on this level.

Decide when and where! Again, it's important to stick with the format and avoid doing any of this on Sunday morning. This phase of doctrine might be the only exception, because this is lecture format, and you may get by with the doctrine section on Sunday morning, if you remember to finish it when you finish. Don't be concerned about getting through the material, as is traditionally done with the standardized lesson series. If it can be done during the week, by all means do so. If it can be done in homes, that too will be an advantage.

Offer it continually and bi-annually! Also plan on offering this phase on a continual basis throughout the year so, as people are being evangelized, they can have an opportunity to join in, and not be made to wait a long time.

Guidelines for Implementing Discipleship groups

In the leader's guide, one can see what a group is like, and the procedures to make it successful. But, how do you get the process started in the church? It is important to remember that discipling is not a set of materials, or another program; rather, it should become the lifeline of the church. Discipling should be <u>what the</u> <u>church does</u> as an ongoing process, as the congregation grows through evangelism and transfer. Each person that comes through the doors will be discipled and cared for.

Starting the process: <u>In the established church!</u> I tip my hat to Ralph Neighbor for saving me some years of misery. I, too, have found that introducing, or trying to help an established church develop and implement these principles of discipleship and shepherding in an already established church, is *almost impossible* - at the very least <u>improbable</u>. Now, let me hasten to add to you as you're reading this, don't give up all hope! I did write improbable, but *not impossible*. It is, of course, up to those who want to stand up and follow the methods of God to take a stand and be courageous in this endeavor by stepping out, taking the proverbial "bull by the horns" and making a commitment to do something about making this New Testament method work in your situation. Now let me warn you, it won't be easy, but it will be rewarding when you allow God's plan to become yours. The problems arise when we allow traditions, pride, and selfishness rule, and not God's will. Just think, my brothers and sisters, what would God think about you if you were the one who stood in the way of your church following His will by using this plan, especially as you see if it is God's plan? Now, I don't want to be presumptuous and say that this is the only plan, the only material, but what is presented in these pages is Biblical and along God's plan. Do not make the mistake of saying, "Oh Lord, I was just protecting what my Dad had started years ago," or, "Lord, I was afraid that false doctrine would slip in," or, "We never have seen it done this way," or like one preacher I met who said to me, "Go prove it and see if it will work someplace else." All these statements are copouts - excuses for not yielding to the will of the Lord. The minister who said, "Go try it somewhere else so that I can see it work first," had little faith. Now in this circumstance, I have proven that it works. I have, over the years, used this method with much success, but this person really was not willing to give up his control, and he was not willing to step out in faith. He may have not trusted me, God's messenger, but his primary failure was not trusting God. It doesn't matter if it has never been done; if God is behind it, and it follows His already-given plan, then it's bound to work. Leaders, be careful that you don't fall into the same pit as those who made excuses with their talents. The one who feared to dare and dream, the one who stood by and settled for mediocre, the one who was not willing to take a risk - all were cast out into darkness. Be careful when you work against God's plan. I know this may sound hard to you, or even may offend you, but if it wakes you up to see that doing it God's way is right, then it is worth the effort.

<u>In the new church!</u> Now in the new church setting, the world is a different place, a different universe, with different rules. It should not be so. The church, whether old or new, must always keep its flame and direction in tune with God so that it never loses sight of its mission and task. I guess that's why, in most generations, God keeps a remnant and the fire

alive so this doesn't happen often. But it does. When man allows his will to rule, then God is pushed aside, at least for a while. God will have His day, and His will shall be done, whether we are a part of it or not.

In the new church, one has an opportunity to build foundations correctly and soundly on the Word of God. It is important to realize that it doesn't take long to establish traditions, so be careful what you bring to the table. What I suggest here is that you begin the church in the homes and with "small group mentality" from the beginning. If you have 16 people who are involved, encourage them to meet in small groups. Let them know that that is just *what you do*. At first, limit groups to eight people. Start them off with the booklet, "Most Precious Thing," to be assured of where they are in their commitment to God. Then, as they join the fellowship, take them through the Steps booklet and incorporate them into a family. At first you will have only one family, but you'll also be developing the leaders and nucleus for the second family. If the church starts with a team, from the very beginning, families can be started when there are enough to do so.

There is a push today for starting new churches with a big bang and outreach into the community. If there is no team or enough leaders and teachers to take care of those who come in those first few Sundays, you'll lose a lot of them, and won't be able to take care of their needs. So, it's important to develop the base, and plan on having two or three different launches, instead of one big one. See the "New Discovery" case study in the appendix for further ideas on this matter.

Implementing the Program in an Existing Cell Group Ministry

Intro: The cell ministry is a growing phenomenon in many churches today. If you already have cell groups or home Bible studies going, it's only a matter of fine-tuning the process.

<u>In an Existing Cell Ministry</u>! The biggest problem you will have is to reeducate those already involved. When a group stays together for a long period of time, it becomes in grown and difficult to break up. One of the problems is that people fail to understand the dynamics of a small group. It's easy, and much less bothersome, to remain the same. But if the group is going to work, you must challenge people with the Great Commission and the need to give others what you have, and the best way to do that is to multiply. If it's a great or divisive problem, simply start new groups, but be sure to have these groups go through the material, or you'll assuredly have problems and division.

<u>Developing a New Cell Ministry from this Program</u>! If you follow this ministry, the groups will be formed in the inception. As you will see, the end result is the development of growing and multiplying growth groups, as a natural outpouring of evangelism and discipleship.

Operational Timeline

First, it is suggested that each person go through the book, "The *Most Precious Thing,* by Dr. Householder. In the new church, it's crucial for everyone to be "on the same page", and that the church team knows where everyone is in his or her spiritual walk and commitment. In an established congregation, this may be more difficult, but still worthwhile for each person to go through, since it helps each believer see what his or her commitment should be like. It will also help the believer know what the new Christian will be learning.

Second, take everyone through the Spiritual Growth Packet.

1. Train leaders (elders and helpers) and introduce them to the packet.

2. Have the leaders first take some of the people through about seven sessions. People should be divided into their respective shepherding groups. This is where the small group experience can begin. Guide the new believers and transfers to go through this material some night in a group leader's home. (See instructions above).

3. All who didn't attend these meetings should be seen personally in their home within a month, if possible.

4. After the first group, the rest of the members are taken through the study as well. A continued program should be in place for taking new people through the study, following their baptism or transfer.

Third, have each person, whether a transfer or "seasoned saint", study the lessons on Christian doctrine. You might have to use more in-depth material or supplement the text with more information for the non-novice. This material can be taught in Sunday school, cell groups, or Wednesday night Bible time. This study may be offered at different times during the year. If a person misses a section, they can catch it up later during another class time.

Fourth, begin developing leaders for small discipleship groups. Some of the people may have to do "double duty" at first, but later it will all level out when others find their place and ministry.

Fifth, training on:

1. Shepherding (periodic meetings with leaders only).

2. Evangelism (seminar with all interested). After shepherding and discipleship programs have been initiated

3. Small groups (with those interested, or as a seminar or a weekend retreat to develop group life and leaders).

Develop contact and greeters' group for Sunday morning (see the Seven Contacts for Life). Develop evangelism follow-up. This is not directly the shepherds' task, but they must see that those who accomplish it are a part of the evangelism team, within each family.

Find a need and meet it. Developing ministry teams based on gifts, talents, interests, and needs you can meet in the community, will make the teams a success. This is of course a broader task than shepherding, but it is the leadership's responsibility to support these groups, and to see to it that these areas are staffed with qualified leaders.

Suggestions: **1. Alcohol abuse**

                 2. Jail ministry

                 3. Hospital visitation

                 4. Mother's day out

                 5. Orphanages

                 6. Birth and death ministry

                 7. Food and clothing pantry

Perspective on the discipleship system! Like building a new building.

- You have a need and share the vision.
- You commit to do the work.
- You get a commitment from the people and stay the course.
- You find someone to help, like an architect, construction foreman, and company.
- You start with the foundation, not the furnishings.
- In remodeling or making an addition, you tie into the old, but do not let the old dictate the shape of the new.
- It takes time, and so does constructing the spiritual building.
- You did not get where you are today in three to six months, so take the time to build it right.
- You have phases, and you know how to deal with them.
- Build the foundations. For a healthy, established church, you have the blocks and materials within the Spirit filled members; you just have to put them together. **For a new church, you have to <u>build</u> some of the blocks and <u>then</u> put them together.**

Phases of the Plan

Phase One: <u>Build the foundations</u>. Set up Family Shepherding Groups, Steps Groups, and Discipling Groups. In the beginning, some people will have to do a little more work, but after the infrastructure is done, everyone will have a place and a ministry. No one person (or even the proverbial 20%) will be doing all the work.

Phase Two: <u>Build the walls</u>. Take the whole congregation through the discipleship material within the "family group" system.

Phase Three: <u>Furnish the building</u>. Equip the whole congregation through finding and providing places to use their gifts in ministries.

Phase Four: <u>Power the building</u>. Develop leadership, mentoring, and apprenticeship for all levels of leadership. Provide a model based upon Biblocracy, not Democracy.

Phase Five: <u>Open the doors.</u> Equip for, and stress, evangelism and growth.

Phase Six: <u>Maintenance, upkeep, and refurbishing of the building</u>. Continue on with the ministries and system. Do not let negative talk or attitudes derail you from the task and ministry.

Phase Seven: <u>Keep the building up to code and up to date</u>. Let the Great Architect continue to guide and move.

PLAN OF DISCIPLESHIP

Stage One: Relationship Building, Parties, Special interest/ needs Fun Events

Stage Two

Stage Three

Stage Four

Stage Five

Stage Six

Stage Seven

Stage Eight

Most Precious

10 Steps

Doctrine

Women

Men

GIFTS

Ministry Teams

Growth Groups

BIBLICAL EVANGELISM
Chapter Ten

Why is evangelism placed in the middle of this book? Shouldn't it be up front? Isn't it the very first place to start? In both the new church and the established church, the answer is, not always. Why?

In a new church, there's a need for evangelism, or *there won't be a new church*. To an extent this is very true, but not if you're making a lot of contacts for evangelism, *but have no foundation to take care of the masses!* In the early church, the masses didn't come until after three years of discipleship and training. Jesus drew together a critical mass from which to launch His church. I suggest the very same strategy today. There should be some effort to gather a group of people, a nucleus from which to work. This basis of discipleship and training should be established before any main push, or plan of evangelism, is implemented. I know this goes against today's practice of sending out thousands of letters and making hundreds of phone calls. If there's a large enough plant team and all the bases are covered, there may be success. However, I would caution against aiming too high, too soon; it could backfire, because you lack adequate ministries in place to care for the initial masses.

In the case of a mother-daughter plant, things should be different. If you can start with 50 to 150 people in the nucleus when you begin the launch, evangelism is a priority. But, that same nucleus should have already been preparing for at least a year - i.e., should have developed its programs, ministries, and staff before the big launch and evangelistic push.

> **In an established church wanting to grow and be successful, new conversions/baptisms will be the means whereby true continual growth will occur.**

In an established church wanting to grow and be successful, new conversions/baptisms will be the means whereby true continual growth will occur. But, as we have seen before, no evangelism should be planned, nor any mass evangelistic events, crusades, or other outreach efforts, until the congregation builds its foundation of discipleship. I usually ask, in the process of giving my seminar in discipleship, if the church has plans for any major outreach or evangelistic campaigns in the next year. Some congregations do have the plans in the works; others haven't thought about reaching out to the lost in years! I suggest they postpone any major outreach until they're ready for the results. (They shouldn't refuse anyone who comes in the door, of course!) If there are individuals who are ready to follow Christ, share the gospel with them, but hold back from having major events and programs. The church that wants to grow through evangelism should devote the next year to getting its people discipled so that for once, those who come through their doors may be cared for. Why continue to go down the same road, failing to disciple those whom you evangelize? As we look at some principles and methods of evangelism, do so, remembering that evangelism is only the first part of our command in the Great Commission to make disciples. Evangelism is *not the end*, but the *beginning* of discipleship. When the foundation of discipleship is firmly established, by all means go all out to reach the lost!

When I was a teenager, learning what it means to evangelize, I would go on our Tuesday night calling program. The preacher would give us cards and a partner with whom to make the calls. "Who are they?" I'd ask my partner. "Well, I don't know, the preacher just gave us the names." Well, we'd then go hunt for the unsuspecting people. We found them, scoped the place out for any barriers or mad dogs, and then made our approach. With palpitating hearts, we knocked on the door in what I call "blind evangelism". Sometimes this method works and is profitable, but most often, it isn't the most productive or user-friendly way of accomplishing this important task.

This chapter is an introduction to evangelism and church growth. Without Great Commission evangelism, there will be no sustained growth. Without sustained growth, the church will die, or become irrelevant to the world. At best, it will only hold its *status quo* and be merely a maintenance situation. Eventually, stagnation or decline will result.

> **How many of us have had a great opportunity, have been led to do something, but then didn't act on it?**

Why don't people evangelize? *Fear* is the number one problem. Let's look at two men and one woman whom God used. The first was Moses. Have you ever been fearful to witness to others? Moses started using his excuses. First was fear of those to whom he was to speak. Second, he was fearful he couldn't speak, but God *wouldn't let him go*. God kept taking away his excuses. What excuses do you or your congregation use that keep you from evangelizing? If your church does reach out, is there success or continued growth as a result of the effort? What excuse might we give, as individuals or as a congregation before God, that we didn't even try to be a witness or evangelize those around us? You may say, "This isn't my gift," and you may be right; some say only 10% of the church have this gift. I think that's a low estimate, but even if it's true, do you see yourself or many people in your congregation using their gift for evangelism? But whether or not you personally have the gift, everyone is responsible to obey the command to make disciples. That is, you may not say the words that bring a person to salvation, but you may have befriended them before, or even afterward, and that's what counts; everyone has friends or may make friends. In doing so, everyone has an obligation to develop relationships so Christ can be glorified; and the person who does so may get to know someone who has Christ in his heart. When this happens, you can be a link to someone's salvation and making a disciple of him/her.

The second man who feared was Jonah, but most of all he had a bad attitude and apathy or disdain for others. God wanted him to go and spread God's forgiveness, but Jonah refused at first. Unlike Moses, who really wanted to follow God, Jonah wanted to run the other way. His hate for the Ninevites was stronger than his obedience to God. Even after they repented and turned to God, he was still a bigot and hard-hearted. Generally, God will not go with us as far as He did with Jonah, to encourage us follow His will. He gives us the freedom to reject His will and, therefore, forfeit the blessings of following Him. How many of us have had a great opportunity, have been led to do something, but then didn't act on it? I have, and I can look back and see that, if I'd gone ahead and followed God's prompting or direction, what a great opportunity and blessing it would have been!

Now, let's look at the woman who was a frequent visitor to the well. Here is a woman who was enlightened and excited - so much so, that she couldn't contain her joy and had to tell everyone she met. Oh, for that kind of joy and commitment today! What if each of us could grasp the implications of the living water that is waiting for us and those around us? Could we hold it back? Would we not also be so excited to share with those who know us and need Him? Let us pray for this fervor. I think sometimes many of us have never truly felt or tasted of that living water to the point that she did, or if we have we have we allowed it to be an afterthought in our lives. I know I have at times, and that is a shame. Nothing is greater than being a part of and/or seeing someone immersed into Christ. We must keep going back to the well of living water each day, and then we'll have the joy and power to be His witnesses.

So don't be as hard-headed or fearful as Moses, and especially not as arrogant and apathetic as Jonah, but be excited like the woman at the well who could do nothing less than share her joy of finding living water that is meant for all. It's not about what we have, how good we are, or how well we can speak or motivate; it's about how much faith we have to allow God to use us and motivate us to live and act for God. In faith, David boldly attacked Goliath. He could have run away in fear, but he came before the giant without his strength, armor, or anything he could boast in but His God. God provided the stones, and David used them in faith. This is how we should approach our Goliaths. It is faith in God's resources, not ours, that will give us the power to follow God's will.

The underlining principle is: The kind of evangelism you win them with will determine the kind of Christian they will become.

If you can accept and understand the above concept box, you'll be well on your way to changing things for the better in regards to evangelism. If your evangelism is shallow, so also will be the results. That doesn't mean God can't take the seed you planted and make more of it. He can and does. But if we are aware of a problem, might it not be good to do things right the first time? You may ask, "What are the right and wrong ways of evangelism? Is it not enough to just do it and let God worry about the rest?" No, for He does give us some directions and illustrations of how to go about evangelizing the lost.

The Four Soils!

The First Soil. The parable of the sower and the seed is very revealing in regards to effective evangelism. In John, we see four types of soil. It is obvious from the text that the soil is the hearts of people, the seed is the gospel, and the sower is the Spirit and/or evangelist. In this context, I think the sower could also be the approach that is taken in the process. It's also obvious that there are four results from the different soils. The question is, "Why are there different results?" Let us explore the four different methods used in approaching each different soil. In the first case, we see a heart or person that is hard and impenetrable to the seed. There may be a few reasons why. First, the person is hard or callous towards the seed or gospel. This may be due to his upbringing. He may have seen or heard, from youth, that religion is not a valid choice. There may have been a negative experience in the past that has hardened his heart to future approaches. This may have been a natural event or series of disappointments that suggested there was no God, or perhaps some Christian in his past was a bad example, or approached him in a harsh or judgmental way. He's become hardened and "turned off" to the gospel. He may simply have had no knowledge or understanding of the gospel and its implications and, therefore, sees no need to accept it. As you can see, there can be a number of reasons why this person was hardened to the gospel message.

In the first case, the person was not cultivated. The hard heart was not worked or softened. In some cases, the person or persons making the approach may have not spent enough time or effort in reaching this individual. They may have shoved a tract at him and **gone on their way.** They may have knocked on the door in an obnoxious way and turned him off. Most likely, no relationship was ever cultivated. Sometimes, a piece of ground is not suitable for any type of planting. Let's say that the soil is contaminated with poison or chemicals. No matter what you do, how you plow, or even if you apply the right ingredients, there will be little or no results. If we've done all we can do to prepare the soil, simply accept the situation and move on, not feeling guilty that the person did not accept God's offer.

The second soil is intriguing in its results. The text tells us that the seed sprang up immediately, but the plant quickly withered and died. Why did this happen? It would seem that this person had some type of belief, or made a decision, because the seed germinated and a plant came up. The gospel did take effect at some level, and in some way, this soil did have a result. What happened? First, the common explanation is that an emotional decision was made, not based upon good decision-making. That is, no preparation or thought was involved in the evangelistic process, or the process was manipulative at best. The method of presentation may have been nearly _hypnotic_ to the point that no real connection was made in the process. Possibly no relationship was built, or the person, for whatever reason, may have failed to make an honest decision. If we can assume the person's decision was valid, I assert that there was a plant, and the seed did germinate, but there was no follow-up after germination. The plant withered away because the soil (his/her faith) was shallow, preparation was faulty or non-existent, and so the plant had no chance of surviving.

The text also indicates there were rocks in the soil; what might they represent? They could represent a lot of residual sins and problems in the person's life, so much so that he/she wasn't ready to deal with, (or wasn't helped to deal with) his/her problems. There may have been rocks of pride, rocks of addictions that wouldn't let go, or rocks of emotions or the past that kept holding on. These rocks stood in the way of the roots taking hold and surviving, and the person made a decision before counting the cost of dealing with these rocks in his/her life.

What could have been done? Again, the approach may have been the problem, as was alluded to above. What could have been done to ensure a successful, healthy plant? One way is to change our methods of evangelism so that people aren't pressured into making decisions based purely on emotions. Those who use these methods are usually "headhunters" or "number builders". Second, it's important to develop a relationship with a new convert, especially right after the conversion, so he can have time to produce some results. Third, it's important to provide a base of knowledge for development of his/her roots. That means there's a need for follow-up and discipleship. This is where most congregations fail in their outreach or evangelism. When evangelism is seen as an event rather than a process of discipleship, the problem may begin. Ill-prepared approaches can be recovered or saved when discipleship is put into the mix. If the person ("soil") was total emotion and no substance, this may be a moot point. Be assured, when there is no follow-up or discipleship, the chance for shallow roots and withering away increases dramatically. Fourth, "rock-gathering" may be in order; that is, we may need to help people remove the rocks in their life. This is usually a great need right after conversion or commitment at whatever level. And once again, discipleship and relationships are important to helping these people stay the course.

The third soil is our next to figure out. It is important that, if the seed is the gospel, it's the same seed in every instance. If the seed's success is tied to the manner of sowing, what went wrong here? Or did something go wrong? We must ask - where are the first two subjects? The first never got introduced to the church. The second one most likely attended a church for a while, but not necessarily so. He may have made a decision and never attended church, or may have attended for a short time. The third subject or soil was most likely in church and remained there, possibly all his life, but in what condition do we find him? The text tells us that this seed grew but bore no fruit. Why not, and what are the implications of having no fruit? First, it says that thorns grew up with the plant, choked it, and caused it to not bear fruit. The thorns were the cares of life; that is, they never really came out of the world. Second, this person never was *light* or *salt;* he never bore fruit by changing his life. He lacked the *fruit of the Spirit*, fruit of righteousness, and good works. He was what some would call *carnal* or *fleshly* Christians. There's doubt if the individual is in a saved state at all! This type may occupy a lot of pews, but may not enter the kingdom of heaven!

So what caused this to happen? This person may have "grown up in the church", but never made a personal commitment. Therefore, he has a false sense of security. He may have, for some reason, joined a body, but was never truly converted, or did it for all the wrong reasons. He may have never really given up the world, and it finally took its toll on his ability to grow as a spiritual individual.

Why did this plant not bear fruit - and why did the world choke it out? How can the church ensure this doesn't happen again? First, we must be assured that our evangelism results in true converts who truly follow Jesus! Failing to get them to this point will cause them to have a false sense of salvation. Change of direction, heart, and lifestyle is what it means to be a follower of Christ. Any less commitment may be cause for doubt whether in fact one is a Christian. I know, to a lot of comfortable people in our churches, this may slap them in the face. Hopefully it does, and wakes them up! It's far better to know the truth and wake up, than go to sleep and wake up in hell. Second, as in previous soils, little or no discipleship was involved with this person. Most likely he was left on his own, and no one encouraged him or held him accountable in his faith. He wasn't made into a disciple and, therefore, was fruitless and barren. You saw what Jesus did to the barren fig tree. Discipleship and accountability will help a person take out the weeds and thorns so he can be productive in his life as a Christian. Any less, and the person may not be what God wants in the last day.

Regarding the first three seeds, what are the implications of the approach; what can be done differently to achieve different results? Might each of the first three seeds turn out differently? If so, what approach might have been taken to facilitate such a result? If the approach had been changed, some of those "seeds one through three" may have moved to situation four. That is, if "soil one" has a "sower" who wants to take time to develop a relationship, show love first, or meet a felt need, maybe the heart can soften to the point that he will be open to see and feel the love of God through you.

> **Left on their own, most people will fail to meet their potential, and some will naturally slip into seed number three.**

The fourth soil is the most prized, where the seed germinates, takes root, grows and bears fruit. This is a true conversion, and at some point, either before, during, or after the conversion, the person was discipled, encouraged, and taught what it takes to grow, and he/she was helped in that process. He or she was healthy because the Word of God became alive and productive in his/her life - fruitful within his/her congregation, and God's spirit was evident in his/her growth and life as a follower of Christ.

Seed number four usually happens in two types of people, assuming conversion is valid and genuine. The first type I call a self-starter and self-motivator. He, on his own, searches, grows and applies the Word of God and therefore bears fruit. If he doesn't find the right relationship or circumstances, he'll either move on to find what he needs, or try to be a catalyst to others, but he will be able to survive in His spiritual life. In the typical congregation, only about 10% to 15% fit this profile. The other person who develops into the fourth seed is one who's been cultivated and discipled by someone along the way, for some period of time (the time-frame differs from person to person.) It may be a Sunday school teacher, a small group leader or just a spiritual "big brother or sister" who mentors and disciples that person. Left on their own, most people will fail to meet their potential, and some will naturally slip into seed number three. To prevent this, a conscious effort must be made on the part of leadership in each church, to be responsible to disciple each person under their leadership. If you do this, you will have narrowed the gap between the fourth and third seeds.

What have we learned in all this? First, the seed must be sown, and evangelism must take place, but it must be done with wisdom and love. Second, the ground or heart of the person must be cultivated, and how this is done may differ for each soil or person. Third, when the seed takes root, further care and discipleship must be implemented to see that the person continues to be faithful to be harvested. It isn't good enough to get a sprout or plant; there must be a harvest of fruit.

Let's look at some examples or theories of evangelism.

Alphabet Evangelism

A's attract A's, and B's attract B's. At the outset, this is not 100% scientific and does not always play out in reality, but this tends to be the case. If there are only individual letters, all we have is an alphabet. It's a place to start, and we need every letter in the alphabet to truly communicate or meet the needs of the church and society. A letter in the alphabet only becomes useful when it's put together with other letters, and they work together to form words and sentences. So it is with evangelism. Successful evangelism comes in relation to other connections and aspects of church life. "Al A" may know "Bobbie B", who knows "Carol C", and so it goes.

Church of Scrabble

The church is much the same way – quite like the game of "Scrabble". You must start with one letter, and add others to make any sense or progression. One person may form a word from a series of letters, and then from one of those letters, a whole new word can be made. Then the words spread and spread. The words, or series of letters, creates other rows of words (people) that would have never been able to hear unless others before had not been added. You may have one word, or series of people, but no one is being added. But then someone adds a suffix, and then suddenly another word, and then another. Do not ever underestimate what one person can do. Have you ever heard of the person who brought Billy Graham to Christ? Most have not, but most people have heard of Mr. Graham and all of those he has influenced for Christ. What if that person didn't take the time to talk with Mr. Graham? Think of all those who may never have heard. I remember playing scrabble, and we all got to the point that we thought nothing else could be added. Then one person put an "s" on the end of one word. From that "s" came another word, then another. Without that letter, the game was over. Therefore, don't underestimate the power of one dedicated soul turned on to Christ to change the world. He was just one letter in the big game, but he may be the key to many others being added to the game.

The Amway Principle

When I was 18, a teacher at school introduced me to a world of circles. I soon found out how these circles meant the commitment of my time and money. The buzz phrase between fellow circlers was, "Are you going to draw any circles tonight?" The question was meant to encourage and ascertain if the other person was going to show the greatest marketing plan on earth to someone that night? Of course Amway was not the only game in town. There were a lot of these types of companies springing up in the early 70's. Amway, whose founders were Christian, is still growing strong. I am no longer in Amway, so this is not a promotion of the company, but the method is the best way of marketing, or even of sharing the gospel.

All of my circles are not in your circles, and I will never be able to touch or meet those in your circles unless you introduce them to me. In the Amway process, one person who introduces you to the company will go with you to introduce your friend. After that, he trains you to do the same for those who are under you, and then you will be able to help them to contact their friends and help them, and so forth into the entire world. If one of these connections drops out, then those who may be under him may never get a chance to hear and receive. The same is true in evangelism. If we follow this simple method of touching one and then going with him to touch one of his friends, and then helping him to help them, we have true evangelism and discipleship. But, thank God, there is no pyramid scheme here. Everyone who decides to follow will have the same access to the top, to the founder, Jesus.

Spiritual Warfare and Evangelism!

What is evangelism? Simply put, evangelism is another word for war. When we are involved in evangelism, we are trying to overcome the enemy's stronghold on a person's life. When you attack another man's castle, you will have a battle to fight. We are trying to persuade Satan's army to defect and join our side. He will fight back anyway he can.

When we're asleep in our foxholes or resting in the trenches, Satan has us where **he** wants us. But when we attack, be assured he will fight back. He is out to win. He is out to destroy everything we wish to accomplish.

Evangelism is our method of war, our front-line tactic. It's where we come in contact with the enemy. That's why putting on the armor and praying for the strength for protection will go a long way in being successful in evangelism.

In order for the church of God to grow, there must be evangelism. If there is evangelism, there are those who are defecting from Satan's army, and he doesn't like that. He will do all he can to fight and discourage or distract believers from seeing that making disciples or being involved in evangelism is as important as any other thing in the church. Satan will even influence whole churches to look inward and become satisfied with where they are and not be interested in evangelism. But, making new disciples must happen if the church is to truly grow. However, the growth is not the real focus; souls saved from damnation and hell should be the motivation. Some churches think they are growing as long as there are people transferring in. You see this "sheep shifting" from one church to another and not true kingdom growth.

A part of both our offense and defense in evangelistic warfare is, of course, our prayer before, during, and after our contact with the candidate. It is in prayer that we gather the strength, wisdom, and protection to tear down footholds in people's lives. It is in prayer that you come into communication with God and His Spirit. It is in prayer that you declare your humbleness to

God and your allegiance to God so that both you and Satan can see that God is involved in the conflict between Satan, the candidate, and God. For if you try to evangelize on your own, Satan will tear you up and hinder God from using you in the process of your witness. Only in prayer will you, the church and those needing to be saved have a chance.

Evangelism: does it really matter?

In today's liberal and politically correct world, Christian exclusiveness is in many places an archaic notion. You're considered narrow-minded and a bigot for believing that Christianity is the only way to God. How incredulous can one be to think they have the only way and the only answer to life's problems? Why does this belief anger the rest of the "god-seekers"? Obviously, if your way is the only way, all others become invalid and senseless. This, therefore, sends the message that you think your Christian view is superior and theirs automatically inferior.

What would it matter if you were a Universalist? Many people would not claim to be universalistic, but rather be referred to as open-minded and non-judgmental. The strict Universalist would not be motivated to evangelize others, since it's okay to believe whatever you want - therefore, to evangelize is in direct conflict with the freedom to believe whatever you want. Many people who have embraced universalism have done so because they want to be included, even though their thoughts about reality are different from "mainline" religious beliefs. In many cases, the belief that there are many ways to God is a copout from real responsibility to "One-wayism" and allows pluralism to be the norm. Pluralism then breeds contempt for absolute truth and promotes the rise of relativism in the mind and actions of the believer and the world.

Why should evangelism matter if you're a Calvinist? If God chooses whom He wants to be a believer and then supernaturally influences and controls the chosen person, why is there a need for an evangelist? The answer would return, "But a Christian doesn't know who will be chosen and, therefore, we must go, allowing God to direct us to the ones who've been chosen." It isn't seeking and saving the lost, but rather seeking and finding the chosen. In reality, the burden then is on God to direct, and if we don't do His work, He'll find others. It really becomes "no big deal" in the reality of things, because in God's sovereignty, He'll find someone to accomplish the task. If everyone's salvation is predetermined, then it isn't important to approach everyone; God will take care of those whom He has chosen.

Can a Christian hold onto his/her beliefs, while at the same time accept other explanations and other ways to God? Although I believe in Jesus as the only way, would a loving God send someone to hell for not knowing any better? Is a loving God really going to send someone to Hell? This is a burning question on many hearts. If God loves, then how can he torture or destroy people in hell? Is this not a contradiction to who He is?

If there is a hell, and if God chooses to punish the non-believer in this way, how should this change your enthusiasm about evangelizing? How burning hot are you for the souls you know? Or, do you say you believe one way, the "only way", but act like the other way may also be true? I pray that God has mercy, but I must act like He will only have mercy on those who follow the True Way, and that I or someone else will have to be the conduit to bring people to that point of conversion and enlightenment. We cannot have it both ways.

Either Jesus is the only way, or as you have heard, He is a liar or a lunatic. If He is *the way*, that should be enough to motivate us. If there are other options, He truly is a liar and not worth following. We are either Universalist or "One-wayist". We cannot live out of two pockets. He is, or he isn't. The choice you make will determine the way you live and how passionate you should be about evangelism or making disciples.

Why do certain cults (ex., Jehovah's Witnesses and Mormons) experience such phenomenal growth? Is it because Satan is blessing their work? Most cults usually have a thread of the truth within their doctrine or beliefs. This half-truth is enough to make their message dangerously acceptable to those who lack a true understanding of the foundations of Christianity.

Are they smarter than we are? It's not really about intelligence, but rather about spiritual revelation of the truth. In many cases it's about being blinded by "almost truths." "Almost truths" can soothe people's yearnings for religious experience, but fall short of absolute truth. Often, "almost truths" are more dangerous than believing in "no absolute truth", because there's a false sense of security. It isn't about being sincere in what you believe; just being sincere about something doesn't make you right about what you believe. Quite often, people are sincere but still far from the absolute truth found in the Bible. The problem frequently is about whose authority is right, or if there is any valid truth equal to, but apart from, the Bible. If there is, people might have a reason to add to Biblical truth. Again, if Jesus is the only way, then it is important that we evangelize those who are trapped in "almost truths."

Are these religions growing and being more faithful because they truly believe in what they're doing more than we do and, therefore, sacrifice more to be faithful? The Mormons truly believe they have the truth too, and actually do something about it. One thing they do is to expect their people to share their faith. What would happen with our churches if the young men and women were expected to go all over the world and spread the name of Christ for two years of their lives? The Mormons expect their people to have commitment, and in turn, they're faithful. I've never heard a young Mormon complain about spending two years of his life in the service of his faith. Now, I haven't been privy to every one of their missionaries, but they are at least dedicated enough to their church and mission to obey and go. Their church expects their commitment and it happens more often than not. But they believe in what they are doing. Do we believe enough in the view that there's only one way to God, and the way is Jesus? Do we believe there is one major way for people to know this truth? Should we not be expected to be motivated enough to share the fact that Jesus is the only way to the Father? Does it matter enough to us to evangelize and make disciples?

Do Mormons have a greater grasp of their purpose and the need than we do? If not, why do we not see this greater purpose - and do something about it? We must examine our motives and our purpose for being the church and become more concerned about the mission of the church, not about being complacent with the *status quo* of doing church as usual.

Why do most people in our congregations lack this commitment and fervor to share and be committed? Can it be because we as teachers have not given believers the right tools or examples? I think this is one of the problems. When there's no overall picture of making disciples in the mission of the church, there will be no continued sharing of the purpose and vision of the church. Each generation must capture this mission and purpose, and train and motivate others to carry on the task. We must teach the importance and the urgency of why evangelism should matter. Remember, evangelism is only the first part of making disciples.

So why does it matter? If you decided that Jesus is the only way and who He says He is, then it matters. It is a matter of life and death, the life and death of every soul. What would you do if you had a pill that cured every disease? What would you do when you walked down the street and saw the blind man singing, the limbless man begging, and the deaf person signing? If you had the cure, what would you do? Well, we have that cure in Jesus Christ. What man destroys, only Jesus can permanently restore.

Whatever problem is causing you or your church to fail to be faithful to the Great Commission, you must learn what it is, and then try to be about God's business. If what you're doing isn't working, find what does work. If it's lack of commitment and/or a lack of vision, then let us pray, repent, and renew a right spirit within us.

When it comes to the world, God wants us to be contagious Christians surrounded by people with a deadly virus. He wants us to lovingly infect others around us with the only serum that will attack the virus that destroys sin in our bodies and in the bodies of others.

But how do people react to a virus? They want to get rid of it. The sinner will react like that at first. You want to rid them of their old way of life by destroying it; at first, they will most likely want to resist. We must persist, because it means the death of their old ways, and this is seldom ever easy. Old ways are comfortable and predictable. To change from self and Satan to service takes courage. Change is a very scary process for many people. If I change, will the new way be better or worse for me? Will I want to return? Do I really want to give up my friends and the way of life I know? We in the Church must realize that it's worth the fight and the effort to persistent in combating the virus of sin. We must not let our lives be so affected by the world, sin, and complacency that we become immune to our mission and purpose.

2 Peter 3:9 commands us to put on the mind of Christ. What does that mean in reference to evangelism, or making disciples? It means to think the thoughts of Christ by hating sin and loving people. It means to have the LOVE for the LOST as He did. If we love, as He loves us, evangelism or making disciples does matter. Does it matter to you? Do the lost matter to you?

Who is in control?

As I said before, how you win people will determine how they live and grow (or not grow) as Christians. In my booklet, *The Most Precious Thing in the World,* the intent is on making disciples, not just having people make decisions to receive or say a rote prayer. The concept that Rick Warren's book, *The Purpose Driven Life* proposes in Chapter 8 can lead a person to have a false sense of salvation. I do not minimize the contribution that Rick makes. I have read "The Purpose Driven Life" two times and will probably read it again, but his one little paragraph on salvation was so Biblically misleading that people may go away saying, "Lord, Lord", *never knowing Him,* and *never really committing* as a disciple or true follower for life.

Most evangelicals today use the formula of "Pray this prayer and receive Jesus", or in the churches in which I grew up, "Take Him as your personal Savior." Who is in control when a person receives or takes something? It is the person receiving or taking who is in control. If, on the other hand, I were to ask you, "Are you willing to follow Jesus as Lord and be His disciple?" then who would be in control? Of course, it would be Jesus whom you are committed to follow. Let us not minimize the power of words in our commitments. If my basis of commitment was on *receiving*, and I did not receive what I thought, then it would be easy to "take my toys and go home". This is what happens so many times in our evangelism. Salvation becomes a one-time event, and when the prayer is said, "then I am saved and I have fulfilled my obligations". In fact, the new disciples' responsibilities are just starting, but that is not usually evident to most people who come to the Lord in this manner. The prayer becomes a "magic potion" protecting them from the fire of hell, but no real lifelong commitment is made in the initial process - or if it is, it's secondary to the process. This lack of process or commitment happens because of the way we teach them in this salvation experience.

Furthermore, the idea that we "take Him as our personal Savior" is also a harmful idea. We do not take Him; He takes us. Again the focus is not on us, but on Him. He also is not our personal Savior; He is everyone's Savior. What I am trying to say is that our relationship with God and Jesus is not a selfish one. We're not in control; we do not choose Him before He chooses us. He came for us, He died for us, and it is Him receiving us into His arms, not us receiving Him. Can you see the difference? It is Jesus who makes the first move, and we respond to His invitation, not Him to ours. But, this is the impression that is given when we use the phrases "take Him" or "receive Him". Let's stop using these powerful words and images and use the ones that will rightly describe the process in our following Jesus as His disciple.

It is true, as the Bible says, that He draws us, but not at the expense of our free will. A person can be drafted to be on an NBA basketball team. The association makes it known that they want that person on the team, but that person still chooses be on that team. If he chooses to sign with the team, he chooses to abide by the rules and stipulations of that team. If he doesn't want to join, he can choose not to play. The same thing is true with us being on Christ's team. He chose us, but we must choose to join and follow Him, or we will not be a part of the team. Now, we can "wear the hats" and say we're on the team, but never show up or sign the commitment contract. The same thing is true with our relationship with Christ. We can say we're on the team, but never fulfill our part to follow and obey Him as **Lord.**

On the other hand, if the commitment and understanding is that you become a follower, then when asked to follow something Biblical, what is asked will be a "no-brainer", for that's what you initially committed to. Those who did not come to the Lord this way, (which includes most of us), can now choose to make that commitment. This is why I suggest that the whole church study and go through my booklet, *The Most Precious Thing in the World,* so that each person can have a chance of making that commitment to be a disciple. When you make this decision, then everything you must do will be a result of this initial commitment. If you choose to follow Him as a disciple, you will want to confess, repent, be baptized, and even follow Him in His Word, and let Christ and the Holy Spirit begin the changing that needs to take place in your heart and actions.

Bonhoffer wrote about "Cheap Grace" being a problem even in his time, and that has not changed today. What is cheap is how we acquire our grace. It should be obvious that grace should not be cheap because it cost Jesus His life, and our commitment to Christ should not be cheap in the way we make that commitment. I am not talking about works to pay for it, but rather the type of commitment it takes. He requires us to give all, as He gave all. Our lives in complete obedience to Christ as Lord, not as Savior, are required. Salvation is the result (gift) of Him being Lord of our lives. Anything else, and we cheapen His grace.

I will let you in on a secret at this point, if you have missed the concept along your way in reading this book. The whole purpose of this book is to encourage and somewhat equip the reader to disciple. This book, along with the whole *Walk in Discipleship* series, is just one way to see that *seed four* is the dominant seed, and not seed three, which is typical. Of course, this is not the only aid or set of materials out there and of course, it's your choice. But if you do nothing, then surely nothing will happen.

God's Intent and wish for His church!

"Therefore if anyone is in Christ, he is a new creation; the old has gone, the new has come! All this is from God, who reconciled us to Himself through Christ, and gave us the ministry of reconciliation: that God was reconciling the world to Himself in Christ, not counting men's sins against them. And he has committed to us the message of reconciliation. We are therefore Christ's ambassadors, as though God were making His appeal through us. We implore you on Christ's behalf: be reconciled to God." 2 Corinthians 5:17-20

Does God have any other plan? No, you are it! God is now speaking and reaching out to the world through us His church. When it fails to happen the church will not grow and the world will have no chance to be reconciled. This reconciliation must first start with man on man then God to man. We are the conduit for the world to God. HE HAS NO OTHER PLAN! This being the case, then how should we change our attitudes and efforts in our churches? How should it change what you and your church do on a day-to-day basis?

The "Most Precious" and Evangelism

What is the most precious thing in the world to you? This is the first question I ask in my book, *The Most Precious Thing in the World*. The answer you will discover is the restoration of man, with God, through Christ. If that is the most precious thing, then evangelism is the most important thing we can do in the church. Is this true? It depends on what type of evangelism. If it is the easy believerism that we issued earlier, then I say, "no". If evangelism is seen as the introduction to discipleship, then I would say, "yes". If our most important thing is our restoration with God then that is not a one-time event, it is a life long relationship. You don't just start a relationship with God and then say I am in, don't need anything else, I am saved, I am Ok. This is not what we see in the New Testament, and surely not God's intent.

This is what makes the book *The Most Precious* unique. It's goal is to ask a person to make a commitment to follow Jesus as His disciple, not just pray a prayer and think that is all you do. After a person makes this commitment and is baptized, they then begin their first session in discipleship. This first session is session Five in the "Most Precious" booklet. This process completes the full circle, and helps the person begin and keep their commitment to be a disciple. But if they decide not to be baptized after session Fur then by all means do not go on to the next lesson. Go back and explore why they chose not to be committed. More about this is in the *Guide to The Most Precious*.

I suggest that every person in the church should go through this book. Why? I explain in my seminars that you have potentially four types of people in your church. The first are those who may have grown up in the church and never truly made a commitment to be His disciple. The second are those who have transferred in and have not made that commitment. Then third, there are those who are just seeking and they need to become disciples. And lastly, there are those who need to experience the book to renew their commitment, and hopefully discover if they may be candidates to become *Most Precious* sharers in the future.

As Jean-Luc Picard, Star Trek captain might say, "This is our prime directive. Make it so." Is making disciples your prime directive? Is it the prime directive for your church, if not, why not? If the church is going to grow, it will be done through the making of disciples. As we have seen, that process begins with evangelism that centers on becoming disciples, not just on saying a prayer or getting baptized. Again, this is where the tool *The Most Precious Thing in the World*, will be of help in your evangelistic outreach.

How is this approach implemented in your church? There will be a slight difference between an established church and a new church start. Let us now look at the strategy for implementation.

Strategy Level One: In new congregations . . .

1.   **Identify those who have the gift of evangelism.** This can be ascertained in a couple of ways. You can ask if anyone thinks he/she has the desire to evangelize, or has ever taken a gifts questionnaire, or had experience in the ministry to meet with others to discuss the need.

If you're establishing a new church and you are the pioneer minister/preacher/pastor, you had better have some gift in evangelism or you won't get off the ground. Or - find someone to team with who enjoys evangelism, is gifted and has had success in evangelizing.

2.   **Train them with the *Most Precious* book and methods of evangelism.** This can be done during training service like on Sunday night or Wednesday evenings, or on a special night of training dedicated to this task. I would, again, prefer that it is not done on Sunday morning, if possible, because of the time restraint. In the first meeting, ask which night is best to commit to this training. I would suggest Tuesday through Thursday nights. This time later may turn into outreach nights or home evangelistic nights in prospect homes.

3.   **Train them and mentor them in the process of personal evangelism.** I remember the first time I went calling on a family. I was 16 at the time and was teamed up with an older man. I didn't have any training but did have an example. If the above training is done sometime in the beginning, it will be a great help in developing the attitude of the witness. One of the best methods is to have each team member be trained on the field in actual witnessing opportunities. Using the CD/DVD presentation (when available) can enhance the witnessing experience, along with *Most Precious* book and its accompanying leaders guide. On the CD/DVD, you will find some instructions which you can use in your training sessions on how to use the video and book.

4.   **Develop them into a ministry team.** This may seem obvious, but not always. The team should see this approach as the beginning of a ministry. As you go through the process you will find, or the people themselves will find, that some of them will not fit into this ministry. This is nothing to worry about; it is actually what needs to take place in every ministry until each person finds his or her place of ministry. If each person is given the freedom to fail, they will be free to look to other areas where they do fit. Some people may find that they are better gifted, or

may prefer, to take a person through the second step by using the *Steps to Spiritual Growth,* or even the series *A Walk in Discipleship.*

Strategy Level Two (in existing churches)

1.   Identify all those who have been attending but who have not yet made a profession of faith. Visit them and invite them to go through the *Most Precious* book in their home. Again, this all presumes that the family groups have been established and these people have been identified with, in this process. Also, people can be identified through the greeting and follow up program or individual outreach. I suggest this also be done within youth groups as well. After the youth workers are trained, you might divide the youth up into two categories, those who are already Christian and those who need to make a commitment. For those who have made a commitment, ascertain the ones who might be able and willing to share their faith with their own peers. First, take them through the material, and then have them experience witnessing alongside other evangelists in reaching out to the non-Christians and their friends in school.

2.   Have the team who were trained in Level One to take the whole congregation through the book, *The Most Precious Thing in the World,* by Dr. Householder, in a small group setting. Now, some may say "We're already Christians, why do we need to do this?" As we have noted earlier, it is important that everyone is on the same page. Second, it is important that the leadership be sure that each person truly has made a genuine commitment to follow Christ. If the foundation is built including everyone, <u>all</u> will have a firm foundation upon which to build.

3.   Encourage each believer to reach out to his/her realm of influence to share this book in a small group. Now of course, not everyone will want or desire to share the gospel with others. But they can share their friendship to the point that they can introduce people to someone who can share the gospel. This is where, within family groups, you can establish home evangelistic studies within homes of people with hospitality and a desire to spread the gospel.

4.   Be sure to look back to the chapter on Discipleship for more instructions on follow-up after evangelism. If the follow-up is not ready, <u>don't</u> reach out any more into the community until the family and shepherding families are in place. If people are not trained to take converts through the steps, wait until they are.

Strategy Level Two (in new churches)

1. As you gather the nucleus, see to it that each person who becomes a part is taken through this booklet so he may understand what he is committing to in Christ. You do not have to make a big emphasis, especially if there is no nucleus to begin with. You just begin this process from the beginning, and the people simply learn and understand - this is *just what you do*. Again, if you are working with a start-up team, be sure that all understand that discipleship and these methods of evangelism are <u>the way it is done</u>. And it's important that *everyone involved* goes through the same material. If there is any resistance, ask people not to participate. It's better to have fewer to start with, than to, in effect, lay the groundwork for trouble and strife later. Those who've never been a part of church life, or had any former

experiences with church, will either have no idea, or be prejudiced concerning what is to be done. As long as you begin with, and stay with, Biblical principles and methods, you should never feel wrong about standing for them.

2. As you add other phases of discipleship, continue to encourage each new member or believer to reach out to his or her friends and relatives with the gospel. These ministries are ongoing, and should never be stopped. And remember that as the church grows and adds other ministries, these basic first three years of teaching and discipleship are not a one- time study, but rather the continual process for all those in the future who come through the church doors. Therefore, it's important that as new people, or even members, meet and bring new people into the church, they will know that what they were taught will be taught to their friends as well.

3. As in the established church, every transfer should go though this booklet as well, so that everyone will be on the same page, thus minimizing conflict and false doctrine. We have noted this earlier, but please remember that for the sake of those coming, it is valid for the shepherding team to be concerned that everyone is on the same firm foundation of salvation and growth as the others. I know, of course, everyone is not at the same level as others in spiritual growth. But I've seen that when a leadership shows and shares with the new people that they're there to help them in their spiritual growth, you'll not only have better retention and growth, but you'll also see a stronger congregation (and leadership) because of it. That's why it's important to place each person in a family and have him/her visited and invited to be a part of the family unit and small group times.

Conclusion: There's no greater experience than to share the gospel with people and witness to them, or participate in their conversion and baptism. I hope and pray that you, the leadership, and the whole congregation become excited and motivated to make disciples. As the story goes, you don't become a fisherman until you fish, and in my opinion you don't become a happy fisherman until you make a catch. I know that some fishermen, like some churches, say they just enjoy going fishing and enjoy going through the motions, even if they don't catch any fish. But I guarantee you that every fisherman goes fishing with the anticipation of catching a fish, and if they say they don't, that's a big "fish story!"

As you know, Jonah didn't want to go fishing in Nineveh. I know some believers and congregations who act and think like Jonah. They, too, don't want to go fishing for men in their community or around the world. They enjoy where they're going in life; but God has called his church, his disciples, (that is, all of us), to be fishers of men, and women. There's not an option to fail to make disciples and still obey God as a congregation. And since evangelism is the first stage of disciple-making, there's no option but for every congregation to make it a priority. So I encourage you to make it your goal to obey Jesus and His last words to "Go and make disciples of all nations."

In our next two chapters we will explore how discipleship is began and sustained in your church. But each congregation must decide to make it their prime directive.

Shepherding, God's Plan for Growth!
Chapter Eleven

What is Shepherding?

It is obvious what shepherds do. They watch, protect, and take care of their sheep. So how does this apply to the church? Throughout the Old and New Testament, strong images and comparisons are made between shepherds and the leaders of God's people.

In his early years, my stepfather, Ken Vogt, spent some time as a shepherd in the hills of South Dakota. Like others, he noticed sheep have a strange and eerie resemblance to people. The first thing sheep are concerned about is filling their little tummies. During their grazing, they will eat and chew, then take one step forward, eat and chew and take one step forward, and so on. Then when they're full, each one begins his little game of let's see who can slip away first. At this point, one turns his head to spy his shepherd. Then instead of taking one step, he now takes two or three nibbles, looks at his shepherd, and then another two or three steps toward his freedom. The smart shepherd gets their attention. All you have to do is fire a shot into the air and immediately they turn around and begin eating. It is a strange thing that when we are satisfied or have our own agendas, we too seem to slip away *sheepishly*. The leader also needs to be watching and be ready to fire a warning shot in love, or send His faithful and helpful dog to gather them all back and in order.

> It is a strange thing that when we are satisfied or have our own agendas, we too seem to slip away *sheepishly*.

He also told me that when there seems to be impending danger from a predator, the sheep will all rush back to the side of the shepherd for protection. They know they need protection, and that their shepherd will be there for them. The same should be true for God's flock. God wants His shepherds to be there, and for the people to have trust in them. But, if the shepherds have no time or show no concern, then the sheep will run off, scattered, into the hands of the enemy.

Remember: The Master Shepherd will want each leader to account for those under his care. When any lamb comes into a fellowship, it is up to those who lead or shepherd to be responsible for those whom the Lord leads to your fellowship. The more a church shepherds and takes care of the sheep, the more new lambs the Lord will bring them.

What does it mean to "shepherd" in the spiritual sense?

Guide! Sheep are the type of animals that will go astray very quickly if not led or guided. A sheep dog is trained to keep the sheep going in directions that are commanded by the shepherd. The shepherd communicates with the dog, and then the dog gets in a position to direct the sheep to the right, left, or even stop them and send them back the other way. The guide dog is also there to keep the sheep in the fold. If one gets out of line, the dog is trained to watch and see that it stays within the fold. The Great Shepherd communicates with those who are guiding His flock in each local body, giving them the directions, with expectations that the leaders will guide the sheep. The dogs are trained to listen to certain sounds of the whistle. Each sound and length means something different. The leaders today, much like the guide dogs, are to listen to the sound of the Spirit and the Word He speaks through the Bible. It is up to the spiritual leaders to guide the people in the spiritual direction in which they should go. Therefore, if your elders are ever considered as dogs, be sure it is in the positive sense.

Protect! The Bible warns of the wolves that want to devour God's flock. The shepherd who is on the job will see to it that the sheep are not in a harmful situation. He will protect them by teaching sound doctrine and truths. He will be aware of what material is provided for his people to study. The genuine shepherd will equip the people with the means of protection by discipling them and helping them, understand and apply the Scriptures in their daily lives. A novice or new Christian typically lacks the spiritual maturity or strength to know right

> The genuine shepherd will equip the people with the means of protection by discipling them, and helping them understand and apply the Scriptures in their daily lives.

from wrong. He is usually willing to listen and blindly obey. If not given the right protection, it will be easy for the spiritual wolves of this world to attack such individuals, and lead them astray.

Feed! The sheep must be continually taken to green pastures so they can feed. The sheep in your flock also need to be taken to the Word of God for continual feeding. It is only in the Word that each person can grow and become mature in the faith. This is why the elder or shepherd must be able and willing to teach, helping each person become mature in his/her faith and daily lives. Again, if he has no desire, time, or ability to teach, then he should not be an elder.

Groom! The sheep need to be groomed and shorn each spring. Now most people will say this is for the benefit of the shepherd so that he can sell the wool, but this is only a by-product. Shearing the sheep also keeps them healthy and free from entanglement. In the spiritual realm, each sheep needs to have the old coat or life removed. Attitudes and habits that are harmful need to be taken away if each sheep is to grow to be healthy.

Keep them together! Only in numbers will the sheep be protected. When individuals are allowed to wander and go on their own, they will often stray from the faith. It is up to the shepherd to be sensitive and aware of each sheep's presence in services and Bible studies. If he/she isn't attending, then go look for him/her and see what the problem is. If they start to stray spiritually, it is the responsibility of the leader to be there and help them stay within the fold. Unlike sheep, man has a choice and can choose to not follow the shepherd or his helpers; this is sad. But, it is the duty of the shepherds to go look for them and try to help or heal any wounds they may have. Having them involved in the family shepherding system will go a long way in keeping the sheep in the fold.

What happens when there is no organized shepherding program?

People are left to their own. What is harmful about this? Some people think if we provide the right programs and have a dynamic preacher, then that is enough to keep people coming with little or no more effort. Jesus called the believers "sheep" for a good reason; they are in need of guidance and protection. There are many things in the world that tempt and compete for people's attention. Again, I can not stress enough how important it is for the first year and a half to have someone take new people by the hand and guide them in their Christian walk. It is also important to provide a maintenance program that will continue to meet the needs of the flock year after year. This is shepherding.

People tend to stray rather than gather. Like the sheep my stepfather looked after, people have a tendency to stray and go their own way. If someone does not pay attention to each lamb, then it will look for other pastures. It is the responsibility of the shepherds to keep the people in green pastures. If the sheep are not taken care of, they will wander away and enter into another flock, or worse, into the wilderness. Many former sheep in conservative Protestant churches have left and entered into the folds of cults. These cults tend to meet the needs of community and safety, and people are attracted to this. If a church or leadership thinks their people can be held by only the doctrine they teach, then the exodus of their sheep will surprise them.

> If the sheep are not taken care of, they will wander away and enter into another flock, or worse, into the wilderness.

People are usually weak and in need of guidance. Many times, leadership makes the mistake of thinking that people should be left on their own. They're adults and can make up their own mind. This is true to some degree, but unless a strong committed leadership guides them, they will not know in which direction to go. The problem in some cases is that the leadership is in the same boat. They may also have a problem with direction and strength within their ranks. They need to have leaders with the vision and direction that is needed.

Evil spiritual powers are out to distract, devour, and lead away the sheep. The Bible warns that it is important that we not forsake assembling together. There is strength when we are in community and looking out for one another. People are relational, and when we are not there for each other, it is much easier for the enemy to make inroads into people's lives.

How does God view the shepherd that neglects His flock? (Matthew 23:13-28) As you read this passage you can see Jesus' disdain towards the religious leaders of the day. In most cases most congregations are as blind as those who lead them. Many may say they want to shepherd, but most never do. Those who do usually keep their sheep; those who don't many times don't even think about it or plan for it. Again, most leaders do not even think or plan for this process. Whatever the reason, God does not like it. He does not like His sheep unfed or unprotected. He does not like for a group of leaders to not lead or shepherd. As we have seen, the work of an elder or shepherd is to equip and shepherd the flock. He is disappointed with a congregation and its leaders that are neglecting the flock.

He hates even more the shepherd that leads his flock astray. There is no excuse, but there is condemnation for the shepherd that destroys God's people. Time after time, I have seen where so-called elders would rather see their agenda adopted than take care of the flock. When an elder says, "I like the church small," and does not make any effort to reach out to those God brings, God is not happy.

Please think about in today's church, or even your church, any examples or attitudes you have seen or heard that may be like that of the Scribes and Pharisees. How do you think Christ would view many of our church boards and leaders today?

What can be done to change this? I hope no one reading this book has ever had this attitude. If you have, I hope you have repented and turned from this attitude. If the problem is that you have not thought of it, or have never been trained to shepherd, then there is hope if you are willing.

Procedures for Shepherding!

Shepherding: The goal is to have shepherding at all levels, General and Special.

General: Regional groups (large group usually based upon region). This is not another study group, but rather a group that is established solely for shepherding and keeping track of each person's growth and attendance in the church. This group will be referred to as "Family Groups."

Special: Each group and ministry team can have a system where people are cared for both spiritually and physically if needed. Small Bible studies, discipleship covenant groups, special interest groups, or ministry groups can also provide for spiritual shepherding and guidance.

> At all times, shepherding is to be done with the motivation of love for each other, not for control.

Shepherding is not a "big brother watching over you" type of ministry, but a ministry that is concerned and accountable to each other. At all times, shepherding is to be done with the motivation of love for each other, not for control. The positive thing about the former Boston movement was their emphasis on small group discipling. But their demise was their uber control over each believer. It is not those who disciple who should be controlling, but the Spirit. And the Spirit Himself will not control unless each believer gives Him the control. When a discipleship ministry goes from agreeable accountability to strict control by its leadership, then the whole system will become cultic and loving.

Structure of Family Groups!

Size! The church needs to be divided into groups of no more than 25 family units, or around 75 people per family group. Individuals are also considered as one unit. For example, if you have a church of 100, then you could have four shepherding families with four teams of shepherds and leaders. When I talk of a family, I am talking of a group of people who are primarily for shepherding and containment. This is the maximum family number. At or near this point, the group should divide. But from the beginning, the family leaders should be preparing for the division by mentoring and preparing new leaders to take over the new groups. When they divide, it is best to already have a shepherd and apprentice for each of the new families. Now as usual, families have a hard time dividing, but by them being in their own growth groups, then the dividing will be easier. Before division, the two new groups should start meeting separately.

Family leaders! Each group should have at least one elder, an elder/shepherd apprentice, and deacons if there are ministries for them to do within the family. Women should be included in the shepherding category in order to be shepherds for other women. Preferably, wives of the elders and deacons should be involved as a family, but this is not mandatory. If the wives do not have the gifts for shepherding, or the will, they should not be forced to shepherd, but there should be other women identified and put in these positions to shepherd the women.

Apprentice program! No more groups should exist than there are leaders prepared to care for them. This is why it is important to always have an intern or assistant in training. The ideal is to have apprentices in every stage and at every level in the families.

Additions! Each group will have additions based on the new people who come into the church, either by transfer or evangelism. Usually each family will bring people into their family by other family members. Inviting people to seeker cell or new discovery/Most Precious groups, or individual efforts of evangelism, can do this outreach.

Multiplication! When the group gets to a certain point, it should be divided into two smaller groups so each group can continue to grow and not be too big for the shepherding team to care for the people. In the larger family group, the magic number is 75 adults, in the growth groups, 8 to 12; and in the small discipleship groups ,4.

Leader Pool! If possible, the new leaders should be trained within each group. This is the ideal and will become reality as the process and ministry grows. To get the ministry started, you may have to recruit other leaders from other groups. Be sure not to strip the other group to a point that they cannot operate successfully. We will speak more about this later.

Accountability! Big Brother or Sister: Each new believer or transfer, as well as every person in the family, needs to have a big brother or sister. The goal is to provide another level of relationship within the family. This is not for Bible study or instruction, but for accountability and encouragement. Now this can be within the small groups or the person may or may not be a discipler. The person also is not to be a part of the shepherding team or leadership, but is responsible for fulfilling their obligations, and should be more mature in their growth and time than the person they are working with. But on the other hand in some certain circumstances there can be mutual accountability. This is desired when you have two mature believers.

Each family should also provide the place for cell groups and Bible studies in their region. This is not meant to force a person to go to any certain group, but rather to encourage them by promoting the family shepherding unit.

Responsibilities for Shepherds

The elder\shepherd is responsible to see that each person is growing spiritually.

a. 1. Know where each sheep is, _that is monitor each person's Sunday and small group participation_! Know who was and was not in church. Most churches don't want to take the time to do this because it is time consuming, but it is worth it. This should not be burdensome if everyone has someone to look after. If the church is divided into family groups, and within each group there are a number of sub-groups, then no one should slip through the cracks. Now a person may decide to leave or go somewhere else, but if they are looked after, that is more unlikely. There is a caution, however, to those doing the shepherding. Do not be overbearing because the people may feel pressured. Rather, they should feel a sense of being cared for. This is a thermometer to how the person is progressing or if there may be problems. If they miss at least three weeks in a row, there may be a serious problem in the making, and a visit from a concerned shepherd may help alleviate or identify the problem. If a person is involved in a small group, someone in their group will be able to share what the problem might be. Now this does not mean every family leader take a survey each week, but each growth group or discipleship group can keep some attention to their members that are not attending church or group activities. When there seems to be a pattern of missing, then it is important to inform the family leader of the missing person. At that point, then someone can contact the person and encourage them.

b. _Encourage each to be involved in church and at least one study group_. If a person is on fire and committed, there will not be a need to encourage them; they will automatically become a part of the small groups and or fellowship. The new person who needs to develop this discipline, or a person that is having some problems, may need this encouragement or teaching.

Some people are introduced to Christ, but are never encouraged or introduced to the local church. This is usually true for transfers or recent converts that were converted outside your church.

    c. <u>Get to know each lamb</u>, *make periodic visits to see how they are doing and what needs they may have*! Once every three to six months, each person in the family needs to be contacted by someone. Someone on the shepherding team should see members of their group at least once every three to six months, unless there is a special need, or if there seems to be a problem or excessive absence. How can you get to know one another if you do not spend time with each other? Now it is true that some people just are loaners, not ready to get close to others. Again, this is what shepherding is about when you get to know your sheep. People who leave usually do so because they never developed any relationships, or no one paid them any attention. Again, all you can do is reach out. Some will open up sooner than others, but if someone is trying to get to know another person, more times than not, they will be satisfied in their church experience. If the member is faithfully attending a cell/small group, then much of the shepherding should be done within that context. Therefore, a visit or call is important from someone else in the leadership on a periodic basis. It is very important that the person be visited if they are a new believer or transfer. If there is need for the minister to see anyone, notify the staff immediately.

    d. *Provide times of fellowship with the whole family group* to *d*evelop a sense of togetherness. It is especially important as the church grows for each family to get together to foster togetherness. As the church grows and gets bigger, it is important that small to medium-sized groups meet together to have fellowship. It is suggested that you have a time available once a quarter, or at least twice a year, and more often if desired. This is not for study or to replace any other group in the church, but just for fellowship and family identity. Once every three months, have a fellowship time. This is where we are talking about community. The thing many churches have lost in this world of change is this special togetherness. The family group is about getting to know each other. In this day, it is becoming more difficult to develop this type of Biblical community. Everyone is busy and tied up with their own agenda. But, the church that makes the effort will succeed more times than not. At some time during the year, you might get different families together and play games. This works well with families that have recently reproduced.

    e. <u>Mentor at least three men or women</u>. This is important, and in the strictest sense, the main service of the elder. Teaching and mentoring is the backbone of shepherding. If the elder/shepherd is not willing to teach or mentor, he disqualifies himself from the position or ministry of elder/shepherd. This can be done within the ministry of discipleship. Every elder/shepherd needs to be discipling at least three men, and the women shepherds at least three women. The ideal occurs when the shepherd's key leaders and apprentices in the family are shepherded by the shepherd. Developing relationships from the top to bottom will ensure that no one goes without being shepherded in the family and the church. Yes, it takes some work from everyone, but no one person is strapped with all the responsibility.

    f. <u>Be alert to problem areas</u>. As with any problem, be smart and realize that it is the responsibility of the shepherds to notify the ministerial\pastoral staff when there is a need for a special visit, or a problem they cannot handle. Failing to do so might cause even more problems. None of us can have all the answers or meet everyone's needs 100% of the time, so don't try; ask for help. Most leaders never know that there are problems in their members' lives until it is too late and they have gone elsewhere. In some cases, people do not care or want to make the effort. In other cases the attitude is, "Great; it is better that they have gone." It is true that some people are just troublemakers and want to disrupt the church and other people. In this case, when they do not want to be a part of unity and harmony, then try to work with them, but do not let anyone destroy the unity. Now, if they are speaking the Word in truth, then maybe the rest need to listen. Remember, if there are any complaints or problems you cannot handle, inform the pastor/staff. If you do not, what may be a little sore could turn into a destructive cancer. I would say that 85% of all problems in the church are not doctrinal, but personality conflicts. "Nip them in the bud" before they can create a major problem.

g. Be confidential and trustworthy in all your dealings with others. By all means, what happens in any situation is confidential unless life is at risk, or rebellion is a severe and continual problem against the Word of God. If any shepherd or leader is involved with a disciple who is involved in a grave sin, the shepherd or leaders should first try to counsel and convince the brother or sister to cease their actions and repent. If they refuse, then another leader should be approached with the problem; either the senior family shepherd or the senior minister. If the person still refuses to repent and change, then the matter should be brought before the whole eldership, then the church as whole, but only to the church as a last resort and for disciplinary procedures. Up until it is taken to the whole church, the proceedings are confidential. Not even wives should know. Now a caution is in order. This is not for revenge or witch-hunts, but for a person that is involved in a grave sin and will not repent. What is a grave sin? Any type of immoral act or situation that will spiritually harm the persons involved or church as a whole should be dealt with as soon as possible. There must be proof before any action or procedures are taken, and in the case of an elder, there needs to be at least two witnesses. Remember, the whole purpose is to help the person not be destroyed. Once there is repentance, there should be forgiveness. See 1 Corinthians 5 and Matthew 18 for more guidelines.

h. Be responsible for keeping some type of record on each sheep. It is suggested that a file be maintained on each person and family to track where the person is in their spiritual growth, not to spy or be used to badger or humiliate. Again, all this information is confidential within the leadership and shepherding team. If each group leader keeps in touch with their group members and, in turn, their ministry leaders, the task will be easier.

i. Go find them! Visit or call after the second or third absence. Again, this may seem over the top, but the results will be phenomenal; just try it. If you touch base and know people are going to be gone, or know their workload, then you will know how to handle each situation. Now, of course, you can become cultic if you try to coerce or control the situation. This you do not want to do, but a loving concern and a quick phone call will do the trick. As relationships are developed the church becomes a family, with each person looking after the other. Most congregations think, "Well, if they want to come, that is their choice, and if they do not want to come, we do not want to offend." It is true that you can go too far in both directions. You can be so removed that no one calls or shows they care, or you can be too far out there and offend. If you serve with love and as a concerned brother or sister, you will be there when others need you.

J. See to it that the deacons are doing their ministries and you are doing yours, the bottom line is take care of the flock's needs. Deacons are responsible to care for the physical needs of the people in their group. The deacons and ministry team leaders are to be responsible for any physical need, while the elder cares for their spiritual growth. Deacons are also to help the elder\shepherd visit with the people in a practical or ministry capacity. If there seems to be a need for spiritual help, refer them to the elder/shepherd. A physical or practical need is to be taken care of by a ministry team or deacon. The elder/shepherd is ultimately responsible to see that both needs are met in their family. This is not to say they are to meet all the needs. Now this does not preclude an elder from helping, but do not make this your major use of time. If it is more your desire to help in this way rather than in teaching and shepherding, maybe you need to be a deacon, not an elder. Remember to bring all needs that your shepherding team cannot meet or handle to the minister/staff.

K. <u>Prepare them to survive</u>! In the process of protecting the flock spiritually, the elders/shepherds are responsible to see that each member has the opportunity to be equipped and to know what it takes to survive in this world. That is done by ensuring there is an educational/discipleship program that prepares the individual to be able to stand up to the world and its temptations, and to those in the world that preach and teach false doctrine. One of the first things is to deliver and be responsible for the delivery of the Spiritual Growth Packet to each member and new member in your family. Why? This is the first step in preparing each person in his or her spiritual disciplines, and it shows each new person that someone cares and that they are a part of a family or community.

Shepherding Families

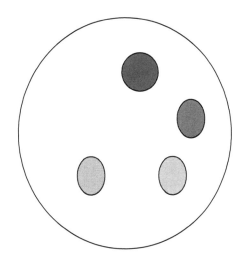
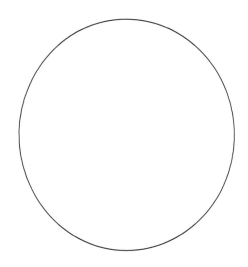

In summary each family has:

1. One shepherd family leader (elder and wife is Ideal But not if wife is not qualified.)
2. Under-shepherds in apprenticeship
3. Deacon/deaconess over ministry teams or needs
4. Growth group and discipleship cells of various kinds
5. Evangelistic seeker cell groups
6. No more than 75 people
7. Opportunity for Christian doctrine and other ongoing instruction
8. Periodic family fellowship times

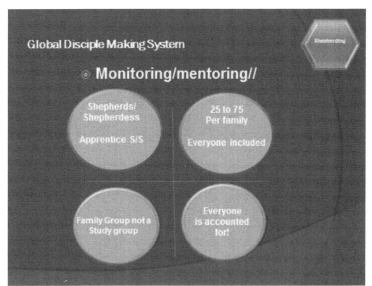

1. <u>One shepherd family (elder and wife).</u> Remember, not all shepherds in the ministry will always be elders, but every elder must be a shepherd. That is just who the elder is, a shepherd. In this shepherding ministry, it is ideal to have a family group with an elder and his wife as the lead shepherds. In an established church where qualified men are ready and gifted to shepherd, the process of establishing these family groups is easy. Where there are no qualified leaders or shepherds, then most likely the church is new or small. In this case, the preacher or church planter must be the shepherd until he can develop them. For example, there is a new church I am working with in developing some of these ideas. They are 30 members strong, four months old, and yet to go public. The church planter and his wife are the shepherds. Their goal now is to find a couple of prospects that they can mentor to become involved in the shepherding process. Let them work with you, and then periodically give them more and more responsibility. It will take time to disciple and bring the fruit to the top.

The lead or senior shepherd is not to be responsible to do everything, but as with any leader, it is his responsibility to encourage others to help and do the work alongside him.

Let me give a disclaimer. Not every wife will qualify or desire to be a shepherdess alongside her husband. Although this is ideal, it is more important to have the right person in the position. Therefore, if she is not, then you must look for another woman that will be a shepherdess in the family group.

2. <u>Each family has under-shepherds or apprentices.</u> This includes wives and women in these groups. This is one of the most important elements in the success and growth of the church and the family groups at all levels. As we have said, the growth of the church is based on how many levels of shepherding are going on. The next generation or the continual growth is in proportion to those who are equipped and ready to take on these leadership roles. This process needs to be started from the beginning of the family groups and be a continual process throughout the life of this work.

3. <u>Deacon/deaconess involved in ministries groups.</u> If there is no ministry for the deacon to fulfill or be involved with, then there is no need for a deacon. Remember also that the ministry should be based in the person's giftedness. No ministry needs, no deacon; no gift in the area of ministry, no deacon. This is where many churches have established a harmful tradition. Being a deacon is a ministry, nothing else. It is not an office or a position over the whole congregation. The deacons again have no place on a deacon/elder board. They are doing a service, and when

the service is finished, so is their ministry. Now most service needs are ongoing, so there is no problem. Refer back to the chapter on leadership to see more on the role of deacons.

4. Growth group and discipleship cells of various kinds. Each family should contain a number of various groups to meet the needs of its members. The difference in these suggestions and other church formats is that the family is to be responsible for one another, and like a family, a number of different groups may be needed. In the plan of discipleship, which you will see in the next two chapters, you will come to realize that people need different levels of maturation, which will require different types of groups. They are also needed to fulfill different purposes in the person's maturity. The four-man or woman groups are needed for the development of personal growth and accountability, and the larger growth group will provide continual growth and fellowship.

5. Evangelistic seeker cell groups. In the "Seeker Cell/Most Precious," the emphasis is on the non-Christian. The Christian number should be a minimum of two couples, or less, with the rest non-Christians. The subject and language used should cater to the members' level of understanding and needs.

In some churches that I have observed and participated in, the larger eight to fifteen formats was all there was. In this church, the philosophy was that this group could provide all the needs in the church. It could provide opportunity for evangelism and continued growth by having an open chair for the new person. This is true and works well if the person is a Christian or has had a Christian background, but for the non-Christian and the health of the group, it can be a disaster. For the non-Christian, they are outnumbered and can feel uncomfortable or ganged up on. For the group, they will always be ready to go back to the basics and milk, and that is not fair to those who need the growth and meat. Now, let me say, there are always times when a group can switch gears and bring a person to Christ, but the percentage is very low, and the risk is very high.

In this one church, the church number grew, but the Kingdom did not. What I mean is that over a three-year period of this method, 90% of the growth in the church was by transfer, not by baptism. This is not Kingdom growth, but sheep sharing. More of this will be touched on in the chapter on evangelism.

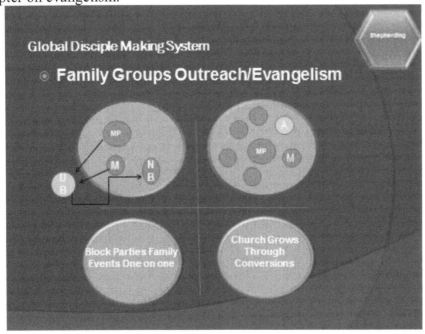

6. <u>No more than 75 people</u>. We have already issued this earlier, but to surmise it is important that the number in a family group is no more than there are leaders to take care of them. The reason for this rule is that if there are more people than can be taken care of then some will be left behind or ignored due to the amount of people.

7. <u>Provide opportunity for Christian doctrine and other ongoing instruction</u>. This is a perfect place to have ongoing instruction. This is usually done in the growth groups or in special study times. Now this can also be done in Sunday school, but in Sunday school, it is obvious that in-depth study is impossible.

The Shepherd family is not one big study group, but rather a family of small groups within in it. The goal is to encourage everyone in the church to be a part of small groups.

Benefits of the Family Shepherding System

If all of these elements are in place, then a number of results may come about.

<u>First, everyone has a place to be, and everyone has someone who is willing to care for him or her</u>. In one church, 40% of the church was typically involved in cell groups. This is really a good start. But, what happened to the other 60%? In this particular church, they were never contacted or looked after if they were not a part of the cell group system. In the family system described above, everyone is visited and included in the family gatherings. No one is left behind. They may not all participate in the formal cells, but they know they are cared for. The chance for them to get involved will be greater if they see they belong somewhere. For some of these people groups you may provide an alternative church Bible study. This is usually the case if it is an existing church when this ministry begins. If it is a new church, then almost all members will be a part of the small groups, unless they happen to be transfers who are not accustomed to this type of ministry.

<u>Second, it is a place to meet one another's need</u>. In this type of family system, we have seen that this type of structure will aid a church in meeting peoples' needs and showing concern for each person in their family. Yes, we are talking about responsibility, and that is what makes the difference between a derelict leader and a responsible one. God requires the second type from His leaders. Now in most cases, men who are in leadership want to do what is right in the sight of the Lord, but they have not been trained or equipped to do so. There is a desire and a goal, but in most churches, there is no framework to help them do the ministry. One such church divided all its members into groups of 28 under six elders, but there was no formal training or idea of what they were to do. In some cases, the leaders were overwhelmed and did nothing. There is a better way. As Jethro taught Moses, layer the leadership, and let each do their ministry. This in no way lessened Moses' task or threatened his leadership, but it did manage it so that he could spend more time in the area of his gifts and responsibility.

<u>Third, it is a place for leadership development</u>. The beauty about this family system is that it provides a place and opportunity to naturally and biblically equip and nurture leaders. When official leaders are needed, you can look at each family and see the men and women who are leading in some way and give them an opportunity to fulfill their full potential. In one of the churches that used our discipleship methods, there was a man that had been approached three years earlier to be an elder and a teacher of 10 men. His first response was, "No, I do not know what to do," so he refused. During this course, he first sat under the teaching of another leader, and after a while was asked to teach a lesson, then more, then to take on his own small group.

After this experience, he was asked again to be an elder and he accepted because he had experience and knew what it was to do the work of a shepherd.

Fourth, it may be a place for future church plants. To some, this scares the leadership, especially if they want to become a "mega church." One church in a former communist country, never to be named, had a minister who wanted to build a mega church. This church was in a city of four million and in need of many other churches, but the minister felt that it only needed one, and that with any more, he feared there would not be enough people to fill them. He really wanted a mega church. I suggested 15 years ago to start other churches, but he did not want this because people could come from all over town to make his a mega church. I just learned he has another church started in another part of town. He preaches at the original church and then rushes across town to preach at the other. He may still want a mega church, but at least he has two locations, and that is a start.

If there is a dream to plant or mother new churches in your city, this is one of the best ways to accomplish it. When you establish a church around these shepherding families, it is no big step to take a number of families in a region and begin a new church. Everything is in place with all the leaders, groups, and nucleus to start a healthy church. If you can start the church with 150 people, that's at least two families, and you will have the momentum to build a strong foundation. Be sure to bring on or raise up new ministers from within. It is important that they have the same philosophy so there will not be any divisions.

True church growth is when the Kingdom of God grows in numbers, not the local church shifting members. Adding new members is not the same as adding new souls. I learned in my doctoral class under C. Peter Wagner that the fastest and most effective way to grow God's Kingdom is by planting new churches.

Guidelines for Contact Ministry

Shepherding begins when the person first comes in contact with the congregation. In God's eyes, sheep are sheep, and when a lamb moves in or comes into a congregation, you become responsible to begin the shepherding process. To the non-believer, first impressions are very important in bringing them to the Lord. You can never take back a first impression. Also, many people have been turned away from God and the Church because their first impressions were very negative.

If you do not know the person, then show some interest. Get their name. They may not be a first-time visitor but still not feel like a part of the family. This is the goal: make them feel a part of and welcomed in the congregation. There needs to be people that are evangelists, as well as people with the gift of hospitality helping with the contact stage. Some of you will just make the first contact. Some of you will make the second contact during the first week. Some of you will do the evangelism. Sometimes a person with the gift of evangelism will not be a greeter but will go with you on Thursday, or on another visit, and share the gospel.

A person that stays in the church after a year usually has made at least three friends in the first month of coming. This is the goal, and this goal is bigger than the greeter program. But the goal is not only to be friendly when people come in the door but also to make relationships. The whole church should be encouraged to find a person they do not know and make a friend.

Generally, you go to your friends first and huddle in your groups. I know when I am at church I usually have people I want to talk with and it is usually not people that I don't know.

Don't expect the pastor to be the close friend of all. He can't talk with everyone or greet everyone deeply on Sunday.

If the person is not rushing out the door, then at least one person should get to know the person a little, get their name and number, and take them to get some tea if they want. If they are invited friends of a member, then the friend should follow up also. It would be good for the friend to introduce them to someone else in your family.

SEVEN CONTACTS FOR LIFE

1. Minister or staff member Sunday morning, if possible
2. Sunday morning with visitor packet
3. Regular member Sunday morning
4. Letter from Minister on Monday (explore how you can get the address)
5. Call or visit by contact/family group member
6. Visit made for relationship or teaching (by contact member, evangelist, pastor, and/or seeker cell or growth group leader, and by appointment only)
7. Visit by minister, evangelist, and Shepherd family leader when person is baptized or joins.

These contacts above are only suggestions, and they may or may not all be made in the first week or two of a prospect's first visit. But, as many contacts as possible and as soon as possible will determine how successful you are in showing the person how much you care.

Now for the most part, those visitors who drop by are usually already believers who have moved to town and are shopping, are dissatisfied where they are and are also shopping, or those who have been absent and are now, for any number of reasons, reaching out again in search of a congregation who cares. Very seldom is the person a total heathen and non-believer; they just don't drop in very often on their own unless they have been in a relationship with a member and someone has used the method of inviting the person to come and see. If it is a person who has been invited, then the one who invites should, if at all possible, be there to help them get in touch with others in the congregation.

TEN COMMANDMENTS OF GREETING

Why should a section on greeting be in this chapter on shepherding? When is the first time most sheep see and come in contact with the sheepfold? It is as they walk into the place of assembly of the church. The greeters and those who are motivated or trained for this ministry are at the front line of keeping and getting sheep into the fold. Therefore, it is important to have these ministers of welcome properly trained and motivated to be there for those coming in. To be successful, greeting is more than just standing at the door, giving a bulletin, and smiling; it is having a genuine concern for those who come into the doors of the sheepfold.

1. Pray that they will see God through you.
2. Enjoy what you're doing that day.
3. Acquire, repeat, and remember their name.
4. Inquire if someone invited them or they came on their own.
5. Introduce them to someone else.
6. Take them to the refreshments if available or possible.

4. <u>Remember</u> guests come before friends.
8. <u>Do not share</u> the gospel at this point; get to know who they are.
9. <u>Invite</u> them out for tea or coffee in the future, if possible.
10. <u>Fill out</u> contact card after visit.

It is important to remember this is teamwork. One person on any given Sunday will not and cannot do all these things. It will take a team of people who see this as a part of their ministry. Some will not be gifted or desire to be a part of this in the congregation, but all must be friendly and cordial. Some of the things above will be done before service and some afterwards. Usually it is a rush for people to get to service on time, and, of course, sometimes they are in a rush to leave. This is where you use your wisdom and training when approaching people. If a visitor is a guest of someone, then that someone should be the link to others.

In a well-functioning family, shepherding is going on in different levels at the same time. In most cases, people are coming to Christ through the families. The family is the highest place for relationships, and a fact that relationship building keeps people involved and coming back.

<u>Using the Booklets, "The Most Precious Thing" and the "10 Steps to Spiritual Growth"
as Shepherding Tools!</u>

If you are using the booklet the "Most Precious Thing" as your evangelism tool then you know that in the last lesson a person commits to being an obedient disciple. In your first visit after their conversion, remind the new convert of this and that the family leader is there to help them in this commitment. This then leads you to the second book, "Steps to Spiritual Growth" by Dr. Householder. This book can be used as a first step to shepherding and discipling your new and established members.

After a person's conversion, taking a person through the booklet *10 Steps to Spiritual Growth* is the first step of discipling and shepherding. Within two weeks of the person's baptism, one of the elders and/or shepherds, along with an apprentice or other leader in the shepherding group, should visit the new member with this booklet. It is suggested that the preacher not participate in this visit. The preacher should have already made a visit if possible, especially if he was not involved in the conversion. The concern here is that the new believer be in contact with his new shepherds and shepherding family. The more relationships that are developed with a person, the more these contacts will solidify the believer's place in the body. It will also provide an opportunity for the new believer's introduction into the family that will be responsible for their initial growth, as well as for getting them involved in the body's life.

The same procedure should also be carried out with those who join by transfer. They need the same material and introduction into the shepherding family as do the newly converted. This information is also important so they will be on the same page as everyone else in the body. Visiting the transfer and including them into the family also gives the shepherds an opportunity to know what the person has been through or what they need to help them grow.

It is even suggested that each transfer be taken through the booklet, "The Most Precious Thing." Why? First, you do not know who they are and if their commitment was a valid one. Second, you will be sure that they will be on the same passage as everyone else that has become members by conversion or transfer.

With an established church, you can take the opportunity to make a visit in every believer's home in the church. These visits will provide a number of benefits. First, it is important that the shepherding elder or team within each group or region visits each member periodically. Giving this booklet will offer an opportunity to provide a service and visit with each believer. Second, it will give each person a set of materials that will help in their spiritual growth. Third, it will get everyone on the same page. Each person should have the same opportunity to put into effect the spiritual disciplines contained in this booklet. Furthermore, if the established members do not have the same tools, then some problems might arise when new believers outgrow older members.

With the established believer, there should be an effort by all shepherding families to visit every member in their group within the first three months of using this booklet in the shepherding program.

The goal is to get every member, both new and old, into small groups to apply this book to their life. After going through "The Most Precious Thing" this is the next step in the shepherding program and discipleship development.

The Minister's/Preacher's Role!

The minister or preacher can reinforce all this by periodically referring back to the "Steps" booklet in his sermons or lessons. For example, the minister can encourage the people to fill out their evangelistic list and reach out. He can use the titles in the section on "Scripture for Need" as sermon titles and encourage the congregation to read the passages under that title in the book before the next week's sermon. He can preach on the disciplines and refer back to the book. A sermon series on the promises in Philippians or truths to stand on can be used. If so, then encourage the people to refer back to the booklet. This all reinforces the tool in people's lives. Also, it is important to give the people an opportunity to share their testimonies that they have worked through in the book.

Conclusion

Where have all the shepherds gone? Most churches that I have come in contact with either have no means of shepherding, or if they do, it is many times an empty shell of a program. Shepherding as you have seen in this chapter should be the center or heart of the churches health. God has indeed intended shepherding to be the main place where people's needs will be taken care of. If we do not know where the sheep are then we will not know how to take care of them, and keep them in the fold. Therefore it is God's plan for growth. For in true shepherding people will grow spiritually and they will be more committed to staying in a church that cares for them, and thus the church will have continued healthy growth.

Is shepherding all there is to keeping the backdoor closed? Shepherding is important for looking after God's flock, but in discipleship, that flock is groomed and fed. It is like comparing the fence and shelter with food. Successful shepherding will have within it ongoing discipleship. Just knowing where the sheep are and taking care of them are related, but different. In the last two chapters, you learned about discipling and how to implement it in your congregation.

Worship, Fellowship and Growth
Chapter Twelve

Who is the audience?

Have you ever left a worship service, or found yourself at a local restaurant (or even around your dining room table) and heard someone say, "I just didn't like the worship today," or, "The music wasn't the kind I like," or, "The sermon was boring," or any other disparaging, negative comment about the worship experience? Unfortunately, many people who go to church today go for what _they can get out of the experience_, and if the experience isn't to their satisfaction, or if their expectations aren't met, they'll be looking for another place to worship - or complain about! Some are simply chronic complainers - about everything. Others do really want a worshipful time; unfortunately, what goes on at some churches appeals to no one.

> **If He is the focus, we will be less concerned about our wishes and wants, and more about being in the right mood to worship God.**

In this "hyper-technological" world of consumerism, it's hard to please many people who come into the sanctuaries of our churches. Why is that? Most people go to church looking for what they can get out of it, sitting there week after week, _being the audience;_ and by being the audience, if they're disappointed, they feel they have a right to complain - because they're the audience! A sermon tape by Ron Dunn opened my eyes to this problem a few years ago. We fool ourselves if we think we're the audience. _God is the audience._ It is <u>God</u> whom we go to worship. What matters is not our going to be pleased, but that we go to please God! If He is the focus, we will be less concerned about our wishes and wants, and more about being in the right mood to worship God. When we understand this important concept, then we can truly worship God. The reason some people may never come to this realization is that most churches fail to make this their emphasis in discipling or teaching. This topic is rarely taught. Why? It's apparently assumed that worship is merely "something you come to", like other events. It's far more than this; it's where we _come in contact with God_ in a corporate setting. It's vitally important that we help believers with this part of Christian life. The second problem is, some believers may have a very shallow relationship with God. If our relationship is shallow with anyone, the time we spend together will be shallow. Third, some people may have no relationship at all. Unfortunately, some people sitting in the pews are not true worshippers because they've never been born again in the first place. This is hard to deal with because they may think they're okay, when in fact they aren't. Getting them to the place where they will admit this is hard to accomplish.

If each participant in corporate worship would think about the reason for being there, we would be well on our way to truly having authentic worship. The bottom line is, if the focus is on God and not ourselves, we're on our way toward pleasing God and developing a deeper relationship with him and those with whom we worship. This in turn will help the church to grow, first individually, and then corporately.

> **Remedies: 1. Worship leaders must make an effort to relay this concept.**
> **2. Truly evaluate your motives and relationship with God. 3. Focus on the basics and try to dispel distractions. 4. Prepare yourself before you worship.**
> **5. See yourself as a participant, rather than an audience.**

Real Worship

Have you ever been in a worship service that seemed sterile and ritualistic? There may even be different styles of worship, or styles of music. It is a known fact that all styles of music will not be loved and cherished by everyone. Although I'm from the hills of Tennessee, I don't like some of our country music; however, for some people, a gospel country hymn is a piece of art that moves them to worship the Father.

It's not the music or the style that determines the worth, but the worshipper's heart. I've heard what was, in my opinion, some awful, off-tune butchering of gospel songs. I couldn't worship because of the "fingernails-on-the-chalkboard" effect; but those who were singing from the heart and soul were praising the Lord with all their might, and God surely thought it was beautiful, or at least appreciated and blessed.

> **Being sensitive to whom you are trying to reach will help you reach them more effectively.**

You must fit the style of music to the culture you want to reach. There are many leaders who fail to remember this when planning or establishing their music or worship program. This component is very crucial in new church works. If the majority of people in your area are from the south (and aging), you might consider using southern gospel, or hymnal-type music. If your surroundings are a younger population, then more contemporary music may be in order. Being sensitive to whom you are trying to reach will help you reach them more effectively. Now, it may be that if you are in a leadership role, or even the worship leader, you may have to provide music styles that may not be your favorite, but you know it is the best to reach your surrounding area. You know whom you're trying to reach with the gospel. Now, Paul may have been a country boy who enjoyed "Judean hillbilly music" but tolerated big-city style "Jerusalem jive" for the sake of the gospel. When he worshipped in the city, he became all things to all men so as to win them to Christ. You see, Paul knew that music was a tool, not a thorn. He would have given up Judean hillbilly music forever if he had to, so that everyone with the Jerusalem jive might be saved.

> **Remedies: 1. Prepare yourself to worship corporately with the right frame of mind and mood. 2. Agree with yourself that you are there to worship Him, not to be pleased through entertainment or type of style. 3. Worship leaders are there to serve, not to perform. Make God the focal point. 4. If you don't like the style, then find another place to worship; if you cannot, then don't complain or be a problem.**

Why Worship?

Because He is Lord! "Worship the Lord with reverence and rejoice with trembling." (Psalms 2:11) In the western hemisphere, it's hard for us to comprehend the concept of Lordship. The closest we could come to understanding it, is in the English monarchy. Nowadays, it may be more of curiosity than a true homage. Another example is the homage Catholics give the Pope. When anyone is in his presence, you can see worship taking place because they see him as God's holy representative, their father (papa). Now of course, non-Catholics see this as wrong, because we should worship or pay this type of homage to no man but Christ or God. But, if you have ever witnessed people around the Pope, then you can get a glimpse of what the attitude should be like when worshiping the true Father. It doesn't matter who we are, none of us should stand for any type of worship towards us, or any other man or woman. Peter would not have stood for it, and neither should any man today. What I want us to see is the example that He is the true Lord. He is over us and deserves our worship just because of who He is.

Because He is worthy! "Worthy are you, our Lord and our God, to receive glory and honor and power; for you created all things, and because of Your will they existed, and were created." (Revelation 4:9-11) This is clear! The Bible says that none of us are worthy, not the Pope, Mother Teresa, Mother Mary, or anyone except God and His son whom He declared Lord over all. Every person, who ever lived, except for Christ, was a sinner and, therefore, disqualifies him or herself from being worthy of being worshiped. Did we create God? Did we save God? Did we love God like He loves us? The answer to all this is NO! He alone is worthy to be praised.

> *We exist* because of Him. When we realize He is the reason why we exist, that should draw us to worship Him.

Because He is creator! "And he said with a loud voice, "Fear God, and give Him glory, because the hour of His judgment has come. Worship Him who made the heaven and the earth and sea and springs of waters." (Revelation 14:7) *We exist* because of Him. When we realize He is the reason why we exist, that should draw us to worship Him. This is why many people don't want to acknowledge there is a God, for then they might have to make a decision one way or the other. But if we accept that he is Creator, then we should worship Him as such. I'm afraid that most of us who'd say, "Yes, we believe He is", don't go the next step, and worship Him for it. Let us come before the throne of our Creator and worship Him with all our hearts.

Because we should love Him! "You shall love the Lord your God with all your heart and with all your soul and with all your might."(Deuteronomy 6:5) Without this love, there is no genuine worship. But don't be accused like the church in Ephesus, "But I have this against you, that you have left your first love." (Revelation 2:4) Jesus was very frank with the people of this church. They had given up their first love and moved away from true worship and commitment. Do we truly love Him? If we do, it will be seen in our worship of Him, both in our individual and corporate worship. You can see in the pages of David and Solomon's writings a love for God. As I write this, I too have to look into the mirror and say to myself, "Do you love Him as you should?" Do we really know what this "first love" is all about? If we had it, why did it go away? Did we really have it in the first place? Being with that *special someone* kindles love. I'm afraid that, for most of us, we only visit Him on Sunday morning, and then only half-heartedly. So we must either fall in love, (or fall *back* in love) with our Lord, or we're just fooling ourselves about our true relationship with Him, and therefore, our worship is empty and useless to Him and to us.

24/7 Worship

Have you heard or said things like, "Come Sunday morning to our worship service," or, "Let us begin our worship time," or, "Now is the time for us to worship?" Of course, there needs to be a starting time for when we begin corporate worship. But, it is important to realize that a Sunday morning, or a group gathering is not the only time of worship; at least it shouldn't be.

Paul tells us to do things like, "Rejoice always," or "Pray without ceasing." These are common things you do, or should do, in worship. So, do we cease worshiping after we are outside the confines of "worship service" on Sunday morning or night? I don't think so. We should worship as the new saying goes, 24/7. That's 24 hours a day, 7 days a week. Of course, that's hard, and sometimes may seem impossible. But, if it's a goal that's in the forefront of our minds, we'll waste far less time.

> We don't *begin* to worship; we *continue* to worship with fellow believers. 11:00 a.m. isn't the time to begin; it is time to continue to worship, only this time, together with fellow worshippers.

We don't *begin* to worship; we *continue* to worship with fellow believers. 11:00 a.m. isn't the time to begin; it is time to continue to worship, only this time, together with fellow worshippers. It's more of a *lifestyle* of worship. If we have a worship attitude 24/7, when times are sad, or things aren't going so well, how do we handle those times? In sad or unknown times, how do you react? Do you have a positive attitude when you don't know what's around the next corner? Do you praise Him and worship Him for who He is, not for what He gives? Can we as children of God develop a relationship that's "24/7"? It's hard for most people to be open and vulnerable with God all the time. We're in the flesh, and so we spend time dealing with the flesh. That being true, how can we worship, even in the mundane, day-to-day events of life? Our frame of mind or Spirit is a key. The way we react and believe will affect our worship. If God is everywhere, and we're in His presence all the time, should we not think about our worship or relationship? When we do, it should make it easy to worship.

Heart and Soul of Worship

Mindless worship! How many times have you stood (or sat) singing a song, and it dawned on you that you didn't even *have a clue* what you were singing? Do you ever sing old songs without thinking about what you're singing, or what the song is saying? This is possible when it comes to singing any kind of song - chorus, praise song, whatever you want to sing. If you don't think about what you're singing, how will it minister to you; how can it communicate the truth to you? I find myself sometimes thinking of how I sound, or whether the person in the next row is on or off key, or how I can harmonize with someone who's singing near me. Oh, but am I worshiping? No, my mind is somewhere other than on the one to whom I'm supposed to be singing. Let's stop fooling ourselves, and start thinking about what we're doing, and about whom we're worshipping.

Heartless worship! If there is no heart in what we are doing, there's no worship. In this situation, you may or may not be thinking about what you're singing, but there's no real emotion, or let us say "heart" in the worship or singing. Now, of course, singing is only a part of the worship experience, but whatever we consider as worship, the same frame of mind and spirit must be present. This is also true when we're praying, listening to the sermon . . . and *especially* during communion time. It should be obvious that God doesn't care for mindless singing, praying, listening or meditating, but "heartless" worship or singing must be even more disgusting to God.

What do I mean by heartless? Let's ask what is "heartfelt" worship. Man's worship that's truly dedicated and in tune with God will begin deep in the heart. It is important that each worshipper truly have an emotional, as well as a mental, relationship with God. God made our emotion of love; do you think He created it merely for brotherly love and not for Godly love towards Him? Can we approach Him and be void of emotion? I think not. If we have no emotional connection with God and His Son, maybe we have no connection at all. Maybe we too have lost that first love.

Christ's view of worship! "But an hour is coming, and now is, when the true worshipers will worship the Father in spirit and truth; for such people the Father seeks to be His worshipers. God is Spirit, and those who worship Him must worship in spirit and truth." (John 4:23, 24) *In Spirit and truth* is what Jesus declared. Wow, He seeks those who worship Him. What a wonderful thing to know. We cannot fool God. We may fool others around us, but God is looking into our hearts, seeking true worshipers. No longer is the focus on the place, but the Who. And this is still the same today. No matter who you are, where you are, or whom you are with, Jesus wants the experience to be "worship in Spirit and truth". It's not the style of worship, but the heart of worship, that counts.

What does it mean, spirit and truth? Who or what is the "spirit" in this context? God wants us to be truthful about our worship towards Him.

The next step is to understand the meaning of "in spirit." First look at that with which it is contrasted. It's in contrast to The Law and Jewish worship. It's usually contrasted from outward "works" to inward devotion, that is, when a person focuses on worshiping from the heart rather than depending on outside activities of worship. God never wanted His people to make sacrifices void of the heart, but it's easy to do some activity and feel okay about it. Malachi records how, even under the old Law, God preferred worship from the heart more than sacrifice. The same problem with some worship exists today; we can offer up songs of praise, without truly praising. We can offer up offerings or gifts that are not truly from the heart and spirit. When each believer worships from his spirit or inner man in truth, he's truly worshiping God. We may fool our-selves, and even others, into thinking that we're worshiping, but if we're honest, we're just going through the motions. In many of our times of worship, both corporate and private, we fail to worship truthfully and with a genuine spirit. Once we find this out, then how do we live it? In Psalms 85:11, one can see both aspects. "Teach me Your way, O Lord; I will walk in your truth." (Psalms 86:11) This is worshiping Him in truth. If you are not walking with Him, how can you fully worship Him? "Unite my heart to fear your name. I will praise you, O Lord my God, with all my heart." This is worshiping Him in spirit, in your spirit. This is unnatural for those who are not in the Spirit, for we need His Spirit uniting with ours to help us in our worship. We need to be dependent upon Him in all things, even in worship. It is an intimate relationship, requiring dedication of all we are.

Worship American Style

What is American style, or is there one? Does the American church "have a market" on style of worship? If you travel, you'll realize that no one church has a corner on worship. We cannot, nor should we, make an issue that we alone have the right way. This can be a problem even between denominations.

I've been going back and forth to Europe since 1975, even working there full-time from 1994-2000. I remember how intense and joyful worship services were in '75, '79, and in the early '80s when I visited then-Communist countries. During that time, I saw worship services last two to three hours. They then would have two or three preachers - not just because there were visitors, it was their way of doing things. Now, over ten years after the fall of communism, worship is different than it was. When I first went to Europe, I thought their worship was special and excitingly different; today, except for the language, you'd think you were in an American-style church. You know, a few songs, one sermon, and let's go home. Why did this happen? Well, it was because of the influence and generally the support of western, and especially American, money.

> **Therefore, I believe it's a crime for any missionary to go into another culture and try to change their way of worship, or look down on how they worship.**

Therefore, I believe it's a crime for any missionary to go into another culture and try to change their way of worship, or look down on how they worship. Again, if worship is from the heart, then in God's eye, it's valid and true. The important thing to remember is that the style of music used in worship cannot be invalid in and of itself, as long as it is from the heart and is held sacred by the worshipper.

Division and Worship

What causes problems in worship? This should not even be a question, but sadly it is. If we can find the reason why, maybe we can find a way to help alleviate the problem. We alluded to these problems in an above introduction, but how do they cause division?

Selfishness is probably the biggest reason for these problems. When we major on our wants, it may be at the expense of the wants of others in the congregation. If we are all so concerned and lobbying for our way, we come into conflict with others and their selfishness. "I want my favorite kind of worship, and others want theirs" This is bound to cause conflict if we try to make it so, or complain and "go home with all our toys". In 1 Corinthians 13, we see that true worship is centered in love. Without love, anything we do is tainted, and at times, nullified.

> **Remedies: 1. Remember who did the sacrifice; so don't be selfish with your wants. 2. Do unto others, as you would have them do unto you. 3. Be willing to give up some of your personal wants for the sake of the body.**

Wrong or misled expectations! What do we expect when we go to church? Should we expect anything? In many cases, people expect to be entertained, as we've already said. Now, if asked, they would say, "No, not me," but when the service is not entertaining, they complain. Or, they may expect a certain style, and when their preferred style isn't met, there's disappointment or complaining. This should not be. We should expect to give our best in everything we do. When we sing, pray, give, preach, or teach, it should be our best; that is what God expects, and so should each of us. But, when we expect others to meet all our wishes and wants, we may be asking too much. If we are complaining about others, are we doing any better? Are we even doing anything at all? It seems that those who complain the most are those who have a lot of time on their hands, because they're expecting everyone else to be perfect.

> Remedies: 1 Don't expect of anyone else what you are not willing to do. 2. Don't expect others, including self, to minister outside areas of giftedness. 3. Don't expect to be entertained or catered to, but come expecting to worship and give of self.

Thoughtless experience. How many times have I caught myself thinking of something or someone else and not truly worshiping in the moment? I used to say when leading singing, "I want everyone singing," but then I thought about it and changed my encouragement to, "I would like everyone thinking about what they are singing, and then singing from the heart as well as the mind." What would your spouse or friend think if you were talking with him/her and your mind or thoughts were someplace else? He/she would think that that's rude. Well, God is no different. We're being rude to the Creator, if, when we worship, our mind or heart is not thinking about Him. Division occurs when we aren't thinking about the One who deserves it.

Unconverted heart. This may be at the root of a lot of the problems, but I hasten to say, even converted souls may produce these problems. Those with unconverted hearts within the church are bound to be selfish, divisive, and controlling. If undetected, true worshippers will be hard to find, for in division, worship is neutralized, and even the converted Christian is tainted and led astray.

In all this, we can see how churches may hinder growth, both individually and corporately. True, genuine, unselfish worship will produce individual growth as well as numerical growth. People will sense this growth, and want to be a part of it.

What can be done to prevent division from starting? All across America, worship has become a source of division. For example, one church was growing, being led by an innovative young minister. This was an established church, with many worship traditions. These traditions (one primary style) had guided this church from the beginning. But, as this minister moved the church forward, in his heart he hoped to make it grow even more. He understood that many progressive churches were growing, by changing from traditional worship styles (hymns) to more contemporary choruses, so he set out to find the best musicians and worship leaders, to take worship to "the next level". Once he and his worship team were assembled, he planned to implement his strategy. At this point, the congregation had two services, and his intent was that they be identical. He had announced that change was going to occur, and then the day came. The two ladies, who'd been playing piano and organ for years, were replaced in one week with a praise band. This sent "shock waves" through those who were used to the old way, but the attitude of the leaders, when complaints came, was to say nicely, "Like it or leave." So, a lot of old faithful ones left. The conflict was resolved later by offering a traditional service first, then the contemporary in the later service, but many people had already left. The conflict also resulted in the minister's leaving.

As we've already seen, no style is wrong in and of itself, but it is obvious (or should be), that you need to proceed slowly and *communicate, communicate, communicate!* Communication is not merely telling someone you're going to do something or change something, but rather it's obtaining feedback and coming to a consensus, when possible, while moving towards change.

> **Suggestions when changing: 1. Do not change just to be changing or because a few people want it their way. 2. Take it slowly and include those who have been involved in the old way. 3. Blend styles together by using both hymns and choruses, both are acceptable to God. 4. If not, then have times or different services that use both. 5. In everything show love, and, by all means, this should never be a source of division. 6. Teach that all styles of music are good. Try using the hymns in different styles.**

What can be done to heal the church? Not everything that's done in church will be supported and agreed upon by everyone. Whenever you have people (especially carnal-minded people) in the church, you'll have strong opinions and disagreements. But a strong leadership that's in tune and focused on its mission will more likely help in diffusing the situation. Some people will not like anything that goes on in the church, and you cannot please everyone. So, do you always cower down to them and give up what you're being led to do? No, especially if your plan is Biblical and the congregation is following the commands and directions of the Bible; but leadership may not be communicating or fulfilling its part. If there are those who complain - or even stop coming, it's up to the shepherds/leaders to go to them and see what the problem is. Many times, if you let people share their frustrations, you usually find out that there was some miscommunication or lack of communication and the problem can be dealt with. The worst thing to do is to ignore the problem and hope it will go away. Usually, those who are disgruntled will bring others down with them. Another thing to remember is that when a person has a legitimate suggestion or complaint, listen. If the problem has been the fault of the leadership, admit it, ask for forgiveness, and change. For example, if there's no follow-up or calling on those who have problems, the leadership should apologize and ask for forgiveness for neglect of duties. The need is for compassion and communication.

Preventing division in the new church. I know it must strike at God's heart that some-thing that is to be the most wonderful and unifying experience turns out to be divisive and destructive.

It's important to remember that worship is relative to the goals of the church. That is, if your community is primarily Southern whites who like country music, hymns will probably minister to them better than upbeat choruses and pop-style music. Now remember, either style is acceptable as long as the worship is from the heart, so it is important to educate and teach these principles to those who are involved. In a new congregation, you can pick any style and go with it, but if it's an established church, you have to be sensitive to all who are involved. If you're going to make a change, you must communicate the reason why. The only reason there's a need for a change, I would think, would be to reach out to the lost in your surrounding community. Still, there must be consensus and vision to make it happen. If you have to have two different types of music or a blended service, you may stave off any problems. It's when one side wants its way at the expense of the other that problems will arise.

WORSHIP AND GROWTH!

It is obvious that worship is a major factor in the growth of any church. Worship is a major reason at the forefront of any growth or decline in the Church. Often, it's in worship that gives people a "first glimpse" of the church as a whole, and upon which they make a decision of whether or not they're interested in coming back. This is a major factor for Christians who are looking for a new church home.

Most people today are looking for entertainment. Quality is important, because you're representing God, and we should give Him our best in anything we do, but I'm afraid it's not quality that drives the church in many cases, but variety. We are a generation of "quick, fast" entertainment. We are a people of stimulation, and if we don't get it here, we'll go somewhere else to find it. Sadly, there is some truth to the complaint that some congregational worship is boring, and lacking in Spirit. If a congregation has a heartless and/or mindless worship, perhaps even God doesn't want to be there! The solution is not one or the other, but both. God wants quality *and* genuineness in our worship, and when both are present, they'll aid in the growth of the congregation as well as of each individual. It's important that one see that worship is not the only key to growth. If one thinks this, his/her growth will be shallow and short-lived. There will also be a great potential for turnover as well. If good preaching, warm personal friendliness, and a good youth program don't accompany the worship, the church still won't grow as it could and should. The worship service is important and will attract people to your church, but if there is no substance or love, the growth will not be sustained. People are seeking quality in sound and presentation, and although important, they're seldom primary or long lasting. So, don't make the mistake of thinking that worship is the cure-all, but it is important in the growth and health of the congregation, as long as it does not become the primary focus.

Plan vs. Spirit! A possible problem that may arise in some churches that are trying to develop the best and most professional service, is that *the plan leaves out the Spirit*. We can organize and orchestrate each second to the point that there's no room for the Spirit's participation. I've seen it both ways. Some services go on for hours without any sense of organization or plan, everyone sharing and singing at will. Others have every second planned out, thus leaving out any opportunity for a Spirit-led service. I think both approaches have their pluses, but also their negatives. The first approach can produce chaos, shallowness, and a possible breeding ground for false doctrine. Paul did say everything done in the church must be done in order and love, but not to the constraint of some congregations. In the second style, there is no room for sharing, or for the Spirit to bring something to the service that was not planned by the worship leaders. One reason for this is that we've become so time-conscious, we don't want to risk going over the traditional time allotted us in the pulpit, so we sacrifice opportunity for any outside "interference" from the Spirit! Now, some would say the Spirit is involved in the planning, so the Spirit is involved. Some ministers preach this way, reading from their notes they have previously prepared, and never stray from the text. Still others prepare nothing, saying they depend on the Spirit to give them what they're to say. When I preach, I'll prepare and ask for the Spirit to guide in that process, but I don't read from a manuscript. Almost every time I've preached, I'm amazed how the Spirit will give me ideas and illustrations I had never thought of before, but that complement what I had prepared earlier.

o   Furthermore, we need to be professional, so if a person isn't polished, he shouldn't share. This does happen, and I think sometimes God looks down and says, "You're missing it." There must be a balance, but if we lose the participation of the Spirit, we might miss something He's trying to say and do in us and/or for us.

One solution is to have a planned time for sharing, either at a night service or growth group time, if not possible on Sunday morning. The only legitimate fear is that someone may take control and abuse the sharing time. The responsibility of the leaders, of course, is to "pull in the reins" if it gets out of hand. There's nothing wrong with having guidelines for worship service, as long as they don't get in the way of the Spirit showing up. Look at I Corinthians 12 to 14, and you can see the problems their congregation had. Paul took time to both admonish and encourage them to be orderly and have a purposeful worship.

Growth also occurs in worship when prospects experience friendliness when they come to the times of meeting. It's sometimes seen as a "courtship" phase. It's important to realize that you can have *everything right* with respect to your worship, but if there is no love or outreach to those who come, the whole event becomes merely a performance instead of a worship experience, and most people won't return.

Youth also have a great deal to say concerning their parents' return. If youth aren't motivated (or in some cases *captivated*) you'll have trouble keeping them interested, which may negatively impact their parent's decision about coming back. This is why it might be wise to have children's worship that's at their level of attention and interest. Most youth (especially the younger ones) have an attention threshold that's shorter than most adults. A 10-minute "sermonette" will do more than a 30-minute one. The important factor is, is it at their intellectual level? If they can't understand what's being said, they'll "tune out" and get bored, and that's the death knell! Bore the children, and they'll influence the parents (not to return), who want their children cared for. God and His love *must* be communicated to the children on a level they can under-stand and experience, for if you lose them at these stages of life, you run the risk of losing them forever! Some, however, have the attitude that "they need to be in adult services so they can be disciplined to sit and behave." NO! The important thing is to learn how to obey and love the Lord, and the adult service is most likely not the best place for this to happen. If your children's worship is done right, all the elements of the adult service can be duplicated on children's level of understanding. You have prayer, communion, songs, devotionals, and discipline to sit still, but in a style and simplicity they can grasp. If this is done well, growth will happen at all levels.

The type of music used often affects emotions. Style and type will make an impact on one's decision to return or to stay, and thereby, what type of people you'll attract and keep. It's common knowledge that you will usually attract a certain kind of people based upon the style of music and service you offer. If you're trying to attract Latinos or blacks, expecting them to listen to slow, non-emotional hymns will simply frustrate and bore them. (To be truthful, it would me, too!) So if you wonder why you aren't growing in a multi-ethnic area, or reaching out to those in your community, look at how you worship. Of course, no one church can meet all the needs, wants, and wishes of every worshiper. That's why we have so many churches with so many different styles, and you know, that is okay with God! Let me state again, it's the heart that counts with God, and if the style will help a person worship correctly, then God is pleased.

Tradition. For transfers, this is a crucial point. They "filter" what they see in the new church through what they've experienced in the past. They make their choice on what they see first, and usually that means worship. True, they also see other facets of the church life, such as the preaching, and this will sometimes override any abnormalities of worship. But for the most part, what they see and experience in worship will go a long way toward whether they stay or go. If they're really uncomfortable, or not sold on the congregation's worship, it would be good for them to keep on going, rather than disrupting your worship and church. I'm not saying that this applies only to the hymn tradition. The same is true for a person who grew up in a contemporary tradition; a hymn service would be just as foreign to him. The sad thing is that many people miss out on a lot when they give up on any style. I guess I'm weird, but I like all styles and can worship in all styles. In one style, I can contemplate and bow down, and in another, I can get excited and joyfully praise. If it's done from the heart, any style can be a worshipful experience.

HOW TO WORSHIP?

How does God want us to approach Him?

With a clean slate. "Keep back your servant from presumptuous sins, let them not rule over me, then will I be blameless and I shall be acquitted of great transgression. Let the words of my mouth and the meditation of my heart be acceptable in your sight, O lord, my rock and my Redeemer." (Psalm 19:12-14) When God is pure and holy, those who approach Him must too, be holy. But how, then, are any of us able to approach such a Holy God? There are two elements in our approach to God. The first is basic, in that none of us can come before the Father without being clean and holy. The only way anyone can be pure enough is that Christ Himself makes him or her pure. This is where each of us must start by being cleansed by the blood of Christ. This is where the slate becomes clean before God. The second element is that we must keep the slate clean. Christians can approach God because through Christ we have access, but we can close the door by our continued sin. It only takes our confession and repentance and our slate is clean again, if our confession is genuinely from the heart. God does not want us at His table if we don't want others at ours.

Bow down with humility. "Come let us worship and bow down, let us kneel before the Lord our Maker. For he is our God..."(Psalms 95:6,7 138:2) Pride is one of the biggest hindrances to our worship. We cannot approach God with a prideful heart. There is no place for our will or pride in our worship of God. True worship is done in humility. A part of worship is realizing our place in respect to the almighty God. God demands our humility; our worship demands a humble heart every time, at every moment. This type of attitude takes a partnership with the Spirit, as well as our effort and thought, to accomplish this on a continual basis.

No hard hearts! "Do not harden your hearts, as at Meribah." (Psalm 95: 8) Do not harden your hearts; be open to His admonishment, correction, warning, and encouragement. Be willing to listen to His voice. This is part of worship. One of our greatest gifts to God is our willingness to listen and respond to God's wishes and will. If we come before Him, we must come before Him with open hearts and ears. We cannot worship if we close our minds and ears during worship. It is impossible to worship with a hard heart. Openness to God will bring true worship. God knows our hearts, and that pleases God in our worship.

With fear and awe! "Therefore, since we receive a kingdom by which we may offer to God an acceptable service with reverence and awe; for God is a consuming fire". (Hebrews 12:28, 29) These ideas of fear and awe are forgotten concepts today in many churches. I have always thought that Christian fear is "awe," but as I think about it more, the two concepts are different. *Awe* is a sense of wonderment towards the God and Creator of the universe, just like a little boy taking hold of his father's gigantic hands and being lifted into the air. We must capture this "awe" in our worship and daily life. The "awe" that our Father in heaven has all in control in his big hands should produce a sense of "awe." It is like the first time one sees fireworks; you hear from the crowd sounds of "awe" with mouths wide open. So should our response to God be.

Fear (God is a consuming fire) on the other hand, is more of a respect or in true fear of His "awesomeness" - that He is not only a compassionate God, but a just and righteous one, and that if we come to worship with selfish and wrong motives, we should fear that He will not be pleased by our attitudes and worship If we continue without this awe and fear, we might lose our first love. Fear is a precursor to guilt and repentance, which is the forerunner to confession and salvation. Without all of this, no worship is valid

NUTS AND BOLTS!

The Participants. In the Old Testament, the emphasis was on the physical temple. It was where you went to find God, or at least know where He resided. That focus has changed, with the emphasis now being upon us as believers, as one of the places where God resides. We are the temples of the Holy Spirit. *We are* the place where God meets. Jesus said, when two or more gather in His name, He will be there. The place is not important. So it is not important that we go to a certain temple or a building, but that when "Holy Spirit temples" meet together, (wherever that may be) God is present. Therefore in worship, if each believer realizes he/she is a Spirit-filled temple, meeting with other Spirit-filled temples, we may have a richer and truer time of worship. Maybe even our attitudes about others would be less divisive and more spiritual.

Therefore, the first task of every worshiper is to see that he is ready to worship in Spirit and in truth. This is a personal thing that each soul must deal with. You may want to pray before you come into a church service to prepare for corporate worship. If you haven't been meditating and worshiping during the week, it will take a while to get into the Spirit of worship. If you have been struggling in getting the kids ready, or arguing on the trip over, then take some time in the car to say a little prayer. The main thing is that God must be the main focus, and sometimes that takes effort on our part for it to happen.

The Sanctuary   Much has been said about the importance of the worshiper and the one being worshipped, and that the place is not that important in regards to our worship. But let me say, when you have a healthy view about the buildings where you meet, and the true building in which He meets us, you can take a look at the physical place where you gather. God is a God of order and beauty. He has created, and has given us some of that creativity. He is not pleased with half-done projects or mediocre efforts. Therefore, wherever we meet, be sure the place is clean and in order. We are setting examples for others, and that is important. Whether you have a 20 million dollar edifice, or a modest one-room building, make it your best - not out of selfish pride, but in honor to God.

The types of services! You may have different emphases and styles of worship, as we have mentioned, but there are also elements of special communion and meditation - or just a sharing and praise time - or just teaching - or just fellowship with one another. In each of these events you can stress that you can be worshiping God through your actions and devotions. Do not limit your worship just to Sunday morning, either. Have other times and events of worship! As we have already stated, worship should not be confined to traditional times or methods. Most people, who worship on Sunday morning in traditional ways, may allow other types of worship in the evening, or on other days. Experiment; worship can take place in many different venues and situations. Can you think of other times where you can worship? When you ask yourself this question, you can begin to explore the possibilities for the times and locations of worship.

The flow of service. I mentioned above about being too stringent (or too loose) in your service. Whether you have every second planned or are "freewheeling" it, let the time flow and be under control of the Spirit. Boring or ill-prepared events or parts of the service have no part. These will drive people away and cause a stumbling block. In this highly technological society, leaders must do everything they can to avoid hindering a person's worship and growth.

ELEMENTS OF WORSHIP

The Song! (Psalm 95:1) I have touched a lot on our styles of songs and how important it is to sing and worship from the heart and the mind. In all aspects of worship, God wants it done in reverence, joy, sincerity, and love. A sweet song from the heart of His children does so much for the heart of God, and the heart of man. When there is true worship in song, you feel it, and identify with what is being sung. That's why it's important that you worship from the heart. If your mind is elsewhere, your singing is not to God, and is like "fingernails on a chalkboard". Your singing may have beautiful tones and harmony, but without the mind and heart, it is nothing to God. This should be our goal: to sing, pray, and worship with our whole soul and mind.

The Prayer! Everyone would probably agree that prayer plays an important part in our worship. It is where we talk to God. Prayer should not be a formality, or a mere habit; it is the place where we have the time to praise Him and talk with Him. Now, of course, we are to pray without ceasing, but this is corporate prayer, and God has some requirements. Do not pray publicly to show off. God can see our hearts, and know if we're trying to make a show of our praying. If this is your motive, it is better to refuse to pray publicly, or repent. Do not pray with mindless, vain repetitions. I have heard an elder week after week say the same prayers. This is not worship; it is vain, because it does not come from the heart, but from the memory, so you won't make a mistake. It isn't true worship. Prayer is the place where we call God and petition Him to be a part of our meeting. Prayer must be reverent, thoughtful, and from the heart - each time you pray.

The Communion! What to do! What not to do! Communion is a central aspect with Christ. He made this evident with the Last Supper. In some churches, communion is the center or focus of the service. Now, we are not going to get into a lengthy discussion on how often you have communion, but it is important to look at the example of the first church. It seems in Acts 2 that each Sunday, they gathered together to partake of the Lord's Supper. I think this is a good example to follow. Some churches that have communion once a month or quarter state that they do not want to wear out the event by having it every Sunday. Then why do we pray, preach, sing, and take up offering every Sunday? Can't we wear these other things out, too? This is a copout. The central theme of Christ is His resurrection and His work on the cross. The partaking of the Lord's Supper reminds us of what He did for us on the cross and our need for communion with Him. This is the place where we can take the time to come and meet Him. You can go through an entire church service and never sing, preach, or pray about this important act. You run the risk of allowing the most important thing for us to remember and worship Him about, being swept away. Communion can never get too used or over done, and this is that time to focus on this main work of Christ. Let us say you have communion once a quarter. It is hard to make arrangements to be sure you will be there, and what if you can't? Then you have to wait another three months. This is not fair to the people, and it is not fair to the New Testament practice, and robs both God and the worshipper of this opportunity. The tradition of the Apostles should override the traditions of today.

The Offering! (I Chronicles 16:29 and Psalms 95:8) God loves a cheerful giver from the heart, a place from which we worship. Furthermore, when we give offerings, we are paying homage to the Great Giver. We are worshiping Him by humbling ourselves to give up a portion of what He has first given us. So if we can think on these terms, we can enjoy the time of giving more joyfully and graciously.

The Fellowship! Fellowship is another important aspect in worship and assembly times. The Word tells us not to forsake the fellowship with brothers and sisters. We need each other, and we need to encourage one another, for the days are evil and difficult to live in. The Bible tells us to treat each other with respect and love while in the meetings (I Corinthians 12-14). The reasons some churches fail to grow, or keep people coming back, is that true fellowship isn't taking place in the church. When a visitor or new convert comes into the fellowship, are they welcomed, or spurned? In many churches, people go directly to their friends and bypass any new people. If you aren't a part of a group of friends, it is hard to "break in". This is sad and should not be. The congregation can have great preaching and singing, but lack fellow-ship, and people will not return. The church is about relationships. If it's hard to make friends, or the church is not friendly, people will be turned away. One weekend, I decided to go to a church nearby instead of my home church because I got up late. I walked in, took a seat, listened to the sermon, got up, stood up for awhile, and then finally left. *Not one soul* came over to me and greeted me. What a way to kill a church and run people away! Outreach must be intentional and sometimes planned, but it should be natural to reach out, and that should be the goal of some of the people in each congregation if the church is to grow.

The Purpose! What is the purpose of the service? Or maybe better, what is the *theme* of the service? What are you trying to give to the people to take with them? This is usually decided either by the preacher alone, or the preacher and the worship team or coordinator. In some cases, there is no theme or purpose, other than "having church". In others, the music is one theme, the sermon yet another. Worship works well when everything is done together. That is, the song and praise time complements the sermon theme, (or at least some do.) The more you try to narrow down the theme, the better the people can grasp the central focus and, therefore, go away with a message in heart and mind.

The Sermon! Why should you worship during a sermon time? Since God's word is being spoken, worship should be in the mind of the listener. Worship is to be in a humble or reverent state of mind. Therefore, when the word is being preached, it is another aspect of your worship towards God. Be respectful. God is now speaking to you in this part of worship time. Now, of course, I've heard and read some sermons where you wouldn't find God at all, only a social agenda. This, of course, is not what I mean by a worshipful type of sermon; in a worshipful message, the word must be respected and worshiped because it's direct from God.

The Invitation or altar call! To do or not to do, that is the question. And if you do, then how do you do it, and for what reason; that is, what is the focus or purpose of the invitation? Also, how you do it is important. Is it high pressure or low? Many churches today have done away with the invitation, which I think is a mistake. This is a time where brothers and sisters can share where they are in their struggles and growth. It is a time where we need to offer the opportunity for confession and healing. The Bible suggests that we do this. Don't be afraid of going overtime, for this is one place where true ministry can take place. The Word also says that we must make public professions of our faith in Christ, and this is a great time to allow that to happen. In some churches the old fashioned altar call is a call to come and bow before God. It can be a "showplace" for some, but having the freedom to come and bow down can be liberating for those who experience it.

When I preach, I offer two types of invitations, one to the believer, and one to the un-believer. I think on Sunday morning, most of our preaching should be for the benefit of the believers, and evangelism should be done during the week in other venues. So when I preach on Sundays, I give an invitation to the believers to respond and do what the sermon suggests, or if they aren't doing what's being preached, to repent and begin to do so. To the unbeliever I say, "If you are not a follower of Christ, the benefits preached about are not yours; if you want to know more about how to become a Christian, the invitation is for you." Both of these types of invitations are needed, and are important to the growth of the church.

THE DISC and Worship

Mels Carbonel and I were discussing the state of worship in our churches and he brought to light the relationship between the DISC behavioral model and music in Worship. Wow what a revelation. Let us consider some of these factors in relation to Growth in the church.

The first consideration is that songs have their own DISC behavioral models. Let us take a look at some examples. _Onward Christian Soldiers_ would be a D, _Rejoice in the Lord_ would be an I song, _Heavenly Father we appreciate You_ a S song. And _Faith of our Fathers_ would be a C song. These of course are some older songs, so therefore take these examples and principles and look at some of the songs you like and sing, and label them with the DISC. A D song will have a driving visionary, goal-oriented theme to it. That is let us get up and get going. An I song will be one that is fun, upbeat, praise and rejoicing type. A S song will be one that is warm, loving and encouraging. And a C song will be one that is theological, contemplative, and deep.

The Song leader, or those who decide on the song list can make a big difference in how the service is presented. In some churches the minister suggest the themes and either lets the song leader pick them, or picks them himself. The interesting thing is that it is easy for a song leader to allow his/her personality style to affect his/her choice of songs. The D preacher or song leader will tend to like, and lean toward picking the driving visionary, goal-oriented songs. The I, as well, will usually pick what is conducive to his personality. He will get board at the C and S songs because they're not as fun. The true S will be pushed to the edge with a steady diet of D songs, and The *C* will want to challenge the people to think and therefore will get bored with a steady diet of *I* songs. It is important to note that most people are at least a combination of two types, and often three. I myself like all types, but those that push my buttons will be those that follow my *DCI* behavioral mix.

Implications in Worship. How does being aware of the different song personality types affect our worship? OR I should ask, how should it affect the way we worship? Most song leaders think about what they want to say when they pick songs, but not how they want to affect the total person that is in the audience. Now you know what I think about who is the focus in our worship, but there is an element of need for those who are participating or listening. Everyone has a filter they look through and that affects the way they worship and feel about their experience while doing it. It is not a perfect world, but we do need to be aware of how people are moved by what they hear and see. When we take into consideration each person's behavioral types when we craft our worship service, then we will reach out to more in this important experience.

The songs and growth. The songs and sermons that are picked will have a tendency to draw certain people to your church, and vice versa can run others away. As I noted before, let me STRONGLY say, that no one style is better than another, if done from the heart. That being said, the type and style of songs do affect those who come and stay, and therefore will affect your growth. A person who is a *CS* type will eventually get bored and frustrated if all you have is *I* praise songs. I have heard many people say they have left because of this one thing. If you have a constant use of one style at the expense of others, then you will not draw the other behavioral types to your church. What I am saying is this is people, it may not be right, but it is a fact of human nature. This is why you have different denominations. The church service may be the first and last place they come. If they do not like the worship then they will not stay long enough to be converted or discipled. To reach out to all kinds of people, then have a mixture of all these types. Each one can help the church grow spiritually as well. Each of us need to be challenged by *D* songs, excited by *I* songs, made compassionate with *S* songs, and influenced to deeply think with *C* songs. Not only do you attract more people, but you also meet more of their needs.

THE FUTURE

The future is bright. Why? The future is bright because God is involved. When God and His Spirit are involved with committed disciples, great joy and celebration will ensue. The future is as bright as we allow it to be, as we come to God with open, genuine hearts. Be open; be free to let God move you into relationship with Him and others. Inhibitions and prejudice can hinder any congregation from growing and worshiping in God. Division and strife will also destroy true worship. But, where there is genuine, excited, thoughtful worship, the church will be more likely to grow. Remember, worship begins at home in your heart, and then spreads to others, when hearts unite. Both are important to the health of the individual and to the health of the congregation as a whole.

MINISTRY TEAMS
Chapter Thirteen

What are Ministry Teams?

"Come join the army and be an army of one." When I first heard this recent slogan of the U.S. Army, I first laughed, then thought, "That's stupid." There is no army of one. You ask any soldier if he wants to be an army of one, and you will also get the same reaction. The Army has succumbed to the narcissistic society of today, at least in its advertising. But in practical situations where the job has to get done, and lives are at stake, Rambo isn't around; there's a need for a team, not one. There's no such thing as a team of one; two, maybe, but never one.

The same applies in the church. But, in many of our churches, there are "armies of one". Who is this "army"? In many cases, it is the minister or pastor. Some of them <u>like</u> being "Reverend Rambo"; they like the action and thrill of being the hero, the one-man show. But, this is very dangerous for both the hero and the congregation. The hero will find out he is *limited,* he is <u>not</u> all-powerful, and that it's lonely being one. He'll find he cannot be as effective as a team, nor can he accomplish as much as if he were part of a team.

> Ministry is not carried out in a vacuum, but within the confines of community.

Ministry teams are just that - teams, groups working together to accomplish a goal or task. The team's existence is based on carrying out a certain ministry. Ministry is not carried out in a vacuum, but within the confines of community. Now it is for certain that teams are made up of individuals working together. In most teams, people don't do the same things, or hold the same positions, but they all work together for a common goal, each using his/her own gifts and personalities to help the team succeed and accomplish the task.

Why have them?

<u>Togetherness and quantity can produce growth and more results</u>. The churches that usually grow, do so through motivating, equipping, and mobilizing their congregation. The best way to do this is through teams.

<u>Why are teams best</u>? The writer of Ecclesiastes 4:9, 12 gives a hint. "Two are better than one because they have a good return for their labor. ... And if one can overpower him who is alone, two can resist him, a cord of three strands is not quickly torn apart." How does this apply to teamwork today? First, there is strength. Emotional and collaborative strength is important in the success of any ministry team. When you have a team working together, it isn't as lonely "in the trenches" when things don't go the way they're planned. Each of us has ups and downs throughout life's ministry, and when more than one person is in the mix, they can encourage and build up the other team members when they're down or in trouble. If no one is stable, the group may be doomed to fail, but if the leader is mature and sensitive, he can be a great mentor and leader who will hold the group together so they can minister to each other while ministering to others. Second, there is variety - variety in gifts and in personalities. No one, of course, has all the answers or strengths to accomplish an effective ministry alone. Therefore, when individuals invest their lot in the group, the group and the individuals are richer for it. No one has all the gifts to do the entire task as effectively as a team can. In a team, weaknesses and

No one has all the gifts to do the entire task as effectively as a team can. In a team, weaknesses and strengths can be managed, and the team can work from within its strengths

strengths can be managed, and the team can work from within its strengths. Some people may disagree and say they can work better when they do not have to keep the group up and intact. This takes more effort, and they can just do it themselves and do it right the first time. Now this may be true in some cases, but even if it is, if all factors are in place and every team member is using his/her gifts as a team, no individual can <u>possibly</u> do what a team can do together.

<u>It's a Biblical model</u>. There are models of teamwork throughout the Bible: Moses and Aaron, Jesus and the twelve, the 70 by twos, and Paul with his team. Humans are intended to be communal and not islands. In evangelism, or any ministry for that matter, a team can have an advantage over individuals. Now this is _not_ to say individuals can't be effective. Remember, a team is, by definition, a group of individuals working together towards a common goal, using their strengths and gifts for its accomplishment. In some cases, the result of the event is as important as the goal. The goal can, in fact, _in and of itself,_ be to become a team. God wants each of us to work together, and that's why He uses and encourages teams in ministry. For that matter, in a way, the Godhead is a team. Now, I do not pretend to understand the complexity of God and His oneness, but there is a concept or sense of community and cooperation as a team. "Let us make man in our own image." (Genesis 1:26)

<u>It produces new leaders</u>. What do leaders do? They _lead_. How can they lead if they have no one to lead? Through working within a team, people may learn if they are truly meant to be leaders. Now, in some extreme cases, a team may be made up of rebellious individuals; in that event, the most seasoned leader may have to "shake the dust off his feet" and move on. In most situations, however, groups of people are neutral until they see how the leader is going to lead. It is more natural to mentor new leaders in the areas where they'll be leading. The old "traditional" way is: appoint or elect someone and then expect him to lead with no prior experience. This is dangerous – clearly not the best way to produce new leaders. It's important to look back at the chapters on leadership to be sure that each individual desiring a leadership role is given the opportunity to receive the training needed, in order to be the best he or she can be.

Characteristics of a team!

<u>Shared goal and purpose</u>. A group of people gathered together is not always a team. Only when they recognize each other and are willing to work toward a common goal and purpose do they become an effective team. This is no different than ministry teams in the church. If we have Lone Rangers, then the team will develop schisms and difficulty. Satan wants to cause divisions and disharmony. He doesn't have to keep people away from church, he just has to encourage division, and the church itself will be its own greatest enemy. When we go in different directions, a team has problems. It's important to keep the goals and purpose prominent.

<u>Everyone can win</u>. But, everyone can lose if the team fails to work together. It is more likely that, if the team can work together, it will have a better chance than if each individual goes it alone. The only time a team can lose and win at the same time is when some team members fail to appreciate other team members in the process, or envy and strife arise. Even

though the tasks or ministry was completed, relationships may suffer, so be careful to stress both brotherly love and working together.

Sense of community. This is one of the most important aspects, and is most often overlooked. You can accomplish a task and even work well together as a team, but still not have community. Outside the church, this may not be important, but in the church, togetherness is sometimes as important as the ministry, or getting through the material. I said "sometimes"; I did *not* say more important. I say this because it isn't *either/or*; it's *both*. As a team goes together (service and goals), they need to grow together. If their focus is only on growth (a good purpose, for the most part), shared tasks may be circumvented. If spiritual growth is the only focus, close-ness can be realized, but ministry goals may be lost or pushed aside. An evangelistic team may spend a lot of time together and end up growing close, but if their main objective is growth, and not winning souls, they've failed to achieve their main purpose.

Committee versus team.

Different mindset! A committee is about decisions and research, but teamwork is about ministering and doing. A committee doesn't always produce work, but rather decisions *about* work. Every team should do their homework and prepare the best they can, but when a church goes from a *committee concept* to a *team or ministry concept*, people approach and perform the task differently.

Different outcome is possible. The different outcome may be inertia (i.e., nothing) in a committee format, as compared to developing shared goals and gifts to get a job or ministry done in a team format.

Committee is worldly and teams are Biblical. Again, *committee* is a term and concept that is bred from the "democratic process"; this should be enough warning that it's to be avoided as we've already seen in previous chapters on leadership. Although we see the concept of teams in society, it seems that the process of team ministry fits the New Testament model better.

Ministry comes from giftedness.

God has a say. What is so special about giftedness, is that God's Spirit looks down on His church and gives gifts. It's His ability to look down and see what His church needs and whom He can use to fulfill those needs. It's when we step in and force people to assume roles where they aren't gifted that the church runs the risk of going on its own, apart from God's will or plan. It's important that each person and congregation help the flock to discover God's gifts because God knows best in our lives and His congregation.

Not popularity or other haphazard volunteerism. When we allow people to volunteer, we run the risk of assigning people where they shouldn't be. Now, some things can be led by volunteers, like ushering, putting things away after a meeting - any number of activities that may need to get done, requiring no real spiritual gift. This should be encouraged for newcomers, but not if it occupies their time, preventing their involvement in discipleship studies.

More effective, joyful, and successful. The result of ministering from giftedness is that the Spirit is giving the power; therefore, a person will be more effective, and you will see results in what you do. If it is evangelism, then you will have success in bringing people to Christ. This should be obvious, since it is the Spirit who gives the power and ability. If there is no success in what you do, you may not have that gift, or else you need some mentoring in that area. Joy is another by-product of the Spirit's partnership. If you truly have a gift, you'll find that you have joy when you think about or do something in that area. Now joy can be suppressed when you put down the importance of your gift, or there's no place for you to use your gift, or you've quenched your gift by refusing to use it.

How are Teams filled or staffed?

There should be no volunteers in ministry teams without apprenticeship and gift analysis. After discipleship, new disciples can explore via gifts test, confirmation of others, and trial participation with the team. Only the gifted people in specific areas should be on any given ministry team. If a person has a desire to be on a certain team, it's wise to give them a chance to explore the possibility, but first, have them take the gifts questionnaire. If their desire doesn't agree with the questionnaire, caution them that they may sit in on the team, for evaluation purposes, to see if they truly have both the gift and desire for that ministry. This is not to be a control issue or a dictatorship - merely an attempt to place people where they'll be the most fulfilled and enjoy success in their giftedness and ministry.

> Secondly, don't assume that just because a person is an admitted believer he is mature and has been discipled

Transfers also must go through the process of discipleship discovery and/or interview. A person who's transferring in may be mature, gifted, and ready to serve, but be cautioned you may not know who they truly are, until someone has spent time discipling them. They too, like all the others in the congregation, need to go through the process of discipleship. There are two reasons for this expectation. First, you may get a person who's been a problem elsewhere and will now bring the problem to you as well. The church doesn't need that. Secondly, don't assume that just because a person is an admitted believer he is mature and has been discipled. So, it is the responsibility of the leadership to see to it that all members go through this process for the benefit of both the individual and the congregation at large. Anyone who refuses should not be in any leadership role whatsoever.

Through meeting or interview by team leaders or elder. Once team leaders are in place, they should do the interviewing.

Those who are chosen to lead should come from the gifted team members. This should not be a person appointed from outside who lacks the gift to be in that team. Team leaders can be called deacons, deaconesses, or team leaders; the term "deacon", however, is not an "office" _per se_, but a leader in ministries. No ministries - no deacons; but have as many deacons as ministries. If a team leader cannot qualify as a deacon, should he/she be the leader of the team? He can be on the team, but not serve as its leader. In Acts, we see that those chosen as deacons or servants were already known for whom they were and what their gifts were. This too should be the description of every team leader and team.

How are teams deployed?

Find gifts, then deploy. Provide opportunities and encouragement for members to do something with their gift. I've seen some churches that gave members gifts evaluation, but put no strategy in place to find areas where people might use their gifts. It may have been better never to have learned what their gifts are, than to discover their gifts and not have help or opportunity in using them.

Through apprenticeship. Most of us need to be mentored in our area of giftedness. One gifted, mature saint helping and showing a new saint what his/her ministry is all about, offers the best means of helping people use their gifts. We do this in most other endeavors and professions; it should be done in the church also.

Through experiment. Sometimes, individuals have to experiment and be evaluated. The gifts questionnaire is only a tool to verify or explore in what area a person might be gifted. The results are often very general; usually accurate, but general. They are only good when matched to experience in the body. A person who has been a Christian for only a few months may not have any frame of reference to know what his or her gift may be. God may not even have given them gifts at the beginning. Each person has the gift of the Spirit, but may not be mature enough to have received a Spiritual gift yet. A gifts test is best used when others can look back and confirm, "Yes, I have seen that in you."

Through placement. If one's profile fits in an existing ministry, place them there. Once a gift is identified, find a place in an existing ministry where that gift may be used. It's important, though, to stress that the person is to be in a team and under a mentor at first. If the team is just starting, team members should get to know one another, and their personalities, as they begin to use their gifts in their ministry.

Through creating new opportunities. If no ministry fits their profile, wait, or put others with like-giftedness together, and help them to develop a ministry. If they can individually use their gift, have a system in place to plug them in. If a team needs to be put together, have these new people pray for others to be revealed to help in the ministry. No ministry should be begun unless there are enough gifted people to successfully run it. If there aren't enough to start or staff a team, wait until there are enough to do it. Pray for others to be revealed and gifted.

Accountability?

Each ministry is accountable to the eldership as a whole! Generally, most ministries are led and filled by people who are gifted in those areas. They are led by what the Bible refers to as *deacons*. The important factor is that, when you have a functioning eldership, all who serve in ministry are accountable to the elders. That doesn't mean *controlled* or *dictated to* by them, but accountable to them. Neither the elders nor staff should be micromanagers of every ministry, but rather, responsible to ensure that two things happen. First, that the ministry is being carried out as it should be, and second, that no divisions or problems develop that will harm the group or congregation as a whole. When either of these situations becomes an issue, the elders must step in and deal with the problem. This is why reports or accountability meetings are needed periodically with the elder overseer.

Each ministry or team should have an elder contact, not necessarily a participant. Because no elder has all the gifts, none of them should be expected to be on every ministry team. In some churches, they may not be on any of the ministry teams because they are already on the shepherding/oversight team, that is, the elder ministry team. Accountability is important and, therefore, a contact/liaison person should be assigned. (He is not to be seen as a "big brother", but responsibility is required from both sides.)

Team leaders or deacons should contact elders if any problems arise that may cause a spiritual problem. It's better for team leaders to be proactive when problems arise, and contact their assigned elder with any potential problems or shepherding needs. Now, shepherding should go on within the team as a natural process, but there may be times when the elder should be contacted, should a need or a problem occur within and/or between the members of any team. This will help the team stay together and be in harmony. Making contact with those in authority would also stave off future problems. Also, the need exists to ensure that each ministry team is accomplishing its goals and mission statement. If not, changes in the ministry team leadership may be required.

Elders should step in only if there is a problem. It is an important factor that the elder contact is not hovering over the team, nor controlling the team and its leaders. If the elder is not gifted for this ministry, or a team member, it's best that he not interfere in the functions of a ministry. If there is a problem, it then becomes the duty of the elder or oversight team to take control of the problem before it becomes any bigger or causes damage.

Benefits of ministering from giftedness!

Have a vision! When a person has a gift, there are certain things that come with that gift. In some cases, people have an ability of *visioning* in their giftedness. They can see what needs to happen and how their gift can be utilized in their ministry. Not everyone with a gift has this vision ability; it usually comes with being a leader, but again, this is a result of the Spirit's influence in the believer's life.

Have insight. One of the main things that illustrate the Spirit's involvement is the insight that is given when one has a certain gift. If no insight or ability is present, you may not have the gift, or else the gift is latent, or unused. The insight is what makes the gift important in one's ministry. But, it requires us taking time to listen and be in prayer to receive the insight from the Spirit.

Power to stay committed and on track. With giftedness comes the power of the Spirit to help in implementing and using the gift He has given. If there is no supernatural power, what is the difference between the world's talent and a spiritual gift? So we can depend on the power and wisdom of the Spirit to use our gifts, and if we do not, we will not be successful in what we do for the Lord.

Will be in your comfort zone. When you aren't gifted in a certain area, for the most part, you feel uncomfortable in doing things outside your giftedness. You will be uncomfortable doing some things that are outside your "comfort zone". When this is the case, a person is apt to be more concerned about being uncomfortable, than ministering in the given task or ministry.

Less likely to burnout or cop-out. Most people burnout because they are not gifted and, therefore, are not successful, nor excited about what they are doing. If a person lacks a certain gift and still participates, he/she will have the tendency to quit or burnout after a time. But if it is your gift, you'll more likely be successful and content about what you're doing, assuming there are no outside factors hindering the joy and success.

Minimize discord and problems. The most important place is in a person's own soul. When you are ministering from your giftedness, you don't have the struggle within. You feel a peace about what is happening. You'll have fewer problems because you're more fulfilled in your service. Being placed with your giftedness and desire will also lessen problems between others with whom you're involved in ministry, and others to whom you minister, because if everyone is in his/her place, fewer problems will arise because of the harmony and success of each other's ministries.

Joy! If you have any gift, one of the added benefits should be joy in your participation in that ministry. If you have no joy, maybe you have quenched or not allowed your gifts to be used. But if you're doing something with your giftedness, there will be joy when we allow God to use us.

Will be more successful. It seems to go without saying that, if all of the above benefits are present, it isn't hard to see that each of us will be more effective, and failures will be minimized when each one uses his gift. Furthermore, if everyone is using their gift, then you have erased (or reversed) the "80/20" principle in the church. Just getting everyone involved inherently brings more people (and their gifts) to the table. When this happens, just by mere numbers serving with their gift, the church will grow, and holy success will happen in the partnership between you and the Spirit.

Motivated. Another internal outcome of the Spirit's involvement is that a person will be motivated to serve in that giftedness. If a person is not motivated, then he has either quenched the Spirit for some reason, or he simply doesn't have the gift. The problem comes when churches encourage "volunteerism", which may cause good-hearted people who want to serve, to volunteer in areas that are outside their area of giftedness.

Team Decision Making

Give everyone a chance to share, and honor their opinions. When you work as a team, utilize the team by hearing from everyone if they have something to say. Now the leader must, at some point, filter opinions and help the team arrive at some decisions. No one has all the information or ideas, and there just might be some jewel that members, or even the leader, might not bring to the table. When everyone has a chance to at least make some contribution, they will have more of an ownership and, therefore, may become a better team member in the process. Encourage ideas and dreaming, and incorporate as many ideas as possible. Bring in experts to help in the decision if needed.

Lay down the ground rules of absolutes, or "non-negotiable"; compromise has its limits. There are times in any group, when rules need to be developed and enforced to ensure the team functions and accomplishes its purpose. One ground rule might be that everyone carries through with his or her commitment. Another might be simply being there on time, or finishing what's started. These ground rules can also be known as expectations for the group. When you fail to state or develop these ground rules, the group or team can wander aimlessly, accomplishing no worthwhile results. There can be danger in too much compromise. If a person is so "out there" and obstinate about his/her view that he/she will jeopardize the team, compromise is not an option.

Write down ideas. Encourage each person to write down ideas he may have. Also, when together, have someone take notes or record the session so you can have a record of what is said. Memory is fleeting, and you can lose some crucial inspiration that might just take the ministry team to the next level. If the Spirit is working, His direction needs to be written down.

Table it before you destroy it. If, at anytime, the team is in disagreement or at an impasse, it is better to come back to the issue when everyone can think more and pray about it. The worst thing is to end the discussion in argument or strife. If you've been in a typical board meeting, you've probably experienced it. Remember, don't be the problem, be the solution!

Be honest and open with each other, and hold each one accountable in love and with respect. Unfortunately, people sometimes approach a meeting or decision withholding some key information, or having a hidden agenda. Remember, you're to be Christ-like in all you do, especially in the church.

Know each other's strengths and expertise and build upon them. When you know the personalities of each member of the team, you will know how to deal with each other with tenderness and understanding, as well as have the ability to use each person's personality to help the team-work together. If you know peoples' strengths, you can encourage them to use them, and if you know their weaknesses, you can either help each person become stronger, (not expect them to work out of their weakness), and build upon others to take up the slack in any area. This is why it's important that everyone completes a personality questionnaire to identify his or her strengths and weaknesses.

Do not get defensive or manipulative - even about your pet ideas. It's hard not to get defensive when you bring something to the table that you're in favor of, and it gets attacked. In most cases, it isn't you that is being attacked; maybe what was proposed simply wasn't made clear, or perhaps others see something you don't see. If it's the will of God, and it follows the commands of the Biblical mandates, continue to champion it; however, if you get defensive and impatient, it may derail the possibility of its implementation.

Consensus vs. voting. Voting has a 100% chance of division; consensus (without giving up Biblical principles and mandates) is the best way to go forward, assuming all participants agree that fulfillment of Bible methods and mandates are primary in any decision. Opinions are to be debated and worked on in love and compromise.

Don't be a problem person. If it seems you're always at odds, perhaps you'd better look at your own motives and attitudes. If the "problem person" is someone else, at some point he need to be approached, and not allowed to disrupt and impede progress. Some people will be problems, and disagree about everything. If you encounter someone like this, it's best he not be allowed in leadership; if he is already a leader, he needs to be asked to step aside until he can work with others.

Why conflict arises

Selfish or hidden agendas. This is probably the most damaging, and most unfortunate, of the reasons for conflict. It's also the most difficult to resolve. When a person is selfish, there is a character problem, or a sin problem, or both. To resolve this, there must be some type of repentance on the part of the offending party. In some cases, people may not even realize they're being selfish until someone else draws their attention to it. When this happens, there can be some healing and resolution of the matter. To truly be able to go forward, those with hidden agendas must be open and willing to admit to this type of agenda or dishonesty.

Misunderstanding of the goals and vision. This problem can usually be handled by good, honest communication. If each person is truly open and wanting to go forward and resolve conflict, explaining the true goals will only help in resolution. It's when a person disagrees with the goals that they will continue to have conflict. If both are open, each of the parties can modify their approach to where there is congruence.

Not enough information to make it. There may simply be insufficient information to make a wise decision in some people's minds. When the lack of information is satisfied and no other problem is evident, then all can be resolved.

Personality conflicts between members. This is a hard one to handle unless people understand others' personalities and are willing to accept them as they are to a point. It's true that in each of us, parts of our personalities grind on others with different personalities. These hard points are where mature adults can face them and try to change themselves, with the help of God and other loving friends. Still, just understanding why a person acts the way he does, will help us in resolving conflict. In some cases, persons will not budge or become aware of their problems and change. In other cases, we must let people be people and work with them, but not to the point where the team or its tasks are destroyed. I've played on numerous teams in my life, and those who will not cooperate or get along will either destroy the team or have to be removed. This is a hard decision, but sometimes it must be done.

Not qualified to be in the position. Some people are just not gifted or qualified to be where they are, and this will naturally cause a conflict. It will cause a conflict both within the person and within the relationships around him. There are many reasons why conflict will arise in this scenario. One is that the person is not happy in what he's doing, and that breeds conflict. Also, he may not be good at what he's doing, and that will naturally cause a conflict with others working with him, either on a team or ministry. To be not gifted is to be not qualified.

Different values about the reason for existence of the group. This is a very basic conflict. If this type of conflict exists, there may be no progress. The group must agree on its purpose before it can become effective, or accomplish any of its goals. There's nothing wrong in identifying this reason or purpose, for this determines our participation in groups or ministries. But, conflict will continue if both parties stay together and fight over the values and purpose of the group. Unfortunate or not, this is often how new ministries got started.

Competitive edge. I'm a very competitive person, and when I'm with non-competitive people, this will cause conflict. The only way it will cause conflict with another competitive person is when you have to win all the time and enjoy defeating the other. Others who are not competitive will more likely get frustrated and give up or challenge you. It's better to keep the competitive edge under control, or you may harm your witness with others and cause conflict.

Dealing with Hindrances

Do not have any hidden agendas. Each person must be honest with himself, and not be deceitful in his dealings with self and others. If each of us can start here, conflict will be eliminated. Be honest with self and others about why you're involved. If it's only to get yourself ahead or "do your own thing", evaluate your participation.

Allow no one to be the chairman or top dog. Although a leader is necessary, in order to help facilitate, he should not be a dictator. I've often seen people appointed chairman, and it ruined them. Power sometimes corrupts when we fail to keep the person who's in control in check. But, if we're led and empowered by God and His Spirit, He alone is in the power position.

Everyone must know, agree with, and stick to the ground rules. If you agree to do something or be on a ministry team, then you should be willing to follow the direction and goals. Now sometimes, ground rules or directions aren't Biblically based, or change is needed when it seems there's no success or direction, but it all should be done with love. However, some people are just antagonistic or controlling and don't want to cooperate, and this will only exacerbate the problem, and not solve it.

Everyone must agree that the Bible is final and should not be circumvented to get across an agenda or idea. If this can be agreed upon, a team or ministry can have a basis to work from - a higher authority and rule that will guide, and avoid conflict.

Some things are not absolute, and shouldn't cause division. On the other side, there are times when things are relative, and should be open to debate. If you have the previous point as the foundation, this point may easily be heeded and followed. Those things that are matters of opinion may be right for a certain situation, yet at another time not be crucial at all. Here, a good, wise leader can see the difference and not allow division over things that do not matter.

No one should manipulate the process or try to control. If the heart is in the right place, the motives are genuine, and there are no hidden agendas, no one should be manipulative or try to control. Now sometimes, natural born or gifted leaders may tend to take control, because that's their personality, or nature. These individuals need to be patient and keep their tendencies in check, especially if they tend to do them in a negative way. There's a thin line between a leader who leads, and a "control freak". On the other end of the spectrum, those who don't want to be controlled may rebel, and try to take control, or sabotage the situation. Both are wrong and divisive.

Tempers and tongues should be controlled at all times. A loose and mindless tongue can do great damage, and I think we've all been there at one time or another. I know I've said things when "my mind was not in gear", with disastrous results, and I wish I could've taken it back. The tongue, as James says, is like a dagger that kills. Second is the temper. Men and women have destroyed a lot of good things, ministries, or relationships with loose tempers. People don't want to be around a person who cannot control his/her temper. A person who habitually does any of these things needs discipline and/or censure until he/she is willing to change. At the very least, he shouldn't be allowed to occupy a leadership position until these issues are resolved.

Team Conflict Management

Identifying conflict. Most all of us have experienced conflict at some level. Most often, it's between two individuals, and the fallout can be minimal to the two; but, when one or more people are involved, the stakes become higher. If the two people are working together in a group or team, then the conflict is multiplied exponentially.

Knowing your team members' tendencies. This, of course, takes some expertise, concentration, and attitude adjustment to ward off conflict. At the very least, some instruction is needed on personalities and how each personality affects others. Frequently, conflict stems from personality clashes, rather than issues or doctrine. An "attitude adjustment" may be required for some people to be able to set aside their own feelings, insensitivities, and prejudices, so we can look at each situation without the biases of individual personality. This is why taking the personality questionnaire is very important.

Some conflicts are healthy! At first, one may think this is an oxymoron; conflict and health are opposites, or at least they should be. Some people avoid conflict at all costs, and this too can be unhealthy in some circumstances. When the conflict concerns principles based in absolutes, that's a totally different proposition, and conflict should happen. The health in this is simply that the truth might then be confirmed in the minds of all parties. If a person has the truth, he can be assured of his stance. If he doesn't, this conflict may bring them to a crisis point where he can see the truth. Conversion results from conflict between a person's values and lifestyle, and God's. Without conflict, the person may never realize his/her need to change and follow God.

Neutralize those who thrive on starting and fueling conflict. Conflict for conflict's sake is almost always wrong in its intent. Can we find examples where conflict has been used as a tool, or perhaps one of the parties simply knew how to turn a negative conflict into a positive one? If a person is always at the center of conflict, there may be some systemic problem with him that needs to be investigated and worked on. However, don't try to save this person at the expense of the group. He/she may need some special attention outside the group.

Organize around discussion and sharing of views but not arguing. Sharing respects the other's idea; arguing usually doesn't. Arguing denotes a win-lose proposition; I'm arguing to win the argument. On the other hand, sharing is more about finding what the truth is. One is antagonistic, while the other is supportive of both sides of those engaged in the debate.

Sometimes a mediator is needed to help in the process. Frequently, at least at the outset, many people have difficulty seeing past their own selfishness, or blindness to the true problem. In this scenario, someone else, either on the team or outside the team, must step in and keep the situation from escalating.

In some cases, the disrupter has to be banned from the team. When the team is at the point of self-destructing over one person's inability or unwillingness to change, compromise, or work out the conflict, that person becomes a liability - to himself and the team. For the sake of the team or ministry, something has to be done. At this point, an elder (or elders) needs to be called in to help. If the conflict is among the elders, they must self-govern their own according to Biblical principles.

If the process among the elders bogs down or tempers are rising, take a break, re-group, or better yet, pray.

If anyone is not convinced, or is argumentative, his resistance must be explored. If the conflict continues in a number of different issues over time, there is a problem with that person, or maybe with the whole direction of the ministry. Both need to be explored. If it's learned that the goals and foundation of the ministry are on Biblical terms, the person is out of line and should be dealt with, as previously noted. What I'm about to say is very important, but un-fortunately *seldom questioned* in our churches. Do not assume that everyone in the congregation (or even in leadership) has been truly converted. It's easy to fool people if we aren't truly examining one another through this type of prism. So it's important that a person who acts like this be approached with this assumption; *approach them as a non-Christian*!

Conclusion: Unity, love, and success of the ministry are what counts. When the ministry or the team is in conflict, all must be evaluated. If there seems to be no direction or goals, what is the purpose of the ministry's existence? If not to glorify God and follow his agenda, what good is the ministry? These things <u>must be</u> dealt with. Furthermore, assigning the proper *gifted and trained* people in ministries will serve to validate each ministry, and be progressive for God and His agenda for our lives, and the church as a whole.

Decision Making Exercises

- Exploring

- Find as many uses as possible for any given object. Use three examples, and have them with you in the meeting.

- First, have each person in the group to come up with at least three ideas on their own. Then in groups of three or four have everyone share their ideas. Take a couple of minutes each to come up with the answers.

- Explaining

- Give each person a subject or problem and have him or her explain why it could work and why the group should do it!

- Excuses

- Divide the group up in twos or into two groups and give them an idea to defend while the other group finds excuses against it. The next time, reverse the roles, using another subject. If this is a real issue, then have each group take both roles

- Executing

- The idea has been approved, or is near approval, if it can be implemented. Have a group of three come up with ways of implementing a certain idea or project.

- Note: Do these or other exercises from time to time to keep the team members sharp. Even better, every time you have a decision or project, use these procedures to work through the process.

PUTTING ALL THE PIECES TOGETHER
Chapter Fourteen

Missing Pieces Does Make a Difference

I have given you different "pieces" to help the church grow, but in your situation, there may be something in the culture or community surrounding you, that you or your congregation need to meet, but either you can't see it, or have in the past ignored it out of ignorance (or sometimes selfishness). Open your eyes and heart and be willing to look outside the box. Now when I say this, I do not <u>in any way</u> lessen the example of the scriptures, for with most of our churches today, to look "outside the box" means to look at the New Testament pattern and examples. I believe we *have boxed ourselves in* today within the confines of man's traditions and methods, as we've seen earlier concerning the *democratic* church. In some of these cases, it's been "the wrong pieces" that hinder growth. But there is yet another category, and that's "missing pieces" that may hinder our growth as individuals and/or as a congregation as a whole.

Since we've entered into the new millennium, there will be many missing pieces to explore. New technology, problems, and needs will mandate our finding new ways to help the church to continue to grow and be relevant in the years to come.

But the problem is, most churches are comfortable right where they are. Sometimes, they don't even know pieces are missing. Take, for instance, a person born without a certain part of his/her body. Does the person consciously miss it? No, from the beginning he/she exists without it and doesn't miss it. Rather, he/she learns to function in a natural way with whatever he/she has been given or not given. But someone who <u>had</u> a part then lost it would always have to adapt and consciously deal with that loss. He may be able to handle the loss, but there will be some remembrance of that missing part. It's the same in the church. If a church or its leadership has never experienced true growth or fellowship, there will be no yearning, sense of loss, or feeling that something is missing. On the other hand, a person who has seen and tasted what true fellowship and growth are, suddenly losing access to it in his/her church, will feel a sense of something missing in his/her spiritual life. The former person is content to go on as he is; he knows no better. The latter, however, will feel uncomfortable in a non-growing church and may eventually look elsewhere or end up giving up altogether.

Why should I suggest there is a missing piece in this process of church growth? In fact, there are probably many missing pieces, everywhere you turn. But if we don't realize they <u>even exist</u>, or simply aren't willing to look for them, by all means we won't find them, and the church will go along as usual, missing things that keep us from growing as we should. There are a few reasons that missing pieces must be sought out and explored.

First, no one is infallible in this area. There are others who will come, whom God also can - and will - use. There should be different strategies and methods to reach different sections and groups of the world. I do believe the core principle of making disciples transcends all cultures and people groups, but what precedes it, and how it's packaged will make a difference.

Second, the Spirit may have something in mind, due to specific situations and different areas. Other ideas or strategies needed in each situation to make a church healthy and grow may not always be evident to the human eye. The Spirit is in control, (or at least He should be) of our plans and direction. It is He who looks at each church and its community and gives out gifts appropriate for making disciples.

Third, not every program will fit every church in totality. Be careful of the Church Growth Guru and the "get-growth-quick" schemes. May I remind you, Jesus took three years to prepare His men and women to serve and lead. We must see that making disciples isn't a program, but IS itself the ministry! If discipleship is just another program it will end or "morph" into another program at some point. Making disciples will fill in all the gaps - IF we let it. When you teach each other how to observe all, all the gaps can be filled.

Fourth, what are you <u>personally</u> missing that may hinder growth? What's missing in you, your church, and/or your family? What are the missing pieces that keep *you* from being spiritually whole? Each individual must ask himself this question, then ask it of the whole church. This is where spiritual leadership comes in and makes a difference. It is when the leaders lead from a spiritual platform, not their own - nor from traditions.

The missing piece may be fervor, compassion, vision, commitment, or stamina to finish things, or perhaps no backbone or faith to stand up for what is right.

Missing faith is, many times, at the foundation of lack of growth and health in the church. In fact, there may be no faith at all; this is a major problem! If there is no faith, people are not challenged - or <u>expected</u> - to grow. With no faith, God's power and agenda are non-existent, and therefore, the church or person will not grow.

Also, lack of vision and ignorance are close cousins. Why do we have vision problems? In many cases, we haven't been given permission to have a vision, or else those in leadership are comfortable living with the status quo and, therefore, aren't looking for anything outside their box. Not everyone, as we will see, is a visionary, but leaders also must be able to transfer their vision so that others can jump on board and follow.

Churches also can try to cram in the wrong pieces by misapplied doctrines or traditions. I don't like puzzles, but those who do like them know that a piece will either fit or not. One cannot put a piece in a place where it doesn't fit; when you do, you'll most likely damage the pieces. In some situations, churches try to make traditions and matters of opinion fit where they have no place.

The right pieces make the church whole. This reminds me of Paul's writings on the body and on the importance of each person fitting and working together in the body, so there won't be any missing pieces. If you have a 100-piece puzzle, but there are only 99 pieces in the box, you can't finish the picture; it will always stick out and be obvious. So should the family of God be, in our estimation. If 80% of the people are only watching, many pieces are missing, causing the church puzzle to be incomplete.

Have you ever said, "If I only had that or this I would _____"? This I call the "Wizard of Oz Syndrome". Each character in that movie thought he was missing something, something that would bring him happiness, or make him complete or whole - "If I only had a_____" But in fact, they all <u>had</u> what they were seeking; they just weren't aware of its presence and potential. The Scarecrow thought enough to know he needed to learn - the first step in any forward progress. Those who think they know it all will soon fall into their own trap of insignificance. The Tin Man felt enough compassion to see a need for compassion. Those who truly need a heart never realize their need or lack of need in that area. The Lion imagined what it would be like to be brave, when in fact, given the chance and the encouragement, he <u>was</u> brave. His doubts kept him from even trying to be brave. How many of us are in the same situation in life? We sell ourselves short, and forget we aren't alone in our quest for courage. We should not forget that the power of the Spirit lives within us, and hopefully, we will have those around us to help us have the courage we need. And, Dorothy longed for a home she took for granted. But each one already had what he/she searched for; he/she just needed to be affirmed and recognized. The family of God also has what we need if we, in fact, have the Holy Spirit, the Word of Truth inside us, and the fellowship of believers around us. We will have the right thoughts because they are God's thoughts. We will have the right heart because it's God's heart that melds with ours. We can have courage to fight the fight and finish the race because we have the Spirit within us to give us the courage to carry on. When we realize who our Father is, and who our family is, then we will always be "at home away from home".

What things have stretched your faith? To what can you point where God has made a difference in your growth and in your church's growth?

Four types of people who are usually found in society and, of course, the Church, that may or may not help us with the missing pieces.

1. **Visionary creator** is at the top of the list. If not for this person, the whole process would stop, or at least deter progress or change. Now one could say Jesus and the Apostles were visionaries enough, and we just have to follow their lead, the Bible, and the Holy Spirit. I would agree wholeheartedly that their foundational vision was and is from God, but I would add the current human element, an element that comes into play in every generation, and at every venue. Why? How we apply the New Testament in our day and time takes visionaries who can look at the current situation and dream how their congregation could be better, or at least Biblical. Some of the visionaries can also create a plan or strategy to make Christ and the Apostles' vision happen today. The visionary may be able to implement it, but in most cases, he is only a catalyst who can transfer the passion to others so they will take up the challenge and get the vision implemented. Therefore, without this type of leader/visionary, no new things will get underway, and the status quo will continue as usual.

2. **Self-starting follower** is next in line of succession; one who can take someone else's ideas and run with them. A few more people are in this category. They don't usually have the ability to be a visionary, but rather have the ability to see the need and the wherewithal to carry out the vision, and in some cases, tweak it and run with the challenge. No one needs hold this person's hand. Although he needs others to work with him, he nonetheless is self-motivated to see that the task is accomplished. Without this type, it's unlikely that new things will be started or sustained. I'll give you some explicit examples in my case studies in the appendix.

3. **Guided follower** makes up most of our leaders, and in this category, will be very helpful and successful in the growth of the church. This person will do a good job, if there is someone who will guide him each step of the way, or at least be around long enough to get things started so that he can continue the process. But, he will not take the initiative to do anything new or come up with new innovative ideas on his/her own, but will continue the _status quo_ until shown something better or different. This is not to say they don't want the best, or don't want their work to be a success; they do. When the self-starter or visionary mentors them, they can lead with great success. But, if they aren't mentored or given new ideas and vision, they'll continue the _status quo_. They have a tendency to take whatever comes their way, or keep the traditions intact.

4. **Non-starter follower** is, for whatever reason, the person who does not follow through with anything, and the description of "follower" is a misnomer. Does this mean he can't - or

won't? Does it mean he isn't motivated, or interested in the project? Then if these things are dealt with, maybe he would follow through. Maybe he hasn't been trained or encouraged in the right way. Maybe he has his own agenda and therefore, isn't interested. What can be done to get this person involved is the question, and the problem. In some cases, it's simply a matter of conversion, conviction, or "get out of the way"! This person, moreso than those before, will be more comfortable with traditions and status quo. For some reason, it's easier to not rock the boat and to continue in mundane rituals for rituals' sake. This type person will not grow a church, or even at times, be interested in whether the church does or doesn't grow. In some circles, we might call this person a "maintenance man". In extreme situations, this person is even *afraid* of growth and may end up sabotaging any chance of growth, for growth may get of hand, and he wouldn't know what to do next. Or, he may just be lazy, and it's easier to let things go as they are. Again, this type of leader would do well in churches that also don't care about growth. Let them co-habit and continue their status quo. Now, how God looks upon a situation like this is up to that preacher, elders, or congregation who find themselves in this continual circle of non-growth. Maybe a look at the seven churches in Revelation is in order.

My whole concern in this book has been to encourage the body to get back to the Bible and the methods contained therein. Our bookshelves are full of self-help and how-to books on almost every subject. I hope this doesn't just become one of those books. In reality, it is to be used to point to the Bible as the guidebook. I hope you will, at least, begin to explore for yourselves the mandates and methods Jesus and the first church planters used to start and grow the church. I hope you see that Jesus' method of disciple making is the primary method we should be using today. His plan is not archaic, but sound and fresh. Jesus did not come just to show the first century church what and how to do things, but He gave a pattern for all time, or at least until He returns. And even maybe then, we'll still be in need of being made into His disciples.

When the church, starting with each congregation, realizes all are living under the status quo of man, and not of God, hopefully they'll wake up. When the leaders wake up and realize what they are all about, then and only then, the church will be led by good shepherds and teachers, not ravenous hirelings.

Oh, how God wants His church to be the lighthouse it should be, the spiritual hospital it should be, and the means of saving mankind by being the harbinger of Christ to the world around it.

So, what are the missing pieces in your congregation and in your life that are hindering you from growth, from making disciples for Christ, from following Him, and from fulfilling His great commission?

Rejoice, for God does not want any individual, leadership, or congregation to have any missing pieces. So, pray and seek God, for He will be found by you if you seek Him with your whole heart. This call to wholeness and growth includes both individuals and congregations.

He will never leave us, nor forsake us, but we can forsake Him. Please let us come to His throne in humility and seek His face, will, direction, and power to be the best disciples and congregations we can be, so help us God. To do this we need to be sure that life of the body is being taken care of.

Need for Body Life

The first time I heard the term *Body Life* was in the book by the same title by Ray Stedman. This, to me, was an important work in the life of many churches around the nation during the early 70's. It brought awareness for the need to take care of the body of Christ through community. Most of what was written was and still is valid today in most of its premises. It is important it be applied within a larger context of church growth strategy. The church that does not have an active body life will find that all the pieces are not in place as they should be.

Elements of an Effective Body Life

The "One Anothers" passages mentioned in Paul's writings take the focus off of self and put it on ministering to, and discipling others. If one part of the body is not concerned or in a healthy relationship with another part, the life of the body will not be vibrant and healthy as it should be. Let us list some of those "one anothers" we see in the Bible.

Love one another! What does it mean to love one another in the church? What can be done that shows the love the congregation has for itself and for others outside the church? If there is no love in the congregation, then how will the world want to be part of your church? If outsiders see that the leadership cannot get along or are always arguing and backbiting, then where is the love? Love starts at home, and that includes God's home. How awful to think that in the family of God, there is fighting and lack of love. If no love is evident, perhaps you have lost your first love.

Encourage one another! Do you find encouragement in your church? One of the most frequent complaints in any given church is a profound lack of encouragement. Now, you may say: "It's the preacher's job, to encourage us from the pulpit". However, real encouragement comes when people take time to get to know each other and honestly encourage one another to be his/her best. Even when a person seems down, a word of encouragement will accomplish much more than criticism ever could.

Pray for one another! Don't underestimate the power of prayer for each other. What should we pray? I encourage you to find out. My book *A Walk in Discipleship* will give you an idea. And, of course, the Bible will be the best place to look, but don't forget to ask others about their needs, and be truly concerned.

Be subject to one another! This may be the least favorite of all. Be subject to whom? Of course to God first, second to your leadership, and third to your mentor or discipler. Why is this important? The concept of discipleship is derailed if there is no subjection to those who are leading. That, of course, puts pressure on the each member of the leadership to be worthy of the subjection of his/her followers.

As we have seen earlier, those who have been gifted to equip have the responsibility to see that this part of the church's life is operating in an ongoing manner. For example, take the above "one anothers" and make them a part of your ministry objectives or goals. Like the prayer, "one anothers" may become the basis of your prayer chain ministry. "Encourage one another" may be the basis for your care and bereavement ministry for those who are sick, in trouble, or grieving. There are many more "one anothers" in the Bible. It would be good for you and your leadership to search them out and try to implement them into your ministry.

The Gifted Ones! Body life minus giftedness is no body life at all. Again, it is important to stress that all ministries and body life functions are based in giftedness and not out of mere programming. In some cases, programs can easily be enacted in a church without this type of basis. Furthermore, with any action or ongoing activity or ministry, giftedness must be at its foundation, as was explored in the chapter on "Ministry Groups".

Who is Responsible for Developing Body Life? We see very clearly in Ephesians 4:11 that it is the leadership's responsibility to ensure the body or congregation is cared for. Any congregation may do all the right programs and studies, but without true concern for the health and maintenance of the body, the results will either backfire, or simply waste away.

What Happens When There is No Body Life? Usually, the church continues to go through the motions, maintaining the *status quo* of "services as usual". Little or no effort is expended, no forethought given about caring for one another, or being spiritually responsible. Only if a crisis arises does anyone ever think about others, only themselves and their immediate family, (and sometimes, not even them!) What happens? Simply, people come in one door & and go out another.

In many churches, the process of leaning on programming alone can actually fragment a program-based church; each program takes on a life of its own, and is not an integral part of the whole. Healthy churches maintain wholeness through being concerned about one another. Here again, family groups, cell groups, and stressing each member's giftedness, can better accomplish this, resulting in more people being watched over and cared for in the long run.

Body Life Must be Intentional, (or Must It?) Will a successful ministry that includes a healthy body life simply "happen" unintentionally, or must there be a need for the right strategy and implementation to make it happen? Sadly, in most cases, body life does not happen without a plan or the leaders' awareness. Of course, without the power of the Spirit in the life of the church and each individual, success will also be difficult in this part of the ministry.

We see in the Ephesus church that they were not able to implement body life concepts without the teaching and training of Paul and his disciples. So seems the case in many churches today. In my traveling and seminars, I have found quite often that body life is non-existent. In all my Bible College training, this type of training was omitted from the undergraduate levels. Most preachers do not go on to higher graduate work where they may come in contact with this teaching, but they still have to make an effort to choose those courses that may be available. Therefore, most church leaders are unaware of, and not equipped to help establish these ministries. Most leaders are instructed in how to keep the status quo, but in regards to having a Biblical-type church, this is not taught at most levels. Indeed, few people have ever been a part of a true model of how the church should be, even in our colleges and training centers; how then can they give the necessary examples or teach methods in order to prepare future leaders?

As we come to a close I want to explore some secrets, myths, and needed realities to church growth. All of us make decisions, and think the way we do based upon the information we have received in past. If that information is inaccurate, our thinking will also be faulty about that subject matter. So let us look at those secrets that will help us grow, myths that may get in the way of our growth, realities about church growth, and things your congregation can do to find those missing pieces.

Secrets of Church Growth!

Secret # 1 - Discipleship is not just another program or class; making disciples is the very fabric of the ministry of the church. I've mentioned this in passing a number of times throughout this book, but this is vital for the success of this type of ministry. Once everyone has gone through the discipling material, you continue it as an ongoing ministry for those who will come into the church in the future, whether by conversion or transfer.

Secret # 2 - Every aspect of the church must be involved in growth and disciple making At every level, and at every station of life of the church, disciple-making should be happening. There should always be, at every juncture, people mentoring others in their areas of giftedness and ministries. This is a philosophy of church life that should permeate every level. It is an attitude that needs to be captured and modeled in the kitchen, in the youth group, from the pulpit, and in every classroom in the church.

Secret # 3 - There are no magical methods to fit all   Having said that, there are basic foundations that must be present. Throughout this book, you've seen foundations laid, which, if followed, would be a beginning in the growth of your church, *but only a beginning*. As the church grows, new challenges will arise that need to be examined. I hope you'll now have a better handle on how to approach every situation. If it's put in the larger context of discipleship and giftedness, success will be easier to achieve. God will guide with His Spirit, and, if we're willing to be led, He'll open up new paths. Therefore, you will have to look for methods that will meet those needs when those times come. But again, I stress that, if you have the foundations of the Bible undergirding you, you'll be able to continue to grow.

Secret # 4 - Time spent with God and others will make disciples Yes, it somewhat depends on how that time is spent and on what happens during that time, as to how deep the growth will be. Just getting together for a once- a -week Bible study because you have always done it is sometimes just a dead end in itself. We can do all the studying we want, but never be changed or motivated to act. It takes someone who can take it out of the can and get it on the table. It takes leaders who will do something with what they learn. Reading *"Go Make Disciples"* and never doing it leads only to frustration or complacency within the body. Studying becomes its own copout by just thinking studying is an end in itself. It is only the beginning, only the preparation stage to the main event. A coach and team members can study playbooks and see training films, but until they put the ideas and techniques into practice and go out and actually use them in a game, they are of little use.

Myths About Church Growth!

Myth # 1 - It is harmful stressing numbers and growth Most likely, this idea came from the ministers and pastors who were at non-growing churches. Jesus stated He came to seek and save the lost and that He desired that none be lost. This sounds like a person who was concerned about stressing numbers and growth. Of course, He saw each person - and the whole- all at once! It's true that, if a church just wants to bring them in by whatever method, shallowness may result. Jesus was - and is - concerned about every person; that's "numbers!" He is concerned about their spiritual maturity and steadfast commitment, and that's growth. To do whatever it takes to get people in and not be concerned about discipling them is *just wrong*. Both must happen, numbers and growth. The numbers will come, and they'll stay, if there are ongoing means for growth through discipleship and body life.

Myth # 2 - It is only up to God and His Spirit to see that we grow This is obviously shortsighted and naive. It's often merely a copout or an excuse to be irresponsible with God's church or people. You cannot truly read the New Testament and not see that the work of ministering is a partnership between man and God. God, without man's or the church's participation, will move on to find another man or church. If you and your church aren't following God, He'll find some other people who will follow Him. Man without God is man trying to do it all on his own, and that will also fail. Even though man tries to do all the right things in the right ways, he will fail without the power of God's Spirit in the mix. In I Corinthians 3:6-9 we see Paul discussing the partnership between Himself, Apollos, and God. Paul planted, or started the church, Apollos watered, but God made it grow. But He would not have made it grow if Paul did not plant and if Apollos would not have watered. Now of course God can do all three with out us, but He at this time chooses not to.

Myth # 3 - All you need is the right kind of worship, programs, and buildings, and there will be growth Some people believe that all you have to have is the right worship and people will come. It is true that good worship today does attract people; and that bad worship can distract a person and they may not come back. We saw in the chapter on worship how important it is and that different styles of worship will meet different people's needs, but to rely on worship to keep people or grow them is a dangerous idea. People can be easily drawn to entertainment, and not worship. If worship is over-stressed, however good it is, it may become the main focus of the congregation rather than continued growth in other areas. What I'm saying is, if the church is growing because of the worship style and preaching style, other needs in the church may be neglected because of a false sense of true spiritual growth within the people's lives.

Some people believe that all you have to have is the right buildings and people will come. Many church buildings in Europe are far more grand than anything imagined in America, but they are cold and empty. Buildings help facilitate to a point, but they won't keep a person coming and sitting in the pew, unless true growth and ministry takes place within the building. The first church grew <u>without</u> a central meeting place. The building can help if growth is already taking place. "If you build it, they will come" is Hollywood thinking, and a disaster in the making for a church who wants to experience stable growth.

Realities of Church Growth!

Reality # 1 - Only Spirit-filled and obedient leaders will be concerned about the growth of the church Why do I say this? I have seen many churches where men are in positions of leadership, and their whole focus is on being in power and holding a position; the health and growth of the church is not their priority. Now, some people shouldn't be leaders because they aren't spiritually mature and qualified. Some people may be spiritually mature, but not gifted to lead, so they should not be leaders. Then there are others who are gifted and mature but have either not been trained or allowed to lead as they should or could.

For this to happen, there must be mentoring, as well as yielding to God and His Spirit. You will be able to see this in the attitudes of the leaders and in the way the leaders lead. This is why it is important to have an apprentice program for leaders before they are ordained or installed as official elders/leaders.

Reality # 2 - Church growth is simple: souls need to be reached, saved, and nurtured We have seen this spelled out in the Great Commission and in the chapters on Discipleship and Evangelism. Look at your church and the churches around you. Take a survey of your church and the others in your community, and ask this one question: of the additions over the past six to twelve months, how many were by transfer, and how many were by conversion? This survey was done in my town, and in almost every case in existing churches, 90% or more were by transfer. This is sheep shifting, not kingdom growth.

If you aren't seeing baptisms, you aren't seeing growth, and you aren't following Jesus' command to make disciples. Don't think it's okay to simply believe, "Well, we'll major in nurturing those who come in and let others do the evangelism." Wrong! You're not fulfilling the purpose for which God intended you. It isn't either/or; it's both. If no new blood is coming in, you'll die. You may say, "Well, we still have all our services, and people are still coming. We're holding our own." Wrong again! Just like Adam, you aren't dying instantly, and still seem to be alive, but you are, in fact, not growing as a body.

Reality # 3 - Those same souls need to be nurtured, discipled, and incorporated into the fold, beginning the day they decide to follow Jesus The second question in your survey of those same churches, yours included: "How many of those people are still in the church today?" You must ask why - or why not. Without discipleship and shepherding in place, as we've seen in the chapter on shepherding, growth or converts will be short-lived. The same is true if the church is based upon programs and campaigns that come and go. Without continued shepherding and discipleship from the beginning, the doors will continue to be open. To just gather people and not incorporate them will be a dead end. This is why it is important to stress becoming followers and disciples of Christ during the time of evangelism. (See my book, *The Most Precious Thing,* for help.) It will make it easier to incorporate new believers as well as transfers after they have made a decision.

In my first preaching ministry, I was blessed by God to baptize 60 souls into Christ in the first year, which resulted in tripling the church in only one year. I was there five years, and at the end of that ministry, 100% of those 60 souls were still in the church. Of course, this was primarily due to the power and guidance of the Spirit, but also that I heeded the Spirit's guidance to disciple those I baptized. Growth and retention don't happen by chance, but by faithful discipleship and incorporation.

Reality # 4 - If the church fails to grow, the leaders will be held responsible. Notice, it says leaders! It takes the whole leadership to make growth happen, and to be productive in Church growth. You may say we do the planting and watering and God gives the increase. That's true; the problem is, most churches fail to plant and water. God will not bypass our planting and watering and still give growth. Many times, it only takes one bad leader to thwart growth; likewise, it may only take one good leader to spur and train others to be responsible and grow, but it takes the entire leadership to come together to make it happen. If the bad leader is allowed to rule, and growth is thwarted or minimized, he and the whole leadership will be held accountable to God. If there is no leader or leadership that steps up and makes a difference, they too will be held responsible. That is why leadership should not be taken lightly.

Now we've seen that growth is both numerical and spiritual. Of course, there are places or circumstances that hinder growth, even when there is a faithful, spirit-led leadership. If this is the case, leaders must continually search to find those hindrances, and ways to help get rid of them.

Reality # 5 - It takes work, time, and the commitment of the whole congregation to keep the church continually growing and to be healthy It takes time and effort to cause growth, and to continue, but is it not worth the results of souls being saved and nurtured? Most congregations don't want to make the commitment to grow a church. That is why 75% of the churches aren't growing today. It takes the involvement of the whole congregation. When the proverbial 20% do all the work, it isn't long before they get burned out or turned off to the work and the church, or they just faithfully plod along over the years, going around in circles.

If everyone makes the commitment to do only one thing, and do it right, based on his/her giftedness, the whole church will prosper and grow. Again, this takes work, time, and commitment from the leadership, and until the leadership commits, it will <u>never happen</u>. We learned in the chapter on leadership that leaders are made, mentored, and matured through discipleship apprenticeship, but, all in all, they are first made in the likeness of Christ through His Spirit.

Why do we have problems in churches concerning what it takes to grow? We can look at the problem from both sides of the leadership coin. On one side, we have the ministers, and the other side, the eldership.

Sadly, I have seen and heard from preachers, ministers, or pastors, that" . . . this is too much work". It IS too much for the individual, but not for God - plus the entire congregation. Make the time - and take the time to make it happen. Some of you may say, "I've tried in the past, only to get 'shot down' by some pseudo-eldership that doesn't have the vision or desire to change." Yes, that's true in many congregations, because they're still a part of the 'democratic system' – which is a _trap_ that needs to be changed . . . but change can happen!

One of the areas that needs change is the leader/elder attitude that sometimes, (not always, but sometimes) creeps into the church. I've seen and experienced this, and if it isn't dealt with, that congregation will be adversely affected. These situations represent the "wrong pieces" in the pie, or congregation. How should a congregation handle such a situation? The first thing to do is to pray that those men realize their attitudes and do something about it. Therefore, I suggest each leader read and pray about the possibility of being a piece out of place, and not being a stiff-necked leader instead. So let us look at what one might look like; if we fail to do this, the church will not grow as it could - and should.

Signs You Might be a Stiff Necked Elder/leader

The elders might say the preacher or pastor just doesn't have a vision or direction to grow the congregation. If you're an elder reading all this, may I repeat myself? Evaluate your eldership and your place in that ministry. What are some signs that might indicate you shouldn't be an elder at this time in your life – perhaps <u>never</u>?

<u>Sign # 1 – If you see the eldership as an office to hold rather than a ministry to serve in, you're approaching your tasks all wrong, and you may be a Stiff-necked elder.</u> The ministry of the elder is to lead by serving and serve by shepherding, teaching, and discipling. If you are there to be on the board, or to be in control of something, it might be time

to evaluate why you're there. It may be time for you to step aside and no longer be a hindrance to the growth of the Lord's church.

Sign # 2 – If you find yourself wanting your way all the time, then you may be a Stiff-necked elder

Do you feel you have to have control? Do you find yourself upset, or lose your temper when life doesn't always go your way? If this describes you, check your motives and your heart. You are NOT where you should be. God is to be in control, not you. It is Christ's Church, not yours, it is He who died for it - not you.

Sign # 3 – Do you "politic" outside the meeting to get people on your side? If so, then you might be a Stiff-necked elder.

Check your heart, and know that this place of service is not for you at this time. The leadership in the church is not another example of a worldly business, it is the bride of Christ. It is not about having your way (unless your way is also God's way). If you can say that what you want is what God wants, make your ideas known. But do it in the confines of the ministry meeting, with an eye on consensus.

Sign # 4 – If you got into this position by nomination or vote, yet don't feel qualified, or if you lack the desire to serve others, maybe this is not the place and time for you

Think and pray, and if this is so, step aside until you're ready. Be advised - you may never be qualified to take on this ministry! Just being around long enough, or having the right connections or money, does not qualify you for the ministry of eldership. You must have the desire to shepherd, teach, and take care of the flock's spiritual needs, not to lord over them as a lawmaker. Think, and be honest with yourself, God, and the others in your church.

If you see the eldership as a place of service and ministry, however, then praise God, for He can do great things through you and your leadership. The church that will grow will have leaders with this attitude.

In addition, let me say that, in the New Testament, the pastors were the elders. They were the ones responsible for shepherding and feeding the flock. When the preaching minister takes on this task or mantle alone, he's doing two things. He is taking on more than he should, and often, that will end in frustration and burnout. Now, it is true that most churches need a champion out front to encourage, lead, and cast a vision, but it is also possible that if you put the right men in the place of eldership, they too can help in all these areas. The second thing that happens when you have a one-man pastor is that the rest of the leaders don't take on the responsibility that they should. Again, the plurality of the right type of leadership will be more effective than just one man alone.

If you're a minister or pastor reading this, realize that churches, like people, have personalities. Being aware of this will help both the minister/pastor and the rest of the congregation. There are churches, and leaders in those churches, who just want to stay where they are and refuse to change. True wisdom comes when you can discern if the congregation is one of those types. If you can discern this, stay away from churches that don't fit your personality or vision, especially when you're starting out in the ministry. More men and women have been driven out of the ministry by this type of church than have stayed in paid full-time ministry. These churches can be called "maintenance" type churches. That is, they want to maintain their style and direction, and they want a person who can come in and help maintain that, and not rock the boat. If you are the type of person who has no drive or vision, who wants to just preach and take care of the people there, and who is not interested in growing a church, there are many of those churches out there. Maybe you're of retirement age and just want to preach and be there. Those are the churches for you. I would encourage both theses types of churches and those types of ministers to come together. I would also say to the church, if you have a man who is applying for the ministry at your church, and you see that he wants to be innovative and a change agent, don't destroy him; simply don't hire him. If you truly want to stay where you are, and you like the way you are, encourage him to go on his way, while you look for a man who's willing to meet your need. Can you be that honest?

Even in this, apprenticeship, mentorship, and discipleship are needed when it comes to new ministers, missionaries, or any professional Christian worker. The success rate will sky- rocket if we can apply these concepts to full-time ministry. To do this, we will have to identify those healthy places, and connect them with those coming into the ministry.

Now, granted, there are some people who try this type of ministry, and yet shouldn't be there. If you are one of those people and if you're open to God, He will show you where you need to be. If you find you are not gifted to be up front every Sunday but that you can be a leader in some other part of the church, great! However, never get "pigeonholed" into one type of service. If God never opens up a way or your heart to any other type of ministry, <u>stay where you are</u>. At times, he may give you other gifts that may lead to other ministries within the church. For example, you may start off as a youth minister, and then find out your gifts lie more in the area of the preaching ministry, or even evangelism. But you may find the youth ministry is where you need to be, and you're there for life. Either way, you can be in the will of God all your life.

What I am saying in the context of this chapter is that if we're going to put all the pieces together that will help the church and individual grow, they must be the right pieces. You cannot mix two different puzzles together and expect to get the pieces to fit. Now, the only anomaly in all this is that God can take a <u>willing</u> "puzzle-piece", and reshape the person to fit - if the believer is willing to let God mold him/her!

As I said in the chapter on new churches, it is easier to put all the pieces together when you are starting from scratch; that is, if you are starting off in the right way with the right foundation. It must be noted, however, that the new foundation will create the end product. If you have a foundation based upon democracy and *Robert's Rules of Order*, you have the potential of placing men in leadership who will be controllers, not servants. If you begin with a foundation of mentoring and discipleship, as the Bible illustrates, you will have a better chance of putting men in leadership who are servants and shepherds first.

Steps for Finding the Missing Pieces!

<u>Step # 1 - What does it mean to put all the pieces together?</u> Maybe at this time you don't feel that you have all the pieces to put it all together. That may be true; that discovery is the first step! As we have seen, each person and congregation must find their identity and allow God's Spirit to help yield to His will and direction.

<u>Step # 2 - Identify the pieces you do have.</u> We have talked about finding one's gifts and using those gifts. Remember, God looks down on each church and sees the people and community and gives the gifts accordingly. It is up to the leadership and congregation to be sensitive and open to the Spirit's leading in finding out what those gifts are.

<u>Step # 3 - Study the Bible to see what pieces are needed, and you'll find what's missing</u>. Some of these will be specific, like teaching and evangelism, but there may be others which aren't so evident. Looking to the Bible would seem to be the best (and first!) place

to look, but many times churches go to the newest fad rather than Biblical methods and principles.

<u>Step # 4 - Do not begin anything new without the right gifted and trained people in place</u> This is especially true when it comes to launching new ministries. You have to have trained, motivated, and gifted people to start the ministry. To do so without these factors will lead to asking for volunteers and, eventually, burnout and dismay.

<u>Step # 5 - Look at (and within) yourself for God's leading and gifting</u> Remember, God can always give you more gifts as you mature, and as the need arises, if you're willing. It may be that you have doubts, and lack faith. If so, lean not on your own understanding, but in faith, on the power of God. You may be lazy and irresponsible; if so repent, and let God move in your life.

Of course, there may be more steps, and these may not be – in your situation - in order of importance or sequence, but they are important to consider in putting all the pieces together to help the church grow, both numerically and spiritually.

Is the Pie done yet?

I like to cook, but I have never baked a cake. But I do watch my wife and know that you need to insert a tooth- pick in to see if it is done. When it comes out clean it is ready. The smell, the taste, the pleasure of biting into that delicious pie or cake is heavenly. That is how God reacts when he looks at His church. Can he smell, taste, and see that we, His church, are pleasing to Him? That should be our goal as a congregation, and as individual disciples.

The question, then, is, "when will we be done"? We will not be done until either we go or Christ comes. The church must keep on putting in the right ingredients, using the right recipe, laid down by the Bible and Spirit. Each piece in the pie needs to be in place. And new pies need to be created all around the world.

God wants to see the church grow. God wants all the pieces together in each congregation working and in unity. And finally God wants each pie to be a pleasing offering given up to Him in love.

APPENDIX

Ministry Team Ideas

Evaluation Forms

Church Models

Case Studies

Bibliography

Examples of Ministry Teams!
Description and ministry

Evangelism ministry. Most Precious sharer

Sharing the "The most precious thing in the world". This ministry is for the sole purpose of bringing people to the saving knowledge of Christ, to help them understand the need to become a disciple or follower of Christ.

Coordinator:

Evangelist

Evangelist

Evangelist

Christian Growth Packet: Every new believer and transfer will be guided through the packet with the intent of introducing him or her to the Christian life and the life of our local church (to be given by the family shepherd or small group leaders). It will include the "Steps to Spiritual Growth by Dr. Householder, Personality questionnaire and study, and one session on "Who are we?"

Coordinator:

Guides:

13/14 lessons in Christian Doctrine! After the person is guided through the New Members packet, then he will be guided through 14 lessons taught by 3 or 4 different leaders, when possible. Whenever a person becomes a Christian, or joins the church, he may enter the class at whatever point the class has reached, and finish with the next "cycle". The class will be given from 2 to 3 times a year.

Coordinator:

Teachers:

Small Group Discipleship!   After a person completes the 14 lessons in Christian doctrine, then he/she will be guided into a small group of no more than 4, including the discipler. The group members will be made up of the same gender. The intent is to help guide the disciple to develop his/her spiritual walk with minimal distraction. (Duration, at least 2 years, but each person is recommended to continue through small groups as a lifestyle.) This is where the disciples will study the Walk in Discipleship series.

Coordinator:

Teachers:

Sunday Service Ministries

Worship Team   The worship service is one of the major ways to either attract or discourage people from coming to the Lord. The worship service sets the mood and tone for our worship to God. So, the service should be pleasing to God, and uplifting to those who attend. To be sure that we are ready to worship each week, we need to have two separate teams ready to lead.

Coordinators   Musicians   Singers   Worship leaders

Sunday physical service ministry!

In this important ministry, a group of people should be available, who are responsible for seeing that needed equipment, etc., is in place before the service and put away at the end of service.

Coordinator:

Helpers:

Communion Service Ministry: This ministry will see that the communion trays and cups are ready for Sunday service. This team is also responsible to help in serving communion to those who are shut-ins.

Coordinator:

Helpers:

During services:

In home visits:

Greeters/welcoming Visitor ministry: This ministry is for the purpose of looking for visitors and making them welcomed. You can include giving out bulletins as apart of this ministry, but have separate teams doing each task. Some need to be on the look out for those new people and then if possible get their name and place or section of town they are living in. This is a great ministry for a small to medium church where everyone knows each person. The larger it gets the more difficult to implement. But if each name taking greeter will get the info and give it to the family leadership team then they can contact them for follow up. OR have brochures to give and encourage them to put in the offering.

I. The intent of this ministry is to welcome every new visitor, and present him or her with a packet.

II. To call or visit every new visitor within a week after the first visit if at all possible, with the intention of meeting needs and introducing them to individuals who are prepared to share the gospel.

Coordinator

Greeters:

Visitors contactors:

Prayer Ministry.

 The community of believers must know the needs of other members, so that we can fulfill the command to pray for one another. The prayer/leader will be sure that the prayer requests are gathered and that they are presented to the congregation, or the worship leader. A prayer chain will be established, so that when there is a need, people can be informed about it.

Coordinator:

Assistant:

Youth Ministry:

 All too often, in many churches, Youth are not a priority. But we at _____ realize that the education and caring for our youth is at the top of our concern. Each group coordinator and team should help the youth to grow spiritually through the teaching of the Bible as well as in fun and fellowship. The youth are the future and our responsibility.

Coordinators: Infants:
                        Toddlers:
                        1-4 grade
                        5-6 grades
                        7-8 grades
                        High school

Fellowship Ministry:

The Bible compels us to gather together and fellowship so that we can better serve and know each other. The fellowship ministry is responsible for planning and providing meals and refreshments for special occasions and for our Sunday teatime.

Coordinator:

Helpers:

Family Shepherding Ministry: God is concerned about the care and growth of each person in the family of God. The fellowship of Christ should be growing towards community. Through the shepherding ministry, people will be under the care of one of the leaders. The purpose is to keep in contact with every member and family so that people's spiritual needs are met.

Shepherds:

Follow-up Ministry: After a person becomes a Christian or member, then the shepherding families are to aid in following up with them.

Coordinator: One who gives to each family leader the names of prospects and new members in their area.

Usually Shepherd team leaders or Apprentices

Finance Ministry: This important ministry will involve the collecting and recording of Sunday offerings, keeping the books, and helping with the preparation of the budget.

Coordinator:

Other Ministries:

Basket of Hope Ministries See www.globalchurchgrowth.blogspot.com for more info.

Jail Ministry

Letter Writing Ministry

Food Pantry Ministry

Orphanage and Retirement Homes Ministries

And any other ministry the Spirit sees need for and your people are gifted.

How are your church's vital signs?
Appendix 1

<u>Circle only one per line and be totally honest.</u> All answers are confidential!

One = never, two = almost never, Three = very seldom, Four = seldom, five = sometimes, six = often, seven = very often, eight = most of the time, nine = excellent all the time.

1. Good Pastoral leadership   1 2 3 4 5 6 7 8 9

2. Biblical Priorities being taught   1 2 3 4 5 6 7 8 9

    and being lived out   1 2 3 4 5 6 7 8 9

3. Evangelistic minded   1 2 3 4 5 6 7 8 9

4. Missions minded   1 2 3 4 5 6 7 8 9

4. Consistently Growing larger   1 2 3 4 5 6 7 8 9

5. Celebration/worship   1 2 3 4 5 6 7 8 9

6. Congregation,   1 2 3 4 5 6 7 8 9

7. Small study groups   1 2 3 4 5 6 7 8 9

 8. Are you a part of one?   1 2 3 4 5 6 7 8 9

9. Mobilized laity   1 2 3 4 5 6 7 8 9

10. Are you involved in Min.   1 2 3 4 5 6 7 8 9

11. Unified Unit/body   1 2 3 4 5 6 7 8 9

If any questions are 6 and below please answer these questions, again everything is confidential: Please write clearly!

Why are these areas scored low?

What can the church do to help improve them?

What does the leadership need to do to help them?

What attitudes need to be changed to help raise it?

What practical things need to be started to help improve it?

What can you do to help accomplish this?

Former Attendee Survey

Name _____

Address _____ Phone. _____

When did you last attend our church?

What church are you now attending?

Are you happy at your current church?

What makes you happy at your current church?

What was the reason or reasons you chose to leave or not return to our fellowship?

What do you think needs to be changed so that we can be a better church?

What things do you see lacking in our fellowship?

What positive things do you see in our fellowship?

Is there any way we can be of help to you, or your family?

If you are not happily attending another church, would you mind if one of our leaders would call on you at another time?

Date of Visit _____ Further comments or observations:

Community Survey

Name _____

Address _____

pH. ___ _____

Number in the Household _____   Number of Children _____

When you hear the word *church* what is your first impression or thought?

Do you think most churches are in touch with the people's needs?

What contact have you had with any church?

Was it a positive experience?

If you found a church that was caring and helpful to people, would you be interested in attending?

Would you like to receive literature concerning our activities?

Would you like to know more about our fellowship?

Date of visit _____   Further comments or observations of interviewer

Project Evaluation Form

Leader/teacher _____

Project or class _____

Date of project _____   _____

<u>Goals Set</u>: List all you can!

<u>Goals met</u>: List those that were met.

Do you feel the project met its intended goals? Why or why not?

<u>Quality of meeting place</u>:

      Was there enough room and were furnishings adequate?

      Were the conditions good? Temperature, light, etc.,

<u>Quality of materials</u>:

      Did the materials give you any helpful new information?

      Were you lacking any materials or suggestions for any additional help?

<u>Quality of teaching or training</u>:

Evaluate the teacher(s)

      Preparedness: Poor   Good   Excellent

      Knowledge of the subject: Poor   Good   Excellent

Attitude with participants: Poor   Good   Excellent

Did you learn any new knowledge or skills due to this project? Give example. (optional)

Have you changed any actions or habits after this session? Give example. (optional)

<u>Quality of participation</u>:

Did you feel that you could freely participate in the group's discussion?

If you could make the project or course any better what would you do differently?

Examples of Family Churches

Mega Church

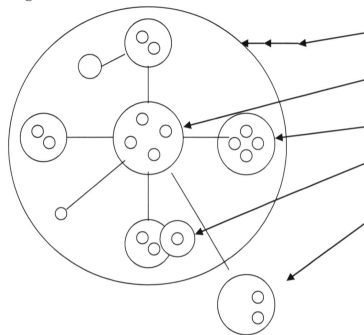

A. City (Jerusalem).

B. Celebration Station.

C. Regional Family Communities!

D. Multiplying Family Units.

E. Daughter Church Outside City
   (Samaria).

New Mega Church

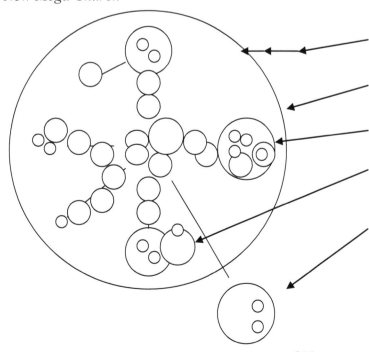

A. Church in a City.

B. Celebrating Corporately.

C. Regional Family Communities!

D. Multiplying Family Units.

E. Daughter Church Outside City
   (Samaria) **Totally Autonomous**

The Mother/Daughter

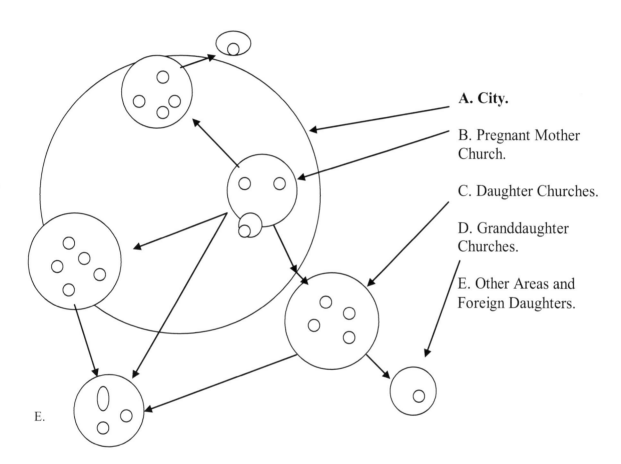

A. City.

B. Pregnant Mother Church.

C. Daughter Churches.

D. Granddaughter Churches.

E. Other Areas and Foreign Daughters.

E.

Case studies

What are the reasons for these case studies? First, see why after the teaching/training there was no success in the church. Also, to see what could have been done better. Third, to see what has been a success, in order that other churches in the future will be a success after the training. This is all to help your church grow - and to see how the churches that are trying to follow the example of The Global Disciple-Making System indeed _do_ grow. Now, it must be understood that, at this point, these are case studies of churches with which I have worked over the past few years. In some cases, the results are my fault; others are the fault of those in leadership who decided not to follow what they had been taught - for whatever reason. A lot of the problems have come from ignorance and trial and error. However, there have been great successes, when all the parts come together. You will find that this system of discipleship works, not because of anything I have done, but because it follows the guide of the New Testament pattern. I hope that, in looking at these case studies, we all can learn better how to make disciples.

Mexico (Everything was not ready.) This was the first Spanish or Mexican church that I trained. The translation of the material was about to be finished when I made plans to train a couple of churches in central Mexico. Well, it came time to make the trip, and my translator informed me that it wasn't quite ready; in fact, it would be another 6 months before the material would be finished and ready to go to print. I made the mistake of going anyway! The training went well, and the churches were excited about the discipleship ministry. I had to promise them that materials would be coming soon. By the time the material was finished, the interest had waned, and I had to make a trip back and try to resurrect the enthusiasm. What I learned at this point was not to start the process with out the material fully being ready. So, now I don't do the full training until all the material is complete in any language group.

The missing preacher! In another situation, I trained a church in the south. I thought everything was set up. The day before I was to leave, I called and talked with the senior minister. He informed me that he would not be able to make it; he had leave town for emergency family matters. But he assured me I should come and do the training. So in good faith I went. It was great. The people were really excited, even to the point that they bought almost $1,000 worth of material. It's been two years now, at the time of this writing, and so far nothing has been implemented. No senior minister, and no go. So I made a policy not to proceed if the senior minister can't make it, even if I have to cancel and never have an opportunity to train that specific church. The fact is, it is a waste of time if the top leaders are not present during the training. Anytime someone misses the whole church training, they are at risk of being a problem or non-participant if the leadership is not all involved and engaging. This, again, is why it is important that everyone is on the same page. This is the case for what ever is tried in the church. This is why many churches have programs which fail, or become simply another program.

Changing of the guard. In one northern town, I trained a church where I thought every thing was in order. In this scenario, I was in contact with the preacher and the chairman of the board in preparation before coming. I went and did the training and equipping, only to find out a couple of weeks later that the minister was leaving, and the leaders all knew it before I came. Once again, nothing really happened, because the church was waiting to see what the next man would do.

Change of leaders/Different philosophies! In one Florida town, I was asked to come and share and train the leadership. I started on Friday evening and ended up on Saturday. I had most of the leadership involved, but not everyone. The leadership decided to let the evangelism minister do a pilot program to see how it would work. He got the ball rolling with about 30 people involved. What happened was great for those 30 people. After 3 months, though, the evangelism minister was let go, but even so, the groups continued to prosper. After another few months the senior minister stepped down and became the Christian school principal and the youth minister took over his position. The sad thing was that the youth minister was one of the leaders *not in attendance* when I did the training. His ideas and philosophy were quite different and he did not see any need in continuing the discipleship. I learned some more things, again, in the process. One thing I changed was: don't train just the leadership and expect the program to get off the launching pad. I then began starting the training on Sunday morning, then continuing with the whole congregation the next three nights. This has proven to be very successful. It is very difficult to transfer enthusiasm from one person or group to another, when the second group hasn't been in on the initial training.

Perfect at first/rogue elder later. Wow, this time I thought everything was in place and every thing was done properly. I started off on Sunday morning, and all the leaders and nearly 90% of the people were in attendance. Over the next two years, the discipleship/shepherding system would prove that it works. Family groups, cell groups, discipleship groups. Raving reports kept coming. But then I got the call from the senior minister that he had been let go, but that they were going to continue the small groups. I then began to explore more closely about the situation. It seems that one of the elders, in the past, had the ear of everyone in the church. If anyone had problems, they would go to him. But in the family group system that I taught, all the family leaders would share the responsibility equally. In this situation, the church had 4 elders, 100 people, and 4 family groups. Well, it worked as it should have, and each family member now went to their family leader if they had any problems or questions. All of a sudden, the "key" elder had lost his total influence over 75% of the people. This, in turn, caused problems between him and the minister, and thus the demise of his position. Everything worked great until some people got off the same page. This illustrates how hard it is to put new wine in old wine skins. All these changes - plus the rogue ruler - resulted in one third of the people leaving the church.

No key person in place! As we learned earlier, success comes when there are key personnel present. If you recall, in the chapter on "Putting All the Pieces Together" you learned there are at least four types of leaders. In two situations, one in Tennessee and one in the Caribbean, this problem of 'key people' surfaced. The churches in both places asked me to come and train their church. I did, and everyone got excited about what was taught. But a problem later arose; when I called, I learned that nothing was being done to implement the program! I found that, in both cases, the main leaders were the type who were not self-starters, but needed someone else to get the ball rolling. They fell into the 3rd and 4th categories. What is needed here is two-fold. One, better follow-up by my ministry, and second, more committed leaders on the field. This has led to major changes and an increase in needs in our ministry so that we can provide better follow-up. But it will still require leaders on the field to be dedicated to seeing the project through and putting things into practice.

Overcoming the past, reaching for the future. What a diverse situation I found myself in, this time in the northeast area! First, the congregation was half Anglo, and the other half was made up of two-thirds Hispanic and one-third Philippino. The surrounding community was even more diverse, which made things even more exciting. Also, in the church, half of the Anglos had come from another denomination, where they'd had some bad experiences with discipleship small groups, so this all made for a great time of training. I found that I had to help heal some spiritual sores of those who'd had bad experiences with discipleship groups. After a while, everyone got excited and motivated to begin to get back on track.

It works, almost! On a Caribbean island, it all comes together, I thought. In this situation, there was a great self-starting leader who took most of what was taught - and applied it! Most, if not all the people, attended the training sessions, and the news coming out of there was great at first. In the first two years, all 90 members were involved in 12 small groups. And their spiritual growth was evident. But there was no growth in numbers those two years. So I explored. The reason why that was the minister decided he did not want to use the *Most Precious* booklet. Yes, there are other evangelistic materials out there. But, I have not seen anything that at this time compares to this book, and it is the foundation to making this system work. What makes the difference is its asking people to be disciples. By not using this booklet the church grew deeply inside by going through the "Walk in Discipleship" but there was no success in growth and evangelism. Try the whole thing, especially if what you're doing is not working or growing. What can it hurt?

Second chance! There are no illegitimate children in God's kingdom. It is for certain, God doesn't care for church splits, or the disunity that occurs in the body of Christ. On the other hand when these things happen, they happen! In most cases it's like putting Humpty Dumpy back together again – it's impossible! As you read in an earlier case study, the one church became two; now what is to happen with the offspring? Like I said, God does not consider the split illegitimate *after the fact*. However the sin of the two took place, hopefully the result will be two God-fearing and loving bodies of Christ. I think this is the case with the daughter here.

In this case, as often happens, the minister was fired, and fully a third of the congregation immediately stopped going to the mother church. Some people weren't going anywhere; some went to a nearby church in another city, but most continued to meet together weekly in their family group for support. This is where I come in, shortly after. I was on my way to Barbados to train a church there and stopped in for a visit and encouragement. I met with the splinter group in the home of the former minister. Now, the atmosphere was heavy, guarded, but excited. The minister didn't know whether he was going to quit the ministry or move on to another place. The group was finding comfort in being together weekly, still going through the walk in Discipleship that I had trained them in a year and a half earlier. I shared that I wasn't there to tell them, either way - whether or not they should start a new church, but that they'd all have to come to that decision. I did encourage them to stay together for discipleship groups so that none would fall away during this rough time of decision. I also told them that if they chose not to continue I'd be supportive, and if they decided to start a new church, I would be there to help them in the process. Five months later, I was asked back to help them in getting things organized as a church.

By now they were in their fourth week of public meeting, and things were going great. They all have the commitment to make disciples, and are unified on the direction of the church through the Bible. Their family discipleship groups held them together, and I think this is the start of a beautiful foundation for Christ's church. Again, it seems that new church work proves the path of least resistance to success in implementing this process of discipleship and family groups.

If you build it right they will come! It is now 2012/13 and God is blessing the work in Cuba. All the pieces are coming together for kingdom growth. The main problem in all the last failures is that the preachers/leaders did not implement the whole disciple making system. But, in this Island the pieces are all coming together. I first came to teach a class in the Bible institute and churches started by Reggie Thomas. While here in January 2012 I presented some of the concepts of the _Global Church Growth Disciple Making System_ to all the ministers for their consideration. My policy is to never ask if I can come and implement it, only present the idea and wait on preachers/leaders to say this is what we want, come and train us. Well, this happened with 3 such churches. My wife and I then came back in September of that year and trained them. We had another exploring meeting for other churches and leaders for future training, and 7 more wanted us to come back and train them. So as I write this we are here training. The report of the first three has one church, which had 22 members when we trained them, and since, have had 16 baptisms using the _Most Precious_ booklet, almost doubling in the first 5 months. The second mission church in that same time period had 5 members. Now after implementing the system and using the _Most Precious_ for evangelism they have had 4 baptisms and now have 12 members. The third church was about 60 members. They have been taking their people through the first two books and are about ready to reach out in evangelism with the _Most Precious_. Now at this juncture 5 more want to get involved, so we are making plans to return to continue the work

What has made a difference in this work than in most of the others? First, the preachers and their churches are willing to commit to implementing the **whole system** step by step and they are having success. The second element is that there are 3 fully committed people working and following up on all the churches that are being trained, and I believe this is the winning combination to success for God's work here. I am just a mouth piece, idea giver for God, and they must do the work to see that it is done in their culture by catching the vision and casting it to others.

Bibliography

Aldrich, Joe. *Life-Style Evangelism*. Portland: Multnomah, 1981.

Arn, Win and Charles. *The Master's Plan for Making Disciples*. Monrovia, CA: Church Growth Press.

Bowland, Terry. *Make Disciples*. Joplin, MO: College Press, 1999.

Bonhoffer, Dietrich. *The Cost of Discipleship*. New York: Macmillan, *1961*

Bruce, A.B *The Training of the Twelve*. Grand Rapids: Kregel, 1971.

Hestenes, Roberta. *Using the Bible in Groups*. Philadelphia: Westminster, 1983.

Householder, Michael R. *A Walk in Discipleship*. Knoxville, TN: Fishnet Publishers, 1985.

Householder, Michael R. *The Most Precious Thing in the World*. Knoxville, TN: Fishnet Publishers, 2000.

Householder, Michael R. *10 Steps To Spiritual Growth*. Knoxville, TN: Fishnet Publishers, 1999.

Little, Paul. *How to Give Away Your Faith*. Downers Grove, IL: Intervarsity, 1966

Ortiz, Juan Carlos. *Disciple* Regal

Pawson, David. *The Normal Christian Birth*. London: Hodder & Stoughton, 1989.

Petersen, Jim. *Living Proof: Sharing the Gospel Naturally*. Colorado Springs: NavPress, 1992.

Staton, Knofel *Check Your Discipleship*. Cincinnati: Standard Publishing, 1982.

Wagner, C. Peter. *Helping your Church Grow*.

Global Church Growth's
Discipling Making Ministry System

You have learned about the "Ministry System" in the second half of this book, now take the time to read, study, and use the materials that will change your life, the life of those around you, your churches, as well lead you to the Bible.

The Most Precious thing in the World!

10 Steps to Spiritual Growth

A Walk in discipleship

To order these books, and learn about more books by Dr. Householder that will help you grow, please contact:

Fishnet Publishers
PO Box 13146
Knoxville, TN 37920
www.fishnetpublishers.com

Or to contact Dr. Mike about this book or ministry of Global Church Growth and its training in the Disciple Making System please see our site at:
www.globalchurchgrowth.blogspot.com

Global Church Growth Discipling Ministries

(GCGDMinistries) is a 501c3 non-profit, non-denominational organization committed to providing training, training materials and support to to various ministries around the world; ethnic, national and foreign alike.

Whether your ministry is a church, a missionary, or an individual; GCGDMinistries would like to help you grow by providing various services.

Click on a link below for details of each type of service or service-track that is offered and how it could help you grow your ministry and help you grow in your ministry.

Services and training Tracks

- Uniquely You Profiling

- Discipleship and Shepherding (Tract One)

- Leadership and Giftedness (Tract Two)

- Evangelism and Church Growth (Tract Three)

Printed in Great Britain
by Amazon.co.uk, Ltd.,
Marston Gate.